BLACK
IN
WHITE
SPACE

BLACK IN WHITE SPACE

[THE Enduring Impact OF Color IN Everyday Life]

ELIJAH ANDERSON

The University of Chicago Press • Chicago and London

The University of Chicago Press, Chicago 60637

The University of Chicago Press, Ltd., London

© 2022 by The University of Chicago

Published 2022

Paperback edition 2023

Printed in the United States of America

32 31 30 29 28 27 26 25 24   2 3 4 5

ISBN-13: 978-0-226-65723-3 (cloth)

ISBN-13: 978-0-226-82641-7 (paper)

ISBN-13: 978-0-226-81517-6 (e-book)

DOI: https://doi.org/10.7208/chicago/9780226815176.001.0001

Library of Congress Cataloging-in-Publication Data

Names: Anderson, Elijah, author.

Title: Black in white space : the enduring impact of color in everyday life / Elijah Anderson.

Description: Chicago : University of Chicago Press, 2022. | Includes bibliographical references and index.

Identifiers: LCCN 2021021095 | ISBN 9780226657233 (cloth) | ISBN 9780226815176 (ebook)

Subjects: LCSH: African Americans—United States—Social conditions. | Racism—United States.

Classification: LCC E185.86 .A525 2021 | DDC 305.896/073—dc23

LC record available at https://lccn.loc.gov/2021021095

♾ This paper meets the requirements of ANSI/NISO Z39.48-1992 (Permanence of Paper).

This book is dedicated to the memory of my mother,

Carrie Bell Hull,

who taught me everything I know—

and encouraged me every day to "be somebody"—

to my grandchildren,

Eve, Isaiah, Arturo, and *Soleil,*

who teach me new lessons every day—

and to my wife and best friend,

Nancy Anderson,

who has supported me unfailingly in every way.

CONTENTS

ACKNOWLEDGMENTS

I want to take this opportunity to acknowledge and thank my research subjects—especially the people of Philadelphia, who were so forthcoming with their observations and their stories about their issues with color. I'd also like to thank the following friends and colleagues, who provided me with support, feedback, and helpful comments from time to time, and who helped me in all sorts of ways.

In no particular order, I note them here as follows: Stephane Andrade, Scott Brooks, James Kurth, Waverly Duck, Richard Alba, Gerald Jaynes, Fred Block, Alvaro Sanchez, Julia Adams, Jeffrey Alexander, Kalfani Turé, Gregory Squires, Jack Katz, Zsuzsa Berend, Vida Bajc, Michael Deland, Randall Sims, Vincent Calloway, Russell Crockett, Angela Crockett, Duke Austin, Vani Kulkarni, Craig Holloway, Philip Weinstein, William Frucht, Marcus Hunter, Nikki Jones, Harold Bershady, Bill Kornblum, Victor Lidz, Annikki Herranen-Tabibi, Randall Collins, Deborah McGill, Linda Haapajärvi, Oliver St. Clair Franklin, William Whitworth, Herman Hawthorne, Marlese Durr, Joe Feagin, Vernon Clark, Anthony Andrews, Lynwood Pettie, Fred

Wherry, Bob Washington, Arthur Paris, Grey Osterud, the late Acel Moore, Linda Wright Moore, Fred Wiemer, Reynolds Farley, Waldo Johnson, Rourke O'Brien, Leighton Hull, Howard S. Becker, Robert Mueller, Patrice Collins, Philip McHarris, Kai Erikson, and my dear friend, the late Renée C. Fox.

For research assistance, I want to thank James Finley, Rasmus Schlutter, Rachel Beshevkin, and Shanti Fader. And I thank my editors at the University of Chicago Press, the late Douglas Mitchell, Alice Bennett, Erin DeWitt, and Elizabeth Branch Dyson.

And last but not least, I want to acknowledge my children, Caitlin Anderson and Luke Anderson; their spouses, Jorge Contreras and Brenna Anderson; and my wife, Nancy—all of whom listened patiently and served as a sounding board around the dinner table. Without the help and assistance of all these folks, and especially the people of Philadelphia, this book would not be what it is.

Earlier versions of some parts of this book have been published in the *Atlantic Monthly*, the *Annals of the American Academy of Political and Social Science*, the *Washington Monthly*, the *Guardian*, the *Sociology of Race and Ethnicity*, and *Vox*. This work, including the representation of certain scenes, is based on qualitative fieldwork, including observations and interviews, and firsthand accounts over the course of many years. To protect the privacy and the confidentiality of my subjects, names and certain details have been disguised.

INTRODUCTION

When Supreme Court Chief Justice Roger B. Taney declared in the 1857 *Dred Scott* decision that the framers of the Constitution believed Black people "had no rights which the white man was bound to respect," he ruled on the state of American society at that time: Black people, free or enslaved, held a place inferior to that of White people, and all White people were above all Black people. This ruling established and reinforced the societal prejudice that White people were simply better than Black people by virtue of being White (Painter 2010; Franklin and Higginbotham [1947] 2021).

After Emancipation, as Black people migrated to towns and cities in the North and in the South, their stigmatized "place" both followed and preceded them. When Black people settled in their new communities, their reception was decidedly mixed; they were resisted and tolerated, and as their numbers grew relentlessly, the local White people worked to contain them, at times violently, in what became the "Black section" of town. These settings where Blacks were relegated were the precursors of the Black ghettos that have proliferated throughout the nation since that time, settings that symbolically reinforced what slavery established: the lowly place of Black people in the public mindset.

Now, in virtually every city in America, there is a "Black side of town," an area where Black people are concentrated, which is generally apart from White residential areas. But the ghetto is not solely a matter of physical location; it is also a symbol of the ghetto's peculiar relationship with the wider White community. In the past, the Black ghetto served as a haven from racism, a place of refuge where Black people could "feel at home" among their own kind. These neighborhoods developed as segregated communities, replete with their own infrastructures and social organization. In time, they would take on a more sinister definition and purpose—not just for Blacks but for the wider society as well. Eventually, the ghetto would serve as a place reminiscent of a reservation, where Black people would reside.

Eventually, the White population developed and elaborated their own sense of group position in contradistinction to the "place" of Black people, symbolism manifested in the physical space of the "Black ghetto." Thus, in the minds of the White majority, and for Black people as well, the ghetto became a fixture of mental as well as physical space. Each generation of White people became socially invested in the lowly status of Black people; they understood their own racial identity in terms of whom they opposed, and this positionality was institutionalized, passed on from one racist generation to the next, and manifested through the enduring principle of "White over Black."

The urban ghettos of America continue to struggle with a legacy of racial caste. Now buffeted by the winds of deindustrialization and a global economy that has left them disenfranchised and socially excluded, these poor Black communities are characterized by high rates of structural poverty and joblessness. Incivility, crime, and violence are all too common. For successful Blacks, who have made their way into the upper reaches of the larger society, but who share the phenotype and skin color of those left behind, contradictions and dilemmas of status abound, as they are at times confused with Black people of the ghetto, whom many White people, and especially the police, are inclined to view and treat as outcasts.

Meanwhile, the wider culture approaches the ghetto with both wonderment and fear. The "ghetto" has become an icon representing for many a derelict lifestyle, encouraging a new form of symbolic racism for which the Black ghetto as an entity unto itself is becoming the primary referent that defines anonymous Black people for the wider society. Thus, in the minds of many Americans, the ghetto is where "the Black people live," symbolizing an impoverished, crime-prone, drug-infested, and violent area of the city. The history of racism in America, along with the ascription of "ghetto" to anonymous Blacks, has burdened Blacks with a negative presumption they must disprove before they can establish mutually trusting relationships with others.

In preparing this work, extending my own body of ethnographic research, I have tried to document the ways in which the most desperate of the Philadelphia Black underclass cope with making a living, and how these coping efforts and their social and cultural adjustments, in the context of existing racial arrangements, define the Black ghetto and the Black people who are presumed to reside there. Also, I am particularly interested in the persistence of racial prejudice and how it has become modified over the last half century, changes that have occurred in the group position of American Blacks and the positional arrangements of groups in American society more generally.

Ethnography is defined as the systematic study of culture, or what Clifford Geertz (2000) referred to as a community's shared understandings. The challenge to the ethnographer is to engage in fieldwork among a population by observing what people do and by listening to what they say to apprehend the "local knowledge" that underlies their community's shared understandings. Ethnographers try to render or represent this knowledge in their writings. To some extent that is what I've tried to accomplish in this book. Hence, the following pages will document ethnographically the circumstances in which Black people make their claims on American society, show the reality behind the powerful stereotype of the iconic ghetto, and describe the ways Black people struggle to address the resulting stigma that follows them throughout their lives, and especially as they navigate what they perceive as "White space."

PROLOGUE

I was born in the South on what used to be a plantation. My grandmother, a sort of village doctor who never accepted payment for her services, was the midwife at my birth. She was a religious woman who lived by the Bible, so she named me Elijah. My mother, who had an eleventh-grade education, was twenty years old when I was born and already had three children.

Her family members were sharecroppers, so she went to the field each day to pick cotton, as did my grandmother and my father.[1] In those days, when crops needed to be planted or harvested, school would let out because that work took priority. My father attended school only to the fourth grade, but in World War II he drove a supply truck in the US Army in England and then in France. After returning from the war, he felt he could no longer live as a second-class citizen in the South. He believed he would encounter trouble there, and a better life in the North beckoned.

The factory jobs of the North were a magnet for rural southerners, both Black and White. My uncles had already migrated to South Bend,

Indiana, and my family followed them there. Once in South Bend, my mother worked as a domestic, working "days" in the homes of well-to-do Whites, and my father, like my uncles, found a job at the (now-defunct) Studebaker automobile factory. For many years he worked in the foundry there. And at age seventy-one, after breathing soot and metallic dust over decades, my father died of lung cancer, though he'd never smoked.

While my parents struggled to establish themselves in South Bend, for the first two years my sister and I boarded next door to my uncle in the home of a woman I called Aunt Freddie, who had migrated to the North in 1910. An educated, proper middle-class Black woman, she read me Bible stories and had a great influence on me.

Eventually my family moved into an apartment in a segregated part of the city. When I started public school at age five, I was one of only a handful of Black students at the excellent Oliver School, the result of a racially gerrymandered school district. By contrast, later, when we moved into our own home in an "integrated" neighborhood that was in effect transitioning from White to Black, I entered a segregated Black school. By the time I graduated from high school, the neighborhood was totally Black.

In the second grade, I learned to read at an advanced level, and the teacher would sometimes stand me in front of the class to read aloud. Not surprisingly, because I was the teacher's pet, my friendships were limited and I felt on the margins.

As an independent child who loved the freedom of being out late at night, I began to run with other boys who gravitated to the streets. I had jobs after school, starting with selling the *South Bend Tribune* on downtown street corners at age ten. On occasion I supplemented my spending money by organizing other boys to take the bus with me to White neighborhoods to rake leaves, shovel snow, or even sing Christmas carols for money.

At age twelve I secured the adult job of setting pins at a downtown bowling alley. Most of my coworkers were winos and homeless men, along with other young boys like me, and I loved being part of the life of these "grown people." Around them we young boys could smoke and curse and act grown-up ourselves with few sanctions. Because setting pins and handling bowling balls caused too many sprained fingers that had to be splinted by the school nurse, I set out to find a "real" job and canvassed the downtown area, looking for work.

On Monday evenings in South Bend, the downtown businesses remained open until 8:30 rather than closing at 5:30. As I canvassed the downtown, I spotted Mr. Forbes, a heavyset middle-aged White man, alone inside his typewriter store. I went in and asked him for a job. "You need some help?" I asked. "What can you do?" "I can do whatever these other boys do," I said.

I'd passed the store many times and noticed a few older boys, both White and Black, working around the shop. After seeing them, I thought I might have a chance.

Mr. Forbes looked me up and down. "Where do you stay?" "On the Westside," I answered, referring to the area of the city where the Black population was then concentrated. "When can you work?" "I can work after school and on Saturdays."

After a few minutes of this back-and-forth, Mr. Forbes agreed to hire me. "Well, I can start you off at fifty cents an hour." "Can you make that seventy-five?" "Naw, you'll need to work your way up." "Okay," I said, "when can I start?" "You can start tomorrow," he said. I shook his hand. "All right." I was elated: this was my first real job, where I would make a weekly wage.

After school the next day I went to the store, and Mr. Forbes introduced me to the other boys, all a few years older, who worked for him.

Over the next weeks, Mr. and Mrs. Forbes would come to know and trust me, and I would come to know them. I would run errands for them like shopping for Mrs. Forbes's groceries, picking up chop suey from the local Chinese restaurant or fetching sandwiches at lunchtime, and on occasion depositing checks and cash in the local bank. Much later, after I'd gotten my driver's license, I even delivered typewriters in Mr. Forbes's new Ford.

The shop was a center of activity, about 350 feet square. The counter was in the front, with typewriters in the display window and stacked on shelves along the sides, a desk, a bathroom in the back, and stairs down to the basement. There was a constant flow of people in and out—customers, students, and older people wanting to rent or buy typewriters. Mr. Forbes was quite the salesman, while his wife typically sat at the desk and took care of paperwork. Their son, Richard, worked there too, selling and renting typewriters or making deliveries. The Forbeses lived upstairs on the third floor of the building.

When things were slow, it might be just Mr. Forbes and his wife and us boys, listening to music on the radio and watching the scene from the large front window. I was very attentive—this was a new world for me. Usually, after arriving from school, I'd empty wastebaskets downstairs and then go to see if Mrs. Forbes had trash to take out. Also, on occasion, I'd paint, fix the concrete out front, and burn trash in the incinerator in the basement, and then settle in behind the workbench to work on typewriters. I'd observe the scene and listen to the conversations as I did my work.

After I'd worked for Mr. Forbes for a few weeks, the police noticed that the bicycle I'd parked outside his shop was a stolen one. I explained that I hadn't known I'd bought a stolen bike, and Mr. Forbes vouched for me: "He's a nice boy." His trust in me was enough for the White officers.

A sensitive man from a small town in Illinois, Mr. Forbes treated me well; he genuinely liked me and became almost like a father to me. He and his wife even included me on family trips to their cottage by a beautiful Michigan lake. I'd do chores around the cottage, swim in the lake, and eat dinner at their picnic table like a member of their family. As the only Black person at that lake community, I was fascinated by this White world, and I noticed what Mrs. Forbes cooked and how their family ate.

Since I worked in Mr. Forbes's shop from age twelve until I graduated from high school, I had several years to observe that privileged world. Of course the customers who visited the store were usually White, as were Mr. Forbes's friends, who would sometimes stop by to talk and socialize. I'd watch the constant traffic in and out of the store and eavesdrop on the conversations. Mrs. Forbes would sit at her desk and do the bookkeeping while the other boys and I would take typewriters apart, soak them in a cleaning solution, wash them down, and reassemble or repair them.

Once, after there had been a fire at the store, we were all working while Mrs. Forbes talked on the phone about cleaning up from the fire. She said, "I never worked so hard in my life—I worked like a n****r." This comment stopped us boys in our tracks. The room grew deathly silent, and we all tried to ignore what had just been said. Mrs. Forbes caught herself but said nothing more. A few days later, Otis, one of the older Black boys, was in the apartment above the shop, changing a light bulb, when Mrs. Forbes apologized for using the N-word. "Oh, that's not a problem. I know you were not talking about me, 'cause I'm not a lowlife," said Otis. "And, Mrs. Forbes, you are a former schoolteacher, so I know you're too intelligent to use that word. It must have been a slip-up."

This was in the late 1950s and 1960s; the civil rights movement was going on, and by the time I was fifteen or sixteen, it was in full swing. People were demonstrating throughout the South, and Viola Liuzzo, a Detroit White woman, was killed in her car in Selma, Alabama, because she was registering Black people to vote. Mr. and Mrs. Forbes and their friends would discuss this incident in the store, and they invariably blamed the woman for not minding her own business. Once in a while we younger people would join in, but the Forbeses often made fun of the demonstrators holding sit-ins, especially when they were dragged away or roughed up by the cops. That seemed funny to Mr. Forbes, who would sometimes mock the demonstrators and pretend he was going to hold a sit-in in his own store if Jim, my younger coworker, and I didn't behave.

This was how I became aware of what race meant to him. This is the context in which I began to learn how he felt about Black people and their struggles for racial equality: that they were a funny, lowly, and distant people who had strange diseases and were different from Whites. Yet at the same time he was friendly to me.

Once when I was fifteen or sixteen, Mr. Forbes's son needed his lawn mowed. It was summertime, and things were slow at the shop. Richard and his wife, Irene, lived across town in a nice White neighborhood. I said, "Okay, I'll do it," and got ready to leave on my bike. Before I went out the door, Richard called out, "Okay, Eli, Irene's there. Don't try anything!" I just waved him off and left.

When someone like Richard said things like that, I was reminded of my place as a Black person in the whole scheme of things. And yet he and the rest of the family were all friendly to me. All these incidents occurred as I was coming of age; gradually, I would pay closer and closer attention to this context and its contradictions.

On occasion Mr. Forbes sent me to other office buildings around the downtown to change typewriter ribbons, giving me an entrée to a host of entirely White establishments. My real initiation into this White world began in Mr. Forbes's store and through the experiences that job afforded me.

Then one day my coworker Jim said to me, "Eli, guess what Forbes told me." I was curious.

"He told me I shouldn't hang out with the colored boy so much."

"No, he didn't say that."

"Yes, I swear he did!"

I was incredulous and continued to argue with Jim about whether Mr. Forbes actually told him, a White boy, not to hang out with me so much.

Mr. Forbes had been my mentor since he hired me at age twelve. Not only had he taught me how to take apart any typewriter, fix it, and put it back together, he also had absorbed me into the life of the store and his downtown office building where he worked and lived. I ran errands for him and Mrs. Forbes, and I knew not only Richard but his wife, Irene, and their young daughter, Beth. I also knew Mr. and Mrs. Weedling, Mr. Forbes's tenants; the lawyers Steve Turoc and Paul Paden; and Mrs. Carter, the wife of Dr. Carter, who gave voice lessons on the third floor and whose trash I emptied when I arrived after school each day. I had cordial relations with all these people. Mr. Forbes and these other adults were the first grown White people I had come to know so well. It was clear to me that Mr. Forbes cared for me as a person, and I was sure he liked and trusted me.

After my conversation with Jim, however, I started to watch Mr. Forbes more closely and noticed racial issues I'd previously ignored. I began to see that while Mr. Forbes trusted me, even loved me, and would do almost anything for me, he placed limits on our relationship. In the caste-like system of South Bend, in which Black people were considered the lowliest, he wanted to protect Jim from my status. In effect, he taught me what it means to be Black in the White world.

Soon after this, my interest piqued, I began to notice even more closely how Mr. Forbes and his friends thought about Black people. They stereotyped them, saying Black people carried diseases like tuberculosis more often than Whites. On Saturdays, when Black women came downtown to shop—sometimes heavyset women in bright-colored dresses and fancy feathered hats—Mr. Forbes would stand up in the shop and call, "Look! Look!" as he and his friends peered out the store's large front window and mocked these women.

I also observed that these men's biases didn't apply just to Black people. Mr. Greene, a tall blond salesman in his late fifties, would sometimes stop by to drink coffee and chat. One Saturday morning when Mr. Forbes had not gone to the Elks Club across the street to play cards the night before, he asked Mr. Greene who else had been there. Mr. Greene replied, "Four guys and three Jews." I overheard this comment from my workbench, and now I began to see prejudice that was directed not just against Blacks but against others too.

I noticed contradictions in Mr. Forbes's behavior as well. For example, I never heard him correct Mr. Greene on that remark, yet Mr. Forbes had Jewish friends. And while generally appearing to accept me and to treat me well enough around the shop, he seemed concerned that my social stigma might rub off on Jim, and Jim seemed to know this as well.

I'd been raised to consider myself equal to anyone, and my parents had encouraged me to see that good and bad people come in all races, but to not tolerate disrespect. My neighborhood friends were not only

Black boys but also White boys like Jim, as well as ethnic White children whose families were recent immigrants from Poland and Hungary, though we children were often more accepting of one another than the adults were; we played together.

I gained tremendous insights during my teen years as I spent time both in my family's home in a Black neighborhood and in the Forbes family's White world. I lived within and on the margins of both spaces during this time, and I became an attentive observer of both.

I never confronted Mr. Forbes about what he might have said to Jim, but as a high school student, and especially during a period of rising racial consciousness, I did question other White men. Once when changing a typewriter ribbon at a large real estate company, I asked the elderly founder why there were no Black people working in his business. He said candidly that his current employees would quit if he hired Black people.

As I worked for Mr. Forbes, I came to realize that he and the other White people there liked me most when I was in my place. In fact, he once told me directly, "Eli, you can go far in this world; just keep your nose clean and don't cause trouble." In other words, "Don't get out of your place." Thus, as a young boy, it gradually dawned on me that in South Bend and perhaps throughout America, there were places where I and my kind might not always be welcome.

• • •

Through these and many other experiences, I became aware that because I was Black, the White world was a problem I needed to come to terms with. I learned that the color line was ever-present, but that it was a delicate and problematic thing, at times almost hidden but bright as day the moment it was crossed.

In some ways this country has made great strides about race since South Bend in the 1960s. But in other ways, the nation has hardly moved forward at all. This book grows out of a lifetime of the professional observations of a sociologist and an ethnographer, and the personal experiences of a Black man in America. Using a combination of ethnography, interviews, and incidents from my own life, I'll show just how enduring the color line is for Black people in America: how "White space" comes into existence and makes life difficult for Black people, and how the negative power of the iconic ghetto is a constant in Black life. In a word, as a young Black man working for Mr. Forbes, I learned my "place."

• • •

Born in a cabin on what used to be a slave plantation in the Mississippi Delta, delivered by my grandmother as the midwife, my family migrated two years later to South Bend, Indiana, where I began my ascent, moving from the Black ghetto to studying at Indiana University, the University of Chicago, and Northwestern University, to teaching at Swarthmore College, the University of Pennsylvania, and Yale University—where I am a Sterling Professor, the highest academic honor Yale can bestow on a member of its faculty. Hence, I have made my way from the symbolic bottom of American society to the symbolic top. Strikingly, the iconic Black ghetto has followed me every step of the way. I have kept memories of my journey and taken qualitative field notes along the way. My long-term qualitative fieldwork in cities along with the lived experience of Blackness have contributed profoundly to the ethnography that is ultimately reflected by this work.

CHAPTER 1

THE WHITE SPACE

Since the end of the civil rights movement, large numbers of Black people have made their way into settings previously occupied only by Whites, though their reception has been mixed. Overwhelmingly White neighborhoods, schools, workplaces, universities, and other public spaces remain. Blacks perceive these settings as "the White space,"[1] which many consider to be informally off-limits to people like them. Meanwhile, despite the growth of an enormous Black middle class, many Whites assume that the natural Black space is that destitute and fearsome locality so commonly featured in the public media, including popular books, music, movies, and the TV news—the iconic ghetto. White people typically avoid Black space, but Black people are required to navigate the White space as a condition of their existence.

Over the past half century, American society has undergone a major racial incorporation process. Toward the end of the civil rights movement, massive riots and civil rebellions occurred in cities across the country, as Blacks grew increasingly insistent and militant (see Kerner Commission Report 1968). It was in this context that the federal government passed far-reaching legislation that made Black people full citizens while targeting for reform racially segregated workplaces, neighborhoods, schools, and universities. These reforms, coupled with a prolonged period of economic expansion, set the stage for the historic period of racial integration and incorporation, including the subsequent growth of the Black middle class, which is now the largest in American history. White society's reception of upwardly and outwardly mobile Black people, however, was decidedly mixed. To be sure, many Whites encouraged and supported racial equality and progress, but many others, consumed by deeply held prejudices, powerfully resisted these changes, which they feared abrogated their own rights and assumed privileges.

The civil rights movement is long past, yet segregation persists. The wider society is still replete with overwhelmingly White neighborhoods, restaurants, schools, universities, workplaces, churches and other associations, courthouses, and cemeteries, reinforcing an implicit White sensibility from which Black people are typically absent, not expected, or marginalized when present at all. In turn, Blacks often refer to such settings colloquially as "the White space"—a perceptual category—and they typically approach these spaces with care.

The city's public spaces, workplaces, and neighborhoods, on the other hand, are thought of as a mosaic of White spaces, Black spaces, and cosmopolitan spaces that may be in various stages of flux, from White to Black or from Black to White. As local demographics change, the image of certain public spaces is subject to change as well, affecting not only how and by whom a space is occupied but also the way it is phenotypically perceived. What Whites see as "diverse," Blacks may perceive as homogeneously White and relatively privileged (see Jackson 1999).

For Black people in particular, White spaces vary in kind, but their most distinctive feature is the overwhelming presence of White people and the relative absence of Blacks. "White space" is a perceptual category that assumes a particular space to be predominantly White, one where Black people are typically unexpected, marginalized when present, and made to feel unwelcome, a space that Blacks perceive to be informally "off-limits" to people like them and where on occasion they encounter racialized disrespect and other forms of resistance.[2] "Deep White spaces" are settings in which Black folk are seldom if ever present and are unexpected; settings such as the rural outskirts of cities like Jackson and Atlanta, or isolated areas of upstate New York, Pennsylvania, and Maine—as well as certain colleges, universities, and firms with no Black people present.[3]

Black space is also a perceptual category, indicated most remarkably when Black people claim and occupy White space beyond its "tipping point," so that Whites avoid the space as "too Black." Hence the space attracts ever more Black people and fewer Whites, sealing its fate for the time being as a "Black space." Over many years, I have observed this racial dynamic at work segregating Philadelphia's neighborhoods, parks, restaurants, malls, and other public spaces. Philadelphia is now the sixth most segregated city in the nation (Logan and Stultz 2011).

While these White and Black spaces may be seen as racially homogeneous, typically they actually can be further classified in terms of ethnicity and social class. "White spaces," for instance, often include not only established Americans of European descent but also recently arrived European immigrants and visitors and others who may be perceived as phenotypically "White" and who therefore fit in more easily with the dominant White society.

Similarly, those inhabiting "Black space" are not always US-born African Americans but may be from Africa, Latin America, Haiti, the Caribbean, Cape Verde, and so on. Accordingly, the racially mixed urban space, which I have referred to as "the cosmopolitan canopy" (Anderson 2011), exists as a diverse island of civility in a sea of racial segregation. Whereas Whites usually stay out of Black space, Black people cannot avoid White space.

When present in the White space, Blacks reflexively note the proportion of Whites to Blacks, or may look around for other Blacks with whom to commune if not bond, and then may adjust their comfort level accordingly; when judging a setting as too White, they can feel uneasy and consider it to be informally "off-limits." For Whites, however, the same settings are generally regarded as unremarkable, or as normal, taken-for-granted reflections of civil society.

In White space, the most tolerated Black person is one who either is "in his place," working as a janitor or a service person, or is vouched for by White people in good standing. Such a Black person is less likely to challenge the perceived racial order of the typical White setting— White people as dominant and Black people as subordinate. When the Black person does not appear in a subordinate role, however, the cognitive dissonance that may occur can cause trouble.

While the anonymous Black person is under special surveillance in many public places in the city, this is especially true in White space. As Black people make their way, they try to be aware of those spaces where they might be subjected to racial profiling, and they readily distinguish among them. They give some public spaces high marks and others low marks based on their own observations and experiences and those of their friends. In many such spaces, Black people can expect to be profiled or to encounter acute disrespect based on their Blackness. And they don't like to be surprised. Many feel that their lives and those of their loved ones are on the line. Thus they may be highly self-conscious and may perceive that they are in hostile territory even when they aren't.

In White spaces, especially on the outskirts of the urban ghetto, Black people can feel alone and self-conscious. Here, Whites may become increasingly defensive, scrutinizing the anonymous Black person and wondering whether he or she is "up to no good." Given this reality, unknown Black people may expect to be surveilled and kept at a social distance and might be pleasantly surprised when they are not.

In times past, certain White spaces were routinely declared off-limits to Blacks, either implicitly or explicitly, and Black people formed cognitive or actual maps based on their understandings (The Green Book [Green and Gertler 2019]). In the South, such race rules were often enforced by the police, or even by White vigilantes who assumed extralegal authority and took it upon themselves to inform and remind Blacks that they were not welcome, at times through violence.

In the North, such rules were usually more indirect. Of course, Blacks who served Whites in traditionally White spaces—"the help"—were allowed to enter. To be sure, lower-status Whites were sometimes unwelcome in such spaces as well, a class divide that persists. But on the whole, White skin spoke for much and continues to do so, and it was often all one needed to be admitted to settings where Blacks were excluded.

THE "N****R MOMENT"

With the civil rights struggles of the 1950s and 1960s as well as the positive social changes that followed, anonymous Blacks can now expect to venture uneventfully into places that are lily-White. They may find themselves to be the only Blacks present there, however, and might be mistaken for someone who works there, such as a janitor. Polite company may not declare this as White space and draw unwanted attention to an "interloper," but some of the most marginal Whites might do so, effectively drawing the color line or actively reminding the Black people of their "place."

In typically White public settings, White people may view almost any Black person present with some degree of unease or curiosity. This moment of racialized disrespect puts Black people in their "place" and makes them feel excluded on the basis of their Blackness—it gives them and everyone observing the situation the emphatic message that, contrary to what the Black person might have once thought, he or she "does not belong." In public spaces like an upscale restaurant, Blacks sometimes get seated by the toilet or the kitchen; when they complain, waitstaff are encouraged to say the unoccupied "better" tables are reserved. If they take the table offered, they might sit through their dinner while the table they were denied remains free all evening. Black informants report many such incidents.

Or a White guard may approach the Black person with a disingenuous "May I help you?" Most Blacks, particularly young males, have heard this question time and time again—not really offering help but asking what they're doing there.

A more accurate question might be "What's your business here?" But this would be too direct, and most protectors of such spaces prefer to avoid a direct insult based on skin color, and possibly a lawsuit. Hearing this question, the Black person is subtly reminded that he is "out of place," that he doesn't belong. Whites may project suspicion of the Black person's willingness or ability to be peaceful, law-abiding, and decent. In certain public places like malls, restaurants, or movie theaters—all interior spaces, often with security nearby—such concerns are muted, but the perceptive Black person knows she or he has been profiled and assigned a provisional status—one false move and the police or security will be summoned.

This is roughly what happened in the April 2018 Starbucks incident in Philadelphia. Two young African American men, who grew up in an impoverished Black community but were now upwardly mobile businessmen, were waiting to meet a colleague at the Eighteenth Street Starbucks. As they sat quietly without placing an order, one of the baristas began to scrutinize them. When one of the young men asked for the code to use the restroom, this seemed to be too much. The barista called the Philadelphia police, who arrived moments later to arrest the young men for what amounted to "sitting in Starbucks while Black."

The other Starbucks customers defended the young men and took cell phone videos; at least one was posted online and made the news. Having been acutely disrespected, the men felt humiliated and deflated. Among Black people, such situations are sometimes referred to as "n****r moments." They are all too common for Black people operating in what they know as "White space," though they don't expect them in spaces perceived to be cosmopolitan canopies. In fact, through this act of racial disrespect, the young men found out the Starbucks was a "White space." This perceptual category can be made known by making Black people feel excluded based on their Blackness, manifested in the frequency and the intensity of such incidents experienced there.

But the n****r moment is not only a moment of acute disrespect based on Blackness; it represents the American color line itself, a line of social demarcation that can be drawn at any moment, but especially when the Black person is navigating White space and is perceived to be "out of place." When such moments happen under the cosmopolitan canopy (Anderson 2011, chap. 8), the reaction is almost immediate; often with an application of social gloss—politeness and smiling—to cover up or repair the damage. The gloss deflects scrutiny of such incidents and gives those under the canopy a chance to recover their equilibrium. Things may then return to normal until the next such moment. These moments can be large or small. The small ones can often be ignored, but the large moments are more consequential and can cause the Black person to review and change his life, abandoning his White friends or the setting in which he made them. Such a moment can even result in his death, especially at the hands of the police, as in the police killing of George Floyd that attracted worldwide attention in the summer of 2020.

Given these challenges, many Blacks approach the White space ambivalently, ostensibly for instrumental reasons. They may avoid it altogether or leave it as soon as possible. In exiting the White space, however, Blacks can feel both relief and regret—relief for having removed themselves from a stressful environment and regret for perhaps leaving prematurely. For the White space is where many social rewards originate, including an elegant night on the town, or can be the source of cultural capital itself—education, employment, privilege, prestige, money, and the promise of acceptance. To obtain these rewards, Blacks must venture into White space, hoping to benefit as much as possible. To be at all successful, Black people must manage themselves within this space.

• • •

Navigating White space is always a challenge. All too frequently, prejudiced people who pervade the White space weaponize their prejudice, marginalizing Blacks or actively reminding them of their outsider status to put them in their place. Ralph's experience is germane.

"Ralph," a Black eighteen-year-old, grew up in a nearly all-White upper-middle-class neighborhood and has attended private schools in a wealthy section of Philadelphia for his entire life. His parents are

well-off and pay Ralph's full tuition themselves. A student of "good character" who makes excellent grades, Ralph is one of the few Black students in his school. He is also a member of the soccer team.

When his team plays other elite high schools in the Philadelphia suburbs, he is usually the only Black player on the field, and he plays the game well. During these games, Ralph is occasionally called n****r, but such outbursts usually come from spectators. Recently, when he was playing in an "away" game, the epithet came from an opposing player. As the clock wound down and his team seemed destined to win, tensions between the opposing teams spiraled into verbal conflict. After one of Ralph's teammates was apparently fouled up the field and Ralph called this to the referee's attention, one of the opposing players retorted, "What are you going to do about it, n****r?" He yelled his remarks directly at Ralph, loudly and within earshot of the coaches, the referee, and the spectators—including Ralph's mother, the only Black person in the stands. When Ralph heard this epithet directed at him, he didn't know how to react.

"Everyone focused on me, and I never felt so alone in my life—my head was about to explode, and I just pushed the guy," Ralph told me later. As the referee approached, Ralph said to him, "Did you hear that? He just called me n****r!" The referee just shrugged. Then the opposing player yelled at Ralph, "So what? Yeah, I said it, and I'll say it again!" The referee and the coaches, all of whom witnessed this exchange, appeared to ignore the White player's comments and Ralph's response.

The spectators—largely the players' parents, teachers, and classmates—looked on impassively, though a few hissed and booed at Ralph. Ralph felt uneasy and very alone, not knowing where he stood with his teammates. His mother felt deeply disturbed and humiliated, but mostly she was sad for her son. After the game, when the tension had died down, the opposing player singled out Ralph's mother and told her, "Your son was in the wrong, you know. He never should have been so close to me." Ralph told me he was glad he didn't see the opposing player approach his mom.

At the end of the game, the coaches suspended the postgame ritual meeting and handshake between the opposing sides. With the confusion,

not everyone understood exactly what had happened during the game;
they only knew there had been unusual tension and that Ralph had
been involved. But even not knowing what the trouble was, Ralph said,
everyone seemed to blame him for the incident. Later an acquaintance
of Ralph's mother said she gathered Ralph had been involved in some
sort of trouble, and she now suggested that Ralph ride home with his
mother rather than on the team bus. His mother refused.

• • •

Black presence in White space is tenuous at best. There are always people who are ready to discourage Black people or to discredit them through association with the iconic ghetto, at times for the aggressors' own self-esteem or advancement. This category includes Whites and others, but some Blacks themselves may try to distance themselves from those associated with the ghetto. Thus the ghetto icon becomes an acceptable hook for racism even without racists (Bonilla-Silva 2013). A particular organization—for instance, a corporation, a nonprofit, or a public sector bureaucracy—may pride itself on being egalitarian and universalistic and may not recognize its own shortcomings with respect to racial inequality. Beyond the issue of security, the public association of Blacks with the inner-city ghetto and the Black person's perennial definition as an outsider causes Whites and others to develop an almost universally low opinion of Blacks as a racial category. White resistance to the fact of Black equality also taps deeper attitudes born of group positional arrangements in which Blacks have historically been regarded as a lowly class (Blumer 1958; Bobo 1999; Omi and Winant 2014). It is from this perceived lowly place that Black people emerge, and its historical and cultural manifestation is the iconic ghetto, now an increasingly powerful racial symbol.

NO GIRLS

In the mid-1970s, when I was a new professor at Swarthmore College, I volunteered to serve on a committee to staff the ABC House, located on a leafy neighborhood street in Swarthmore. ABC stood for "A Better

Chance," a national organization dedicated to providing ambitious young inner-city Black men with a better chance of attending college and succeeding in life. The idea was to select B-level students from inner-city high schools and get them away from their presumably troubled communities, where negative influences like gangs, violence, and crime might overwhelm them, and to bring them to a "good" community like Swarthmore so they could attend a high school where their academic aspirations could be strongly supported.

Why B students? The program assumed that A students would be able to navigate the wider system effectively and make their way to college without assistance. It was the B students who needed to be kept from falling through the proverbial cracks and into the pitfalls of a troubled inner-city environment, so this is where the organization's energy and resources were focused. The Swarthmore committee consisted of a few professors and a few high school teachers from the Swarthmore High School. As a young Black faculty member, I was charged with helping to select a staff that would promote the dream of success and upward mobility for the residents.

One Saturday afternoon in April, a number of us sat in a common room of the Swarthmore English Department and interviewed candidates for these staff positions. We selected a pleasant young married White couple who were graduate students at a local university to serve as houseparents. Their duties would be to "run" the house, making sure that meals were prepared, and to see that the young men did their homework, got home and to bed at a reasonable hour, and got up on time to attend school.

After a while the committee moved along to interview Swarthmore College students and select two to support the couple. One of our interviewees was Josh, a White male student. We questioned him about his qualifications for keeping the boys in line, interested in their schoolwork, and so on. Another interviewee was Tom, a rising Black senior from Chester, Pennsylvania, a nearby town whose name was synonymous with "Black," as in the Black ghetto. We peppered him with questions about himself, including his experience with an arrangement like this, and asked more about his qualifications for the role.

The process was moving along well, and things seemed to be going fine. Tom was a personable young man, and the committee was impressed with his qualifications, his demeanor, and the overall way he presented himself.

Then one of the high school teachers raised an unaddressed concern. He asked Tom how he would get the young male students to do their homework, but also what he might do with them for fun. Tom responded, "Well, I'd take them to the movies. I'd take them bowling. I'd show them around the town."

Then the White teacher became a bit more direct. "That's all well and good, but what would you do for, uh, social life? Or, you know, ah, girls? Of course, we don't really have any girls in Swarthmore."

Tom looked puzzled. He hesitated, then looked over at me, the only other Black person in the room. Our eyes met, and we both realized instantly what the Swarthmore High School teacher was really asking him. There were plenty of girls in the town and the school, of course. The teacher was asking whether Tom would encourage the ABC boys to associate with Swarthmore's White girls. After regaining his composure, Tom said, "Ah, uh, I'd take them to Chester." With that answer the White members of the committee seemed to breathe a sigh of relief.

Chester, about three miles from Swarthmore, is an overwhelmingly Black community, a physical ghetto surrounded by a White suburban ring. Outsiders, especially so many of the White people of Swarthmore, commonly know what Chester means—it's "where the Black people live." With his question about social life, the White teacher was trying to forestall a potential scandal involving young Black men and local White girls. He wanted to know if Tom understood, and he was relieved to hear that he would take the Black students to Chester—in other words, Tom would remind them of "their place" and encourage them to observe it. Tom got the job, but his answer to the Chester question connected the two of us on what it meant for us as Black men in the White space. We both instantly recognized the indirect message of the teacher's expressed concern, for we both knew our place in the racial hierarchy and played along. The ABC students were to be welcomed to the community, but only conditionally—they needed to know and stay in "their place." We both understood that the White Swarthmore High School teachers didn't want the Black boys to date or befriend the White girls. In other words, Tom and I saw the color line, and we both acknowledged it, I through silence, and he through his answer.

Experiences like these go well beyond students in high school and college—and they are still current. Virtually all the Black people I've interviewed and observed know that Blacks and Whites occupy separate and usually unequal places in the racial order, governed by the "master status" of Blackness, and these Black people in White spaces typically lack the moral authority and credibility that their White colleagues are usually accorded. Whites often take such authority for granted and can wield it without needing to think about it. But Black people typically must campaign for such trust, and when trust must be demanded, it loses its grace. This is the dilemma of Black people in White space regardless of status. In the White space, the essential issues are always the same: trust, regard, and moral authority, and Black people rarely have enough. When you're Black, whether you're a lawyer, a doctor, a professor, or a business executive, the Black place is tacitly understood as one of relative subordination, one that many Whites assume to be the natural Black space.

THE BLACK NOD

When Blacks move about in White space, they sometimes encounter other Black people, people who understand on a cultural level not only the peculiar challenges of this space, but also that they are outnumbered by White people present there. Feeling so alienated, they look for allies. In fact, as Blacks move about the White space, often the first thing they note is the number of Black people present. What primarily defines the larger society is the absence of Black people and the preponderance of White people. The presence of familiar faces, or simply other Black faces, brings a measure of comfort.

Being generally outnumbered by White people, Black people feel a peculiar vulnerability, and they assume that other Blacks understand the challenges of this space in ways that Whites cannot. Since the White space can turn hostile at any moment, the implicit promise of support that Blacks sense from other Blacks serves as a defense, and it is part of the reason that Blacks acknowledge one another in this space, with the nod or informal greeting serving as a trigger that activates Black solidarity.

Thus, when Black people encounter one another there—even if they have never met before—they often smile, nod, speak, or even sometimes wink to acknowledge one another's presence or to let their Black brethren know that they "see them," and that they are not alone. While this is not always an explicit defense against the White space as a hostile environment, it offers the prospect, if only symbolic, of support from another knowing person.

In fact, when navigating White space, Black people are on the lookout not just for other Black people—who may or may not prove to be dependable sources of support—but also for other kinds of allies as well. In this environment, Black people are especially needy.

And particularly in these respects, and for these reasons, Blacks tend to feel more comfortable in racially and gender diverse settings than they do in homogeneous White settings that often exclude people like them. The brotherly or sisterly nod may advance to an extended conversation or even a friendship.

Just such a gesture serves as an affirmation that in this anonymity of potentially hostile Whiteness, the Black person may have a friend. After all, if things turn ugly, Whites absolutely cannot be counted on. Most Whites have little idea, and many are willfully ignorant, of the challenges Black people face in the White space.

Black skin on a stranger in the White space is, or at least can be, an important marker, a profound indication of another person who understands. White skin on the stranger holds no such promise. For these reasons, when a Black person encounters another Black person, he or she is encouraged to pay attention, to look at the person directly and to look the person over, to determine as much as possible what can be expected in this setting.

Because of Black people's longtime experience of being on the bottom of the racial caste system in America, a kind of brotherhood and sisterhood has developed based on Black skin. Black people are inclined to make that nod since they are not that far removed from Jim Crow segregation, from the years when all Blacks lived together in Black ghettos.

The nod, however, is seldom automatic; instead, it is given only after consideration. Yet this assessment is made in an instant, and the iconic ghetto—with its negatives and positives—is typically factored in. Meetings with other Black people typically involve a rapid process of mutual assessment.

First their eyes meet. If both "pass inspection," mutual nods likely follow, communicating, "I see you." Those who project negative images of the iconic ghetto will be ignored. This differentiation reflects how today's Black ghetto differs from the ghetto under the rule of Jim Crow. Then the ghetto included upper-class, middle-class, and working-class people as well as the poor. Excluded from White neighborhoods, all Black people lived there, as a caste apart from White society. While that Black community had the problem of desperately poor people, it also included well-educated professional people, supportive social structures, and a focus on decency.

When civil rights legislation ultimately enabled wealthier, more successful Blacks to leave, the desperately poor were left alone in the ghetto. Therefore Black people who are living in the larger society typically work to distance themselves from those Blacks who project the most compromising or negative images of the iconic ghetto. They become concerned about emblems of status they display, including their dress, their speech, and their demeanor. They do so because in the White space, most Black people are acutely aware of the image they project, sensing that their well-being—at times, even their freedom or their life—is at stake.

CHAPTER 2

THE ICONIC GHETTO

For many Americans, the ghetto is "where the Black people live," often stereotyped as an impoverished, crime-prone, drug-infested, and violent area of the city. The urban ghetto is no longer simply a physical space; it has also become increasingly a mental construct, a point of reference that hovers over phenotypic Black people as they make their way in civil society. Perpetuated by the mass media and popular culture, this image has achieved iconic status and now serves as a powerful source of stereotypes, prejudice, and discrimination. The poorest Blacks occupy a low-caste status, and for the Black middle class, contradictions and dilemmas of status are common, underscoring the nation's racial divide and exacerbating racial tensions. Anonymous Blacks must often disprove these stereotypes before establishing mutually trusting relations with others. The iconic ghetto reinforces what the institution of slavery so effectively established: the Black person's lowly "place" in the American racial order, especially in the public mindset.

When Black people presumed to be from the Black ghetto "stray" into White space, they typically draw or attract the White gaze, surveillance, and at times harassment and demands to "go back where they came from."

JOGGING WHILE BLACK

Several years ago I vacationed in Wellfleet, Massachusetts, a pleasant Cape Cod town full of upper-middle-class White vacationers and working-class White residents. During the two weeks my family and I spent there, I encountered very few other Black people. We had rented a beautiful cottage about a mile from the town center, which consisted of a library, a few restaurants, and stores catering to tourists. Early one weekday morning, I jogged down the road from our cottage through the town center and made my way to Route 6, which runs the length of the Cape from the Sagamore Bridge to Provincetown. It was a beautiful morning, about seventy-five degrees with low humidity and clear blue skies. I had jogged here many times before. At 6:00 a.m. the road was deserted, with only an occasional passing car. I was enjoying my run that morning, listening to the sounds of nature and feeling serene. It seemed I had this world all to myself.

Suddenly a red pickup stopped dead in the middle of the road. I looked over at the driver, a middle-aged White man, who was obviously trying to communicate something to me. He was waving his hands and gesticulating, and I immediately thought he might be in need of help, but I couldn't make out what he was saying. I stopped, cupped my hand to my ear, and yelled back, "What did you say?" It was then that he made himself very clear. "Go home! Go home!" he yelled, dragging out the words to make sure I understood. I was provoked, but I waved him off and continued on my way.

This incident not only spoiled my morning jog but nagged me for the rest of the day. Days later I shared it with friends, Black and White. Many of the Black people recounted their own similar tales. But who was this man? What was his problem? Was the incident merely a fluke? Did many other White people here feel the same? And exactly what did he mean by "go home"? Did he assume, because of my Black skin, that I was from the ghetto? These questions remained with me, and over

the years they've inspired my thinking about what I've come to call the
iconic ghetto (Anderson 2011, 2012a,b,c).

And more recently:

As I take my morning jog through upscale White neighborhoods,
White people I meet tense up, especially when I wear a dark hoodie;
they look away and practice "civil inattention," pretending not to notice
me. When I don my Yale or Penn jersey or hoodie, White folk seem more
welcoming, less uptight; they sometimes smile or wave, or they may
say hi. This happens to me repeatedly.

When my jogging outfit associates me with a university, it identifies
me as a certain "kind" of Black person, one local White people might
trust or find comforting, a Black male with a putative collection of
positive attributes or markings that might distance me from the iconic
ghetto. I'm taken as a less scary Black male, as someone unlikely to
commit a heinous crime against this community, a person who has
for the moment passed inspection under what Black people know as
the "White gaze."

The iconic ghetto has a powerful negative resonance, inspiring
prejudices and insinuating them into the workings of the wider society.
They manifest themselves in the activities of everyday life—at the
downtown theater, in the local drugstore or restaurant, and on the
public street. Strangers with dark skin are suspect until they can prove
their trustworthiness, a hard task in the fleeting interactions of the
public environment. People often observe, keep their distance, then
move on, thankful that they got past a risky situation.

During the 1960s, when the civil rights movement culminated in
rioting in urban Black ghettos, these fearsome conflagrations seared
into the minds of Americans the stereotypical image of the Black
ghetto as synonymous with disorder, trouble, and urban distress, if
not rebellion (Kerner Commission 1968; Cobb and Guariglia 2021).
This public image was powerfully underscored in 1992 when riots were
ignited in Los Angeles by the acquittal of the police officers charged
in the beating of Rodney King. And popular media and newspaper
reports have reinforced this image of the Black ghetto as a place where

anarchy and senseless crime are common. Moreover, rap stars like Tupac, N.W.A., and the Notorious B.I.G. have all contributed to the stereotypical power of the icon, as personified by the urban Black male.

For contemporary Americans, both Black and White, the word "ghetto" has generally come to be associated with Black people, powerfully referring to the areas where Blacks have become concentrated over time; in popular parlance, it's "the Black side of town" or "the 'hood." To Blacks and Whites alike, the term is almost always pejorative.

While the larger society's perceptions of the Black ghetto have varied over time from benign to evil/depraved, today it is a place widely considered incomprehensible and dangerous. Murder and mayhem, particularly interpersonal violence among youths, are all-too-common features of ghetto life. The wider society is fed a constant diet of negative reports on this community, which unfortunately are too often accurate.

Even more unfortunate, however, is that the large number of Black citizens who are law-abiding and decent are seldom acknowledged. In fact, these people typically live among those who are often desperate, and they are always under pressure to live conventionally and to thrive in spite of the negative power of the icon. But their lives are often rendered invisible by the sporadic crime, drug violence, and structural poverty that appear increasingly racialized.

For outsiders, the ghetto is more often imagined than directly experienced—imagined as impoverished, chaotic, lawless, drug-infested, and ruled by violence. Like most stereotypes, this image contains elements of truth, but for the most part it is false. Over the years this imagined ghetto has become a kind of yardstick by which all Blacks are measured. Relations between Blacks and Whites outside the ghetto have become complicated by this association (Winant 2002; Wacquant 2012a,b).

About a decade ago, after I arrived at Yale as a new professor, the chair of the sociology department invited me to meet him for dinner at the Yale Club of New York City at 7:00 p.m. on a Thursday evening. Dressed in a blue blazer, I arrived early and took a seat in the lobby. Since it was dinnertime the space was busy, and I decided to go up to the club's library to read the day's New York Times. *As I approached the elevator, there was a crush of people waiting. When the car arrived, I entered and moved to the back to make way for other passengers. Everyone except me was White.*

As the car filled up, I asked a man of about thirty-five, standing by the controls, "Could you press the button for the library floor, please?" He looked over at me and said, "You can read?" The car fell silent. Suddenly his friend, another young White man, came to my defense and blurted out, "I've never met a Yalie who couldn't read." Now all eyes turned to me. Silence. The car reached the library floor. As I stepped off, I held the door and said, "I'm not a Yalie, I'm a Yale professor," and went into the library to read the newspaper.

• • •

The persistence of the way the iconic ghetto shrouds all Black people was brought home to me recently when I traveled from New Haven to Philadelphia by Amtrak's Acela train, making stops in New York City, Newark, and a few other places along the way.

Dressed in a dark suit and tie and a black topcoat, I found a pair of vacant seats and took one. I was pleased to have extra space to stretch out. As the train moved along and made occasional stops, seats filled and emptied. In New York City we waited while the train took on many more passengers. I expected someone to take the seat next to mine, but no one did. The train resumed its journey, and after about fifteen minutes I decided to go to the café car for some refreshments. As I rose and looked over the car, I was surprised by how crowded the train was, since the seat next to mine was still vacant. In fact, it remained unoccupied for my entire trip to Philadelphia.

In Philadelphia I was met at the train by Mr. Goldberg, a well-dressed young White man who works for the University of Pennsylvania. He had invited me to speak at that evening's panel, and as a gracious host, he had arrived at Philadelphia's Thirtieth Street station to escort me to my hotel. We exchanged pleasantries and then made our way to the taxi stand just outside the station.

A middle-aged Black attendant waited on us, and after we stood in line for just a few minutes, he ushered us into a waiting car. Our eyes met. "How you doing?" *he greeted me, smiling warmly. He seemed to ignore Mr. Goldberg.*

"Fine," *I murmured.* "Happy New Year."

"Happy New Year to you, too. You da man!" *he replied.*

"Just trying to maintain," *I answered.*

"I see," *he said, as he closed the cab's door.*

The attendant and I had just experienced communion based on our shared skin color, with the implication that we were part of the same community, though I had never seen this man before. But he clearly saw me as someone he could be familiar with, given our shared color caste and our presumed common plight with respect to race relations: we were brothers under the veil. Through our exchange, we both acknowledged and constructed a solidarity based on presumed common experiences, histories, and future expectations pertaining to our skin color.

Whereas my Black skin had seemed to repel White strangers on the train, it led this Black man to give me special attention.

Returning to New Haven a few days later, I took a 4:37 p.m. Acela train from Philadelphia. I was able to find two vacant seats almost immediately and sat down in one. Since it was Sunday evening, there was a fair number of travelers.

When the train arrived in Newark, New Jersey, the seat next to mine remained vacant. When we arrived in New York, the train took on many passengers who were heading up the Eastern Corridor to return to school, work, or wherever. The conductor passed through a couple of times, announcing that this train was especially crowded and travelers should make room for others. I complied and moved my coat from the neighboring seat.

Soon we left New York on our way to Stamford. At this point the conductor made another pass, and noticing that the seat next to mine was vacant, he asked me if the seat was unoccupied. I confirmed that it was. He smiled and said, "I'll find someone to sit with you." *At that point I stood up and looked around—nearly every seat was taken. I sat back down and meditated on what had just occurred again and thought how it echoed what the novelist John Edgar Wideman (2010) had remarked on: that fears of the iconic ghetto—of violence and depravity—follow Black people throughout their lives, repelling others even when something is at stake, such as a material benefit (like an empty seat) that would easily accrue to them. One of the issues for Black people is that they carry with them baggage of uncertainty—White people don't know how they will be received by Black people, including potentially being seen as racist or being blamed for the Black person's suffering.*

What is so ethnographically interesting about my train ride, specifically that I could ride all the way to Philadelphia and return to New Haven seated virtually alone, is that it exemplifies the tacit racial reality that Black people deal with all the time (see Rawls and Duck 2020).

Subject to such discrimination, Black people study Whites and compare the treatment they receive to the treatment they suppose White people to receive, and often find it lacking. In turn, they become familiar with the ways of White folk, including the gaze, the frown, and the forced smile that is really no smile at all: it is a nervous reaction to an uncomfortable situation they must defuse; reactively, they grimace. The reality is that there is a pattern of social distance between the races. Given a choice, most of the Whites on that Amtrak train simply did not want to sit next to a Black man, no matter how well-dressed he was, no matter how mannerly he might have appeared.

I attribute this to the stigma, the negative difference that Black people typically experience in such overwhelmingly White situations, and that I experienced as a Black man riding virtually alone in the predominantly White train car. On my way back to New Haven that Sunday night, the train was loaded with college students, faculty, businessmen, and others, people we might find in the middle-class suburbs of New York, Philadelphia, Bridgeport, and New Haven. These were not impoverished or working-class White people of limited education and means, people who might have had challenging issues with Black people moving into their neighborhoods, attending their schools, or competing for their jobs.

No, my fellow travelers were members of the educated elite, the

so-called "best of America," people who had attended the better prep
schools and colleges and now worked in top firms and lived in nice,
quiet neighborhoods—sophisticated, well-heeled White people. The
issue staring me in the face on that train was racial caste, a rigid
system of social stratification that effectively places those with a Black
phenotype low down and those with White skin in a superior place.

Moreover, in this analysis the Black man entering the White space
of the Amtrak Acela train is stigmatized, someone who contaminates
the space by his presence. These White people may be able to tolerate
one or two "nice" Black people in their midst, but more would likely
overwhelm their preferred definition of interacting with Black people,
no matter their quality.

THE LEGACY OF RACIAL CASTE

We can distinguish the "old racism" of the antebellum plantation from
contemporary racism. The earlier version was explicit, whereas today's
is subtle and indirect. These two racisms compete, but they also overlap
and reinforce one another, depending on how Americans interpret and
define everyday race relations. It's also true that the old racism deeply
influences the new; the urban ghetto is the modern manifestation of
the legacy of slavery and Jim Crow segregation. The new racism derives
from the wider society's view of that place "where the Black people
live"—that den of iniquity on the verge of self-destruction.

Although the term "ghetto" originally described the segregated
neighborhoods of Italian Jews, in America today it refers to destitute
Black communities where all manner of crime and incivility reign
(Wirth 1928; Duneier 2000).[1] Of course, although such neighborhoods
are almost uniformly inhabited by Blacks, not all Black people live in
the ghetto. But because of this strong association, Blacks appearing
outside the ghetto are often placed on a peculiar probation in which
it is up to them to convince others that they are decent, law-abiding
citizens. And this is where the traditional form of racism and the new
attitudinal racism meet.

Ours is a peculiar era in which White people twice helped vote President Barack Obama into office yet won't allow people who resemble him phenotypically to live in their neighborhoods, attend their schools, or work alongside them as colleagues. In some ways this is similar to the American dilemma Gunnar Myrdal wrote about so many years ago (Myrdal 1944). Certainly, separate drinking fountains and legally segregated neighborhoods and public accommodations are a thing of the past. Today race relations are a lot more complicated. Much racial prejudice and discrimination is hidden or has gone underground, but the effects are significant: in too many work settings, neighborhoods, and schools and universities, African Americans are underrepresented or absent.

As a result of the racial incorporation and desegregation of American institutions that followed the civil rights movement, Black people now participate at all levels of the American occupational structure. Nonetheless, many of these people are treated as tokens, as highly symbolic representatives of the Black ghetto community who often lack the moral authority and legitimacy of their White counterparts.

As they operate in these settings, their challenge is to be consequential despite their racial challenges. Although they operate in places where Black people have traditionally worked in relatively menial positions, interactions here too can be fraught. When Blacks appear in such settings, attempting to pass as full persons, many Whites are tolerant. To a degree, however, Black people are conscious of their provisional status; for many of their White counterparts, the Black person has something more to prove. Many Whites draw the line at full social equality. Such settings are often racially confusing, for things are not always as they seem.

Most public spaces operate with a veneer of racial civility that at any moment can be exposed for what it is. Blacks and Whites alike for the most part act with caution when they encounter strangers with Black skin who seem to be from the ghetto. For the power of the ghetto image, embodied in the mark of color, makes all Black people suspect, makes them people with something to prove as they venture forth in the wider society.

In addition, in the wider pluralistic society, more privileged groups whom Blacks compete with for place and position often regard Black people as beneath them in an effort to enhance and protect their own sense of group position. In this respect, it is in the interest of other groups to perceive poor Blacks as "low-down" and immoral and to blame them for their own circumstances. Nowhere do these attitudes express themselves more powerfully than in the area of employment, where Black people face rampant discrimination associated with their putative ghetto status.

THE ICONIC NEGRO

The iconic ghetto is complemented by the iconic Negro, the image on which many racial stereotypes are built. Over time, the iconic Negro has gone through various incarnations, from the Uncle Tom character of Harriet Beecher Stowe's novel to the clown or buffoon portrayed in a long spate of Hollywood films produced mainly for Whites. Today the iconic Negro is the male criminal bent on destroying life and property.

Stereotypically, he is "big, Black, and scary," someone who might strike fear in the hearts of Whites—and often, in the Hollywood script, meets his demise, dying in a hail of bullets or being beaten to a pulp. In the social hierarchy, today's Black man is assumed to begin from such a low status that it may be difficult for the average White person to appreciate his human qualities. In many powerful respects, the anonymous Black male symbolizes the ghetto, and this image serves as a standard by which all other Blacks may be judged, their credibility hanging in the balance (Welch 2007; Baker 2018).

Consequently, ordinary people often approach an anonymous Black male with some unease, counting his race as a defect he must remedy. His clothing style and other aspects of his self-presentation may be emblematic of the ghetto, further discrediting him. For many in the wider society, the young Black male wearing a hoodie is the personification of trouble. Typically, the Black man is treated as a dangerous outsider until he proves he is worthy of trust. And his Blackness often disqualifies him from White society's superficial standards for common courtesy.

The other notorious and persistent ghetto stereotype is the "welfare queen," an overweight, hyper-fertile, openly sexual, and improperly aggressive Black woman who obtains benefits she doesn't deserve while lounging around and enjoying luxury consumer goods. This image, propagated by Ronald Reagan and other conservative politicians, helped to justify the Clinton administration's abolition of "welfare as we know it"—a key measure among numerous attacks on the social safety net (Edelman 1997). In racially mixed settings, the Black woman with children in tow might be perceived as loud and boisterous, seemingly unfeminine yet sexualized, more bestial than human (Goff et al. 2014; Covert 2019; Lybarger 2019). In shopping malls and on public transportation, she strikes her children and curses them in front of strangers, her face contorted as she barges along among middle-class Black and White people, who sometimes glare at the spectacle in disgust. This icon of the Black woman on welfare hides from the consciousness of most citizens the fact that most families who depend on welfare are White.

The images of the Black criminal and the welfare queen hold a threatening or transgressive status, and these stereotypes encourage the wider society to pigeonhole Blacks and relegate them to the category of "other." These two images may represent, or even personify, a status threat when some Whites observe Blacks who act "uppity."

Occupying the dominant position in the racial hierarchy, and supported by the master status of Whiteness, many Whites have come to expect deference from Blacks who make it out of the ghetto and into "polite society." Some may even still believe that Blacks are biologically inferior and should be grateful for being admitted to racially mixed settings. Behavior that does not fit ordinary expectations may be taken as threatening, and behind that sense of threat, the most insecure Whites fear losing status to Blacks (Blumer 1958).

Although Black people increasingly inhabit diverse positions in society, negative stereotypes persist and adapt to changing social situations. For instance, the ghetto stereotype follows middle-class Black families into the suburbs. Some Whites eye their new neighbors warily because they aren't used to living near Black people. They may think of them as "nice Black people" who are exceptions to their race or suspect they have not arrived through legitimate means. Could they be drug kingpins? How else can you explain a Black man who drives a new Lexus and sends his children to private school?

When Whites encounter Black strangers in public, the iconic ghetto almost invariably serves as a reference point to interpret their identity and the import of their presence, and this may be especially true when the ghetto community is nearby. This association, made in a split second, shapes initial interactions and sometimes never disappears. If the encounter deepens, the Black person has a chance to disabuse the White person of such assumptions, but that always takes work and, often, more time than is available.

Hence, in their quest for decent treatment from members of the wider society, Blacks must constantly manage their identities, adjusting their self-presentation against the stereotype of the iconic Negro. Black people striving for social acceptance may self-consciously use Standard English, mimicking the speech of upper-middle-class Whites, modulating their voices, and self-consciously observing a formal etiquette to project propriety. This self-presentation may come off as stiff and at times pedantic or old-fashioned.

Yet the association of Black skin with the powerful image of the ghetto can easily overwhelm the Black person's best efforts and attract closer scrutiny. As Whites struggle to recalibrate their interactions with the anonymous Black person against the image of the iconic Negro, they may see the person as puzzling, incongruous, or simply out of place.

"George," a middle-aged Black man, describes his children's experience in their integrated schools.

Both my kids had integrated experiences. My son Georgie comes home, and he's at a school in the White neighborhood. It was a magnet school, and mostly White, integrated kids.

So, Georgie comes home one day and says, "We were marching into the auditorium and they started yelling at me, yelling at us to knock the shit out because we were being too loud. And if we were White, they wouldn't have done that."

I said, "Now, where did you get that idea from? We've never had that kind of . . ."

And he said, "I know that."

And then my daughter Ebony comes home, and she said, "You know, Dad, I'm everybody's best Black friend. That's my strength, that's my forte. I'm everybody's best Black friend."

So, even though my kids had a chance through our efforts to integrate, to go into a system where there are White people, and to get some success in that venue, it was still pretty clear to them that because of their skin color, they would always be different in some way. They would always be categorized in that light.

• • •

Many Black males report that they must disavow negative associations through successive positive interactions. To gain the acceptance of Whites, Black men deliberately distance themselves from "big and scary" aspects of the widespread stereotype, behaving as unobtrusively as possible, striving to remain self-contained, moving slowly rather than suddenly, and keeping White people at arm's length. Except among their own kind or with others who have earned their trust, Black people can feel they are always onstage.

BLACK IDENTITY

Out of frustration and in an attempt to rehabilitate their sense of self, in public some young Black men and women actively defy the image of the overly deferential, obsequious Black person. Instead, they present themselves as loud, speak in unmodulated voices, and consciously use "Black English," a dialect that many Whites view as ungrammatical. Deliberately using the markers of the iconic Negro to push back against

Whites' ignorance and control, they refuse to conform to the norms of civility that prevail in White environments, aware that, even if they wanted to, they would never belong, as "Louise," a thirty-five-year-old Black woman, discovered in her youth:

In high school, I told myself I would never use slang because I was like, "I don't want to be one of them," right? This is me trying to separate myself out from the ghetto, right?

Some White kid walked up to me and was like, "Yo, yo, yo."

And I said, "Oh, this is it!" Even though I vowed never to use slang, he still sees me as slang. I was just like, "Ooh, this ain't gonna work."

And even now, I refuse to adjust my language, you know. I am what I am, and I'm still just as capable and smart. I can still be me. I guess that's part of it, right? Like, now that the racial line is so faint, I'd much rather be caught off guard in my own skin than caught off guard pretending to have assimilated.

These young people welcome the confusion of Blackness with a "ghetto" identity because it makes them appear "hip" and "cool." It proves they have not "sold out" to the dominant White society or assimilated into its values, becoming "Oreos." It shows they haven't forgotten where they come from and, by implication, devalued the ghetto.

And some middle-class Black people, as a matter of identity politics, also treat the ghetto as a source of authentication. They go out of their way to actively claim the ghetto by adopting its symbols, including dress styles, speech patterns, or choice of music. In so doing, they conflate a positive Black identity with the ghetto, embracing common stereotypes and falling into the catch-22 that others seek to avoid. They see this as a means of establishing their authenticity as "still Black," despite navigating the largely White middle-class world they feel does not accept them: they want to demonstrate that they haven't "sold out." These people sometimes "code-switch," easily moving back and forth between Black English vernacular and "White" English. For them the 'hood becomes a credential, signifying a peculiar brotherhood of the oppressed that many middle-class Blacks embrace so they can feel they haven't sold out. Thus, the iconic ghetto becomes, paradoxically, both a stigma and a sign of authenticity.

Yet many of these same people spend a good deal of time and energy distancing themselves from the ghetto among their distrustful White counterparts, who need to be impressed again and again. The ghetto follows them into their university, corporation, or medical workplace, and they must wage a constant campaign for a different sort of authentication as bona fide members of their professions.

Thus association with the ghetto may do them psychic good while opening them to treatment as second-class citizens. In using the ghetto as a source of validation, they conflate Black identity with the 'hood. The 'hood becomes a credential, signifying a peculiar brotherhood of the oppressed that many middle-class Blacks buy into. Many also feel some moral responsibility to "look back" to the ghetto—to try to help those they have in fact left behind. Because of their peculiar marginal status between the wider society and their native community, middle-class Blacks can serve as cultural brokers, linking one community with the other and at times interpreting and explaining the ways of one to the "other."

SYMBOLIC RACISM

The old racism of traditional White supremacy is deeply ingrained in a virulent ideology of White racial superiority born out of slavery and the Jim Crow codes, particularly in the Deep South. That sort of racism hinges on the idea that Blacks are an inherently inferior race, a morally null group that deserves subjugation and poverty.

The form of racial prejudice so commonly expressed today is different. While it too was born of America's legacy of slavery and segregation and is informed by those old concepts of racial order—that Blacks have their "place" in society—it also reflects the urban iconography of today's racial inequality: the Black ghetto, a uniquely urban American creation.[2]

While the old-style racism of White supremacy rooted in the institution of slavery still exists, Americans in general now have a much more nuanced, more textured attitude toward race than the nation has witnessed before, and that attitude is not always manifested in overtly hateful, exclusionary, or violent acts. Instead, it underlies a pervasive mindset along with stereotypes implying that all Black people "belong" in the inner-city ghetto and are stigmatized by their association with its putative amorality, danger, crime, and poverty.

But this pervasive cultural association—Black skin equates with the ghetto—does not come out of the blue. Since the days of slavery and Jim Crow, as a result of historical, political, and economic factors, Blacks have been contained in the ghetto. Today, with persistent housing discrimination and the disappearance of manufacturing jobs, America's ghettos face structural poverty, whose social manifestation ties Black people even more closely to the Black caste.

Above all, since to many White Americans the ghetto is "where the Black people live," the misguided logic follows that all Black people live in the ghetto. That pervasive fallacy is at the root of the wider society's perceptions of Black people today. While it may be true that everyone who lives in a certain ghetto is Black, it is patently untrue that everyone who is Black lives in a ghetto. Regardless, Black people of all classes, including those born and raised far from the inner cities and those who've never been in a ghetto, by virtue of skin color alone are stigmatized by the place and victimized by their color caste.

In some ways the iconic ghetto reflects the old version of racism's positing that a Black person's "place" was in the field, in the maid's quarters, or in the back of the bus. If a Black man was found "out of his place" he could be punished, jailed, or lynched. In our day a Black person's "place" is in the ghetto.

If the Black person is found "out of his place," such as treating patients in a hospital, teaching in a university, practicing in an upscale law firm, staying in an upscale hotel, swinging a club on a golf course, or living in a prestigious neighborhood, he may be arbitrarily profiled and treated with suspicion, avoided, pulled over, frisked, arrested—or worse. The rampant police killings of Black people are examples of how this more current type of racial stereotyping works. Someone the White police officer sees exhibiting the emblem of the ghetto—Black skin—is often considered "out of place" in White spaces.

White grievance fuels the iconic ghetto, including an assumption prevalent among White and Black Americans alike, that there are two types of Blacks: those living in the ghetto, who belong to the "street," and those considered "decent," who play by the rules to become successful.

As a result of this pervasive dichotomy—that there are "street Blacks" and "decent Blacks," or "ghetto" and "non-ghetto" Blacks—many decent or middle-class Black people actively work to distance themselves from the ghetto by dressing well and spurning ghetto styles of dress and speech.

One of the most critical implications of this analysis of symbolic racism is that it is based on or deployed against the "iconic Negro" who, others may assume, occupies the very bottom rung of the nation's caste-like racial order. In the urban iconography of the city, this symbolic racism can be peculiarly equal opportunity and engaged in by people of various races and backgrounds.

Through the social process of "distinctive opposition," in which groups realize their identity by distinguishing themselves from those they are opposed to, virtually anyone wishing to be seen as worthwhile may be motivated to claim distinction from this inner-city ghetto icon (Evans-Pritchard [1940] 1969). Such people, including Blacks themselves, are capable of engaging in symbolically racist behavior. In the inner-city ghetto, this shows itself in the recurrent tensions between "street" people and "decent" people and their families. In the larger society, racist Whites are inclined to lump all Black people together and paint them broadly as an inferior caste, distancing themselves from Black people more generally.

CHAPTER 3

THE DEFICIT OF CREDIBILITY

"The Dance"

The iconography of the Black ghetto competes with the plantation system of the old South as a means to define Black people. Given the powerful negative stereotype of the iconic ghetto, especially its putative danger, crime, and poverty, most outsiders, including many Whites from relatively homogeneous residential areas, have learned to be wary of the ghetto's inhabitants. And given the history of the racial injury at the hands of the White majority, many Black people have learned to be wary of White spaces, and of the White people who occupy these spaces, especially those they perceive to wield power there.

When an anonymous Black person enters the White space, often the people there immediately try to make sense of him or her—to determine "who that is," or to figure out the nature of the person's business and whether they need to be concerned. When the Black person is unknown, stereotypes can rule perceptions, creating a situation that can estrange the Black person. In these circumstances, almost any anonymous Black person can experience social distance, especially a young Black male—not because of his merit as a person but because of his Black skin and its indication of "outsider" status in the White space. Thus, such a Black person is burdened with a deficit of credibility, especially in comparison with their White counterparts.

Strikingly, a Black person's deficit may be minimized or tentatively overcome by a performance, a negotiation, or what some Blacks refer to derisively as a "dance," through which individual Blacks may be inclined to show White people and others that ghetto stereotypes do not apply to them personally; in effect, they perform for credibility or for acceptance. This performance can be as deliberate as dressing well and speaking in an educated way or as simple as producing an ID or a driver's license in situations in which this would never be demanded of Whites.

Almost by definition, the Black person performs before a distant, judgmental, and unsympathetic audience of gatekeepers—distant because of the extant racial divide, and judgmental and unsympathetic because their minds are typically already made up about the Black person's "place" and the threat they believe he or she poses to the White space, and perhaps to some of the people standing in judgment. Depending on how effectively the Black person performs or negotiates, he may "pass inspection." But there are no guarantees, for some members of the audience are inclined at times to weaponize their prejudices, to put the Black person in their "place." Moreover, others in the White space may require additional proof on demand.

In public White spaces, like upscale shops or restaurants, many Black people take this sort of racial profiling in stride; they expect it, treat it as a fact of life, and try to go on about their business, hoping to move through the world uneventfully. And most often, with the help of social gloss to ease their passage, they do so (Goffman 1959); however, on occasion they experience blatant discrimination, which may leave them deflated and offended, and which they cannot ignore.

As I noted earlier, White security guards, salesmen, and bouncers often use questions like "Can I help you?" disingenuously—not as a gesture of assistance, but as an occasion for surveillance. Sensing the questioner's ominous tone, a young Black person hears instead "What are you doing here?" Such self-appointed defenders of White spaces prefer indirection over insult in these challenges, if only to avoid the potential for legal troubles down the road. When the anonymous Black person can demonstrate that he or she has business in the White space, by producing an ID card or simply passing an initial inspection, the defending "agents" or gatekeepers may relax their guard, at least for the time being. The Black person may then advance from a deficit of credibility to a provisional status, suggesting a conditional "pass," with the person having something "more to prove."

But as the iconic ghetto hovers overhead, this social plateau simply leads to further evaluations that typically have little to do with the Black person's essential merit as a person and everything to do with his or her Blackness and what it has come to mean in the White space. When venturing into or navigating the White space, Black people endure such challenges repeatedly. In White neighborhoods, Black people may anticipate such profiling or harassment by the neighborhood watch group, whose mission is to monitor the "suspicious-looking." Any anonymous Black male can qualify for close scrutiny, especially under the cover of darkness. Defensive Whites in these circumstances may be less consciously hateful than concerned and fearful of "dangerous and violent" Black people.

In the minds of many of their detractors, to scrutinize and stop Black people is to prevent crime and protect the neighborhood. Thus, for the Black person, particularly young males, virtually every public encounter results in a degree of scrutiny that a "normal" White person would certainly not need to endure. A more subtle but critical version of this kind of profiling occurs in the typical workplace. From the janitor to a middle-level manager, Black people, until they have established themselves, live under the tyranny of the command performance. Around the office building, the Black male worker comes to be known publicly as "the Black guy in my building," and if there are a few such "Black guys" working there who "roam" the premises, White workers at times confuse one with another, occasionally misidentifying the person by name. Given such racial ambiguity, the string of White people standing in line to witness the Black person's performance, or "dance," may encourage those who were once approving or convinced to demand an encore. Thus, as long as the Black person is present in the White space, he or she is likely to be "on," performing before a highly judgmental but socially distant audience. During the performance, by exhibiting "positive" attributes, the Black person presents a front, or social gloss. He or she may take care to dress well, to speak well. Even if the Black person makes this effort, the audience's assumptions are not easy to shake, particularly when he or she is associated with the ghetto (or the 'hood) and is believed to be threatening or dangerous.

In these circumstances, the audience for a Black person's performance has a deep interest in not being impressed; their interest is in defending themselves, which requires thinking of the Black person in a certain way. Conceiving of the person as dangerous justifies the distance the audience displays and has important implications for the perception of Black people in public places, and especially young males. More broadly, this suggests that a new kind of symbolic racism is emerging, one that is strongly associated with the iconography of the ghetto itself, for once the person "passes inspection," he or she can "graduate" to a provisional status. Accordingly, Black skin carries a racial master status that effectively supersedes whatever other status the Black person may seek or claim. Black skin means that one is viewed first as being an outsider, from the ghetto and thus sharing its lowly status (see Hughes 1945; Becker 1963; Anderson 1990).

But through social interaction, Black people may work to persuade others that they do not deserve the treatment commonly meted out to those who might look like them. Hence the distinction between the deficit and the stigma, or provisional status, is one of degree and kind; thus, the deficit status is not necessarily permanent but is malleable, flexible, and can possibly be improved upon, or perhaps discarded altogether—albeit a resolution that is highly unlikely. Once the Black person is able to pass inspection, the deficit of credibility may lessen as others begin to view the person more and more as a credible, competent, law-abiding member of society. And while reaching this milestone is important, it is not the end of the story or the close of the campaign for trust and credibility. In a sense, however, the Black person's work has only begun. Having convinced a few Whites and others of his or her credibility, chiefly by becoming better known, the person must work diligently to continue to behave in ways that put a White audience at ease. In essence, the Black person's credibility is interminably provisional as new occasions of White scrutiny and suspicion require proof at almost every turn.

The impermanence of this position is owing in part to the fact that, in the White space, the Black person will likely encounter many more people who will need to be impressed. In fact, there is often a parade of others needing to be convinced that the presumed stereotypes do not apply. And the string of such people, standing in line to see the Black person's "show," may cause those who were once persuaded to reconsider; to these people, the Black person may need to offer a refresher course. At some point, things may settle down. But because of the competitive fluidity of White space settings, during the current state of race relations, the Black person continues to occupy a precarious status, one that needs constant attention or, from time to time, propping up.

In the nineteenth and early twentieth centuries, when Black people danced in minstrel shows to entertain White audiences for money, no matter how proficient the person's performance, he or she retained the status of entertainer or fool. No Black person could dance well enough to escape Whites' negative attitudes. Of course, there is a significant difference between minstrel shows and contemporary "dances." Back then Black people were performing Blackness; now they perform Whiteness.

The degree of trust a Black person is able to command is to some degree a function of the person's skin shade. If the Black person is light-complexioned, he or she is often trusted more (see Monk 2021b). Light skin may work to distinguish them phenotypically from the mass of Black people residing in the ghetto, and because of this light complexion, these people tend to be more comfortable mimicking the ways of Whites, anticipating the potential social payoff for taking leave of their presumed comfort zone. On the other hand, light-complexioned people in a poor Black community may face challenges from others who use their light skin to discredit them. Hence, certain light-complexioned Black people may overcompensate by presenting themselves as "Blacker than thou" in order to pass as "Black" in the local community—to show that they are "down with the 'hood."

THE MIDDLE CLASS AND THE POOR

Middle-class Black people are typically more familiar with and thus better able to understand the assumptions others make about people like them (Feagin and Sikes 1994), and may be more effective at negotiating their way. And with such understandings, they can work to offset a deficit of credibility with a host of presentation rituals—that is, with an acute sense of propriety. In the wider, White-dominated society, the Black person's burden is persistent, and he or she often acknowledges the need to wage a campaign for credibility. Thus, the icon of the ghetto is one thing for members of the Black middle class—who are often able to "pass inspection"—and another for poor Black people, who typically have greater difficulty. Lighter-complexioned people, too, are generally able to pass inspection more easily than their darker-skinned counterparts; given the relative ease with which they do so, they may be unaware that such a problem exists—or they may pretend as much.

However, because often they are more carefully scrutinized, darker-skinned Black people can become highly attuned and sensitive to slights based on race (Monk 2021b). At the same time, many middle-class Black people are capable of "fronting"—that is, of "code-switching," or smoothly enacting roles and behavior consistent with the expectations of others, depending on the situation (Monk 2021b).

By contrast, lower-class people of the ghetto are more often, but not always, stuck in place and unable to pull off a convincing performance of middle-class propriety. For them, the icon can affect employment, health care, and daily life in ways that both the lay public and social scientists little appreciate. Specifically, the icon hovers, hindering poor

Black people's ability to become employed, increases the likelihood that a police encounter will lead to arrest, and affects the quality of treatment that poor Black people receive in hospital emergency rooms, where diseases may not be given the serious consideration they deserve. Strikingly, middle-class Black people are often easily confused with the poor, which encourages them to be highly sensitive to slights and to meet racism head-on. In observing waiting patterns in hospital emergency rooms, I've noticed that poor Black people tend to defer readily to those in charge and are impressively patient: they are at the mercy of administrators, who hold their lives in the balance (Hughes 1964; Rainwater 1967).

In this fundamental respect, the impact of the iconic ghetto is likely to be highly consequential for the ghetto-dwelling Black person. For unlike middle-class Black people living in the suburbs, poor Black people are unable to deny their residence and its heritage—they really do come from the ghetto. And no matter how hard they may try, they cannot shake off this association. In our highly competitive and increasingly rivalrous society, many Whites, immigrants, and middle-class or "striving" Blacks are inclined to make sure this association sticks. Defining people by the ghetto icon is considered a viable way to know, understand, and distinguish ghetto Blacks. Upwardly mobile or striving Black people may have an immediate interest in making such distinctions, whereas some White people and others tend to employ a broad brush, categorizing all Black people as "ghetto," often taken as an epithet, by placing them at a social distance and treating them as pariahs or outcasts (see Wacquant 2007). The Black middle class vehemently disagrees with this practice, but with limited credibility in the eyes of larger White society, even the well-off are unable to do much about it politically.

Although poor Blacks appear to bear the brunt of the icon's effects, these circumstances present members of the Black middle class with a conundrum. On the one hand, they are Black and therefore have been reared in a race-based society in which the color of their skin has mattered since the day they were born. On the other hand, to get ahead in society—in terms of education and the pursuit of a profession—the modern workplace requires that they behave in universalistic ways, particularly toward members of other ethnic groups. In essence, their "race-based" experience is supposedly no longer relevant to their present everyday professional life. Moreover, even by bringing up the issue of race, the Black person may be perceived as breaking the cardinal rule of a so-called post-racial society. Hence, while millions of Black people continue to live in disenfranchised ghettos, and while the modern workplace is very often a setting of White homogeneity, Blacks are discouraged from advocating for their own people. They are encouraged to remain quiet on racial issues even when others bring those issues up.

To weigh in on racial issues is to run the risk of appearing "racial," a label that works against the Black person in the modern organization. Thus, a Black person's avoidance of the topic, as well as the decision not to advocate hiring other Black people in the workplace, is often instrumental both in nature and design. The maltreatment that Black people experience is often a function of the economic and social marginality felt by those they encounter. In public encounters with Blacks, economically marginal or ethnocentric Whites may be reminded of their own shortcomings or their lack of the material goods that might enhance their sense of well-being. Moreover, when they observe Black people who have such material goods, or even a status higher than their own, they may become disturbed, feeling that their own rights have been abrogated. How did this Black person—his or her color a marker of ghetto status and residence—acquire "all these valued things," particularly material symbols of status, but also economic and social positions of power, privilege, and prestige?

During such encounters, at first blush Whites may determine that people with the Black phenotype are not worthy of respect; they are starting out from the ghetto and therefore need to start further back in the social queue. In this conception, the Black person belongs at the "end of the line," not "where I am, given all the hard work I've done to get here." Such public relations are by nature fleeting. The counterparts typically know little about each other beyond what they perceive on the surface. This surface knowledge may be filled in or augmented by the iconic ghetto and the stereotypes that the ghetto itself inspires.

Despite their immediate association with the iconic ghetto and a host of ghetto-inspired stereotypes, members of the Black middle class are generally able to wage a campaign for respect that works against their presumed deficit. Performing this work can leave them feeling utterly spent and demoralized, but they typically keep this side of themselves hidden from their White counterparts. It may become much too important for them to show that they have self-control, are not whiners, and can "take it well"; many do so successfully, but such performances take their toll psychologically, physiologically, and in other ways. Most often, though, when they relate to White people, Black people present a front, much like what Erving Goffman describes as a presentation of self. To be sure, all people may be inclined to "present" themselves, for many of the reasons Goffman mentions (Goffman 1959).

In these circumstances, in dealing with the racial divide, Black people may feel a need to dissemble. Thus, in some sense, the stereotypes they encounter may not be immediately consequential. The effects tend to accumulate gradually, in time wearing Black people down, sapping their spirit, and turning them into cynical citizens. But many middle-class Blacks take this aspect of their existence for granted. They try to take prejudice and discrimination in stride. Why complain? Many simply rationalize the way they are regarded and the treatment they experience as "a fact of life" or "the hand they've been dealt." While most Blacks do not complain openly to Whites, many others discuss such incidents among themselves, labeling the special price they pay in these incidents the "Black tax." It is a tax they know they are required to pay just for living in America.

In fact, such shared acknowledgments contribute to Black people's background understandings and their dominant narrative of American race relations. In this narrative, Blacks assume that most often White people have the inherent power to prevail over Black people in the ordinary affairs and contests of everyday life. Whenever there is a disagreement or dispute between a Black person and a White person, Blacks expect and understand that the outcome is rigged in the White person's favor. This state of affairs is due to the "deficit of credibility" alluded to above, but it also has to do with institutionalized racism.

As I stated previously, many Black people choose to acknowledge this hazard of their everyday lives only among their own; most want to avoid attracting unwanted attention from their White counterparts— essentially showing that they are wise to the game being waged at their expense. In doing so, they keep hidden a critical problem of daily existence, while resigning themselves to their fate. Hence in quasi-public settings such as the workplace, they "put up with stuff" all day and depart as soon as they are able, only to face it again the next workday; they hope that in time, the situation will improve. Social interactions between Blacks and Whites, in which the power differential is stacked in the White person's favor, are always delicate propositions that require careful management.

For Black people even to attempt to deal with the problem is to risk, as Goffman suggests, "flooding out the situation." Hence Black people often simply defer, dissemble, and, as best they can, try to move forward. Middle-class Blacks tend to have a special set of social skills at their command, along with material resources—money, occupations, and the ability to enact the demeanor required for their relative success. Often, they become effective and meritorious social actors; among their own, they pride themselves on their ability to perform the roles and recite the scripts required to survive in White spaces. Their character and the social resources attendant on it have allowed them to prevail in most social situations. In this vein, the most impressive is the occasional "n****r moment" and other insults they endure. Typically, they can handle such trials and learn from them.

Over time, they develop an exquisite ability to read people and situations, look out for potential conflicts, then handle whatever comes their way—abilities that, for many Black people, continue to be "works in progress." The middle-class Black person who has such special skills can be especially threatening, not so much as a "dangerous" or "fearsome" Black person, but as one whose status and bearing threaten the hegemony of White people in the White space and who thus, in the minds of certain Whites—perhaps the most marginal—needs to be "taken down a notch," to be "put in his place," to be "shown who's boss." In such circumstances, Whites who see such a person might think, "Who does she think she is?!"

Thus, middle-class Black people who have worked so hard to accomplish things and to distinguish themselves run the profound risk of "existing while Black." Such Black people can then suppose themselves to be at risk in almost everything they do—walking while Black, driving while Black, napping while Black, jogging while Black, working while Black, teaching while Black. To the extent that they engage in these behaviors in White space, at times, Black people can feel themselves to be at risk socially, if not physically.

THE WHITE DEFICIT OF CREDIBILITY

Typically when anonymous Black people navigate White space, their social antennae are on high alert. In "the White space," Black folk expect to meet at least three types of White people: those who mean them well, those who don't, and a wide swath of "tolerant" White people with almost no visible racial animus, people they may win to their side. These are people who seem open to friendships with all kinds of people, including Blacks, but who may well be genuinely surprised by their friends' and neighbors' negative reactions when they invite a Black person to their home, recruit a Black person to their workplace, or become intimate with a Black person. For Black people, a primary challenge as they navigate the White space is to be able to tell which kind of White person is which and, when necessary, to take evasive action to protect themselves and their loved ones; typically, gaining such knowledge and understanding is a work in progress.

In White space, Black people may view almost any White person they meet for the first time with a certain wariness; for they may be uncertain about the White person's attitude toward them and of exactly where they stand. Thus, initially, they may display a certain hesitancy and guardedness, and may place the White person in a provisional status, charging him or her with much to prove before earning their trust. Meanwhile, in this setting, they may look around for familiar faces and gravitate toward the few Black people they find. However, this is not without its risks as well; they are concerned not to appear "racial" in circumstances where their appearance as "color-blind" Black people is strongly encouraged.

In the general scheme of things, while in the White space, they know that politically they are on thin ice, and that while the White people in this setting may express open tolerance, they could turn hostile at any moment, their glossy exterior presentation notwithstanding. Moreover, the White people embedded in the White space typically only very rarely have any Black friends, and often know absolutely no Black people. Black people may also presume that the White people they encounter in these spaces, regardless of their politics, are likely to be racially insensitive, if not racist, and thus may be unable to conceive of Black people without prejudice; in face-to-face interaction, Blacks expect the Whites they meet to dissemble, hiding their true feelings about people like them.

Hence, typically, Black people burden these Whites with a deficit of credibility of their own and may implicitly associate them with the menace of the White space, just as many White people burden anonymous Black people by initially associating them with the menace of the iconic ghetto. Hence, anonymous Blacks and Whites begin their relationship with much to prove to each other. While Black people may know and acknowledge these things, for political reasons they may keep such thoughts to themselves, while sharing them only with other Black people, or with those White people whom they have come to know and to trust. And when encountering unknown Whites in such spaces, due to the extant racial divide, full trust may never come.

Strikingly, while perhaps acknowledging these challenges, many White people may bring such presumptions and background understandings to their encounters with Black people and may anticipate being stereotyped as racist or racially insensitive—thus they may become concerned to show that such a stereotype is wrong or does not apply to them. In fact, White people from various walks of life and political persuasion, those who are racially prejudiced and those who are not, may feel obligated to perform tolerance, that is, engaging in what amounts to a performance—their "dance"—or negotiation geared to disabuse Black people, and enlightened White people, of the assumptions that they are racially insensitive or racist.

Their challenge is to convince the Black people and others in their presence that they are not racist or do not look down on Black people—despite their implicit racial connection with or apparent association with the White space.

Social justice movements, including the civil rights movement and now Black Lives Matter, have put the wider, White-dominated society on notice that it has dues to pay, and that there is much work that needs to be done to win the trust of a large and influential segment of Black people and their White allies. This understanding may then be expressed or manifested in shows of civility and tolerance by Whites toward Blacks. In somewhat of a reversal of roles, Black people become the distant and highly judgmental audience for whom a White performance is made.

JAMES

James was an unusual White man with whom I became close friends during my fieldwork in Philadelphia in the early 1980s. He was of Irish descent and grew up in Brooklyn. His family was Catholic and working class, and his folks raised him based on that Catholic morality. His religiously conservative upbringing, his education at a Jesuit college, his military service in West Germany, and the 1960s counterculture were all experiences that ultimately shaped James, making him a person who was open to all kinds of people.

Later James studied for an advanced degree to become an architect, and after working in several different local companies, he landed a job in a major architectural firm in Philadelphia. At the time he was hired, the firm was an extremely White space, a workplace in which the only Black employees were janitors and the like. However, there were at that time many emerging Black architects, including new college graduates from around the nation.

James would seek these graduates out, bringing them to the attention of his colleagues; he would work to recruit these recent graduates into the firm, mentoring them once they were hired. As a result, James's company became one of the few architectural firms with a significant number of Black employees, mainly because James had advocated for them. Unfortunately, this advocacy garnered mixed reviews within James's firm. His sociability and mentoring skills led to jealousy and derision from some of his colleagues.

In time, James's artistic focus changed from architecture to painting and drawing, and his interests in the firm turned to human resources. He was eventually appointed director of human resources, and in this position, he began to directly recruit young Black people and other minorities to the firm. On occasion, he would introduce me to some of these recruits, and I came to know some of them as well. They all had fine things to say about James: he was a wonderful mentor; he was helpful and supportive of them; and he truly made a difference in their careers. Additionally, since many other firms in downtown Philadelphia had no Black people on staff, James helped to increase the number of Black architects working in the city.

CHAPTER 4

THE GHETTO

A Brief Social History

Since the time of slavery in the American South, a powerful but subtle sense of diaspora has shaped the Black community. After Emancipation, increasing numbers of Black families left the plantations for northern as well as southern cities. Although Blacks initially lived near the elite Whites they served, the combination of racial segregation and Black community formation led to the concentration of Black city dwellers in specific neighborhoods even before Emancipation.

Throughout the Great Migration, from the early 1900s to the 1960s, millions of Blacks migrated from the rural South to the cities and towns of the North, the South, the Midwest, and the West. Their stigmatized "place" both preceded and followed them. When Black people settled in their new communities, their reception was decidedly mixed; they were both tolerated and resisted, and as their numbers grew relentlessly, the local White people soon worked to contain them in what became the "Black section" of town.

The settings to which Blacks were relegated were the precursors of the Black ghettos that have proliferated throughout the nation, spaces that symbolically reinforced what slavery established: the lowly place of

Black people in the public mind and the enduring principle of "White over Black." In time all Black people were consigned to the least desirable sections of places they migrated to, often settling "across the tracks" from the White communities (see Spear 1969; Osofsky 1996; Massey and Denton 1998).

In early Philadelphia, particularly in the old Seventh Ward, bounded by South Street on the south, Pine Street on the north, Sixth Street on the east, and Twenty-Third Street on the west—the area W. E. B. Du Bois studied—Blacks settled in the backstreets and alleys among recent European immigrants, people they effectively competed with for place and position, but with whom they also had at times close, even intimate connections. Their homes were typically in these racially mixed neighborhoods that they shared with impoverished Irish, Scottish, and English immigrants, adjacent to the homes of well-to-do Whites, where they and others often worked as servants. In many cases, checkerboard residential patterns prevailed, including buildings, alleys, and blocks that in time became impoverished and all Black or dotted with, say, an Irish family here and a Scottish family there. Over time the area's White population grew larger and became ever more invested in and committed to its own sense of group position. By contrast, the "place" of Black people was anchored in the Black section that was later known as the ghetto (Blumer 1958).

Over time, especially in the minds of the White majority, the ghetto would become a fixture of mental as well as physical space: it would become iconic. Each generation of Whites would become socially invested in maintaining the established lowly place of Black people; these people understood their own identity in terms of whom they opposed, and they typically opposed their Black counterparts. As they competed with these Blacks, their relatively higher position, which they typically struggled to maintain, was passed on from one racist generation to the next. Since the days of slavery, most people had known, believed, or soon found out that Whites were relatively privileged and Blacks were not; that White people were defined as dominant and Black people as subordinate. People who crossed this color line were sanctioned, Blacks more so than Whites, often violently. It was a time of racial conflict over place and space. In those days, skin color served as a bold line, a marker, and a social border that separated Blacks and Whites. And the significance it was given strongly encouraged members of each group to remain among their own kind, but more particularly led Black people to "know" and remain in their lowly social place.

The Black migration was unrelenting, and the nascent settlements attracted newly arriving Black migrants who sheltered in the settings they could afford, where they and their families could expect to feel safe and possibly to thrive.

In time, these neighborhoods developed and expanded as segregated communities; they would later be termed ghettos and take on a more sinister definition and purpose—not just for Blacks but for the wider society as well. Eventually the ghetto would function like a place reminiscent of a reservation, a place where Black people would live and would ultimately be contained. But such areas would be defined as peculiarly negative spaces against which the larger communities could amalgamate as "White" people in defense of their sense of group position (Evans-Pritchard [1940] 1969; Blumer 1958; Ignatiev 1995; Roediger 1991).

In Philadelphia, the "city of neighborhoods," this pattern prevailed and ultimately spread block by block, neighborhood by neighborhood, to other parts of the city. But as the Black sections expanded, in a progression known as "invasion and succession," the White residents typically fled (see Park and Burgess 1925). White municipal governments usually ignored the Black areas, and with limited public services and enforcement of building codes, they were allowed to become blighted slums (see Du Bois 1899; Hunter 2013). As these areas became increasingly segregated, they also became known for their dilapidated housing stock and storefront businesses and had little effective political representation. Moreover, as Whites fled these areas, Black people consolidated their presence, which allowed them to feel protected among their own kind, where they largely lived on their own terms.

As these Black sections continued to expand, newly arriving Black residents filled in the interstitial White spaces and began to encroach on the adjacent White areas, provoking White residents to either act against "the Blacks" or move on. Typically they stood their ground as long as they could, coexisting with their Black neighbors, but eventually they fled. Ultimately, elements of the city's White population embraced the ideology that had supported slavery and Jim Crow, which defined Black people as racially inferior and subordinate in every conceivable way. In time, the unrelenting influx of Blacks discouraged cooperation or integration between the races, and racial tensions inspired sharp and enduring stereotypes, prejudice, and discrimination toward Black people.

But most critically, the ethnic White immigrants developed, elaborated, and embraced an identity as "Whites" in distinction to "the Blacks," powerfully informing their conception of the iconic ghetto and the people who occupied it, but also of their sense of who they themselves were and hoped to remain. As the larger White community made its peace with the growing Black presence, it ultimately worked to contain Blacks while allowing them to carve out their own subordinate spaces within the wider institutional framework.

As the influx of Black people continued to grow, the development of local Black settlements set the stage for their separation and growth apart from the wider White community. When venturing outside these local enclaves, Blacks faced harassment and violence at the hands of Whites, especially youth gangs. Also, racial restrictions, or "restrictive covenants," placed on White-owned properties discouraged the owners from selling to "Negroes and Jews" (see Gotham 2000).

Moreover, for Blacks who defied this discouragement and settled in White areas, violence typically awaited in the form of sticks and stones, the burning of crosses in the front yard, and even setting fire to their new homes (Esper 1985). Such Black people were reoriented to the Black spaces, where they were effectively contained.[1]

Black neighborhoods became refuges where Blacks could get away from Whites—backstage areas where they could relax among their own, especially Black people who ventured into White spaces for work. Blacks could also feel protected by the principle of safety in numbers. And these communities served as a beacon of hope, a haven for Blacks new to the area; they attracted Black people on the move, and sometimes those on the run (see Goffman 2014).[2]

A mutually beneficial relationship often developed between the White and Black spaces as Black people provided labor to the White society and the White society gave Blacks job opportunities. In Philadelphia the Budd Company and many other factories and White-owned businesses were major employers. In traveling to work, however, Black people often passed through White spaces, trips fraught with uncertainty and danger. After leaving work, Blacks were encouraged to return to their own communities. People with jobs bought homes and supported businesses and churches in the local Black neighborhoods. These segregated communities were reinforced and solidified by working-class men and women who labored in hospitals, factories, wealthy and middle-class White households, and local small businesses.

In time, these Black businesses developed, particularly in those niches where Black people could be uniquely served. These enterprises included insurance companies, beauty shops, barbershops, hotels, taverns and speakeasies, restaurants, caterers, and funeral homes. Blacks sought them out and supported them. The nascent ghetto was born out of these small enclaves. Eventually Black communities grew large enough to support and expand their own institutional structures. The ghetto community provided social nurturance apart from the dominant society, with its own social system of checks and balances, its own distinctive social order (see Cayton and Drake 1945).

George's family owned one such community business:

My parents owned a small business, a small mom-and-pop store, grocery store in the middle of that community. My dad raised the capital to buy this business by hitting the numbers. There were no banks, no venture capital funds, no association or cooperative that he could go to and easily get the money he needed, so he hit the numbers—poor man's stock market, Black man's stock market—and bought a small business in the middle of a small community that transitioned from White to Black in southwestern Philadelphia. We were part of the community. We supported community organizations; we hired young people from the neighborhood. The old lady who got her food on disability and got her check once a month, we gave her credit until she got her paycheck, and then she came and paid it. We delivered her food to her so that she could eat. We looked out for people.

And all those fifteen years, when there was crime and organized mayhem going on all across the city, all around us, we were never robbed or violently assaulted in any way. The community supported us and accepted us.

• • •

As they developed, these Black sections of the city had their unique challenges. Because of their status as "where the Black people lived," almost by definition the wider White society considered them inferior in quality of life, politics, and economic clout. And their municipal services were seldom if ever equal to those in the White community. The Black church became a social locus, and political representation emerged as a force and inspired a rich Black cultural tradition (Lincoln and Mamiya 1990). Social and political leadership groups were nurtured and formed primarily as a service to the local community, but also to reckon with the White powers that be, to lobby for the interests of the Black community.

If at first the White community seemed unconcerned by the expansion of the Black community, over time it came to view the Black presence as a problem it needed to contain. Black communities suffered attacks, some physical and some political, as socially restrictive laws were passed. There were outright calls to restrain the Black community, which defended itself by drawing residents together and giving migrating Blacks a haven from the racism of the wider society. Over time, depending on the size of the town and what it had to offer Black labor, these small Black enclaves grew into massive urban ghettos. The larger and more successful such Black communities grew, the greater became the Whites' efforts to suppress them, particularly when Whites saw Blacks as a threat (Madigan 2003; Albright et al. 2021). Through successive White political administrations, policies pushed the Black ghetto further into poverty and disenfranchisement.

Over time the iconic Black ghetto reinforced what the institution of slavery had established: the "place" of Black people at the bottom of the American racial order, a peculiar place in this society. This place, of course, had its roots in chattel slavery, and in this new incarnation, it was widely taken for granted that Blacks were to live and work in a world apart from and subordinate to the White society in almost every respect, from the law and politics to economics. Blacks were simply not to enjoy the full duties, obligations, and rights that accrued to their White counterparts.

Moreover, the civil law was understood to favor Whites over Black people. Blacks were on their own, left to settle their disputes informally and to care for their own civic needs. In the Black community, city services were not always forthcoming, and local building codes often were not applied uniformly (Hunter 2013). What this meant practically was that swaths of the Black community were left to become blighted and vulnerable to the criminal element. Black sections changed fundamentally from havens for Black people to slums that were increasingly impoverished, unattractive, and dangerous. With this ghettoization, Whites' perceptions of such communities changed as well: from regarding them as benign to considering them increasingly dangerous, impenetrable, and threatening. A self-fulfilling prophecy was set in motion.

By the early twentieth century, Blacks and recent immigrants were consigned to dilapidated neighborhoods near the urban core, and working-class Whites were moving to the inner suburbs, aided first by mass transit and later by highway construction and broader car ownership. The cycle of blockbusting, White flight, neighborhood succession, and redlining that became notorious in the 1960s was already at work by the end of World War II (Sugrue 1996; Massey and Denton 1998; Rothstein 2017). Blacks responded by creating myriad cross-class social and religious institutions and a vibrant cultural life, and there they found acceptance and security that to some degree countered the hostile discrimination they faced outside their community. A uniquely American style of racial segregation, even apartheid, developed that not only relegated African Americans to second-class citizenship but also confined them to delimited, ghettoized spaces in the city.

SOCIAL CONTEXT

The history of race relations in this country—from slavery and Emancipation through the two world wars, and from the migration north to the civil rights movement—has left many Blacks feeling permanently slighted if not still oppressed. This account relates the Black experience in Philadelphia from Du Bois's day to the present, placing in social-historical perspective the position of Black people as well as the social processes they now navigate in the city.

In 1899 W. E. B. Du Bois made sense of the social organization of Philadelphia's Black community by developing a typology of four classes: the well-to-do; the decent, hardworking families who were doing relatively well; the "worthy poor," who were working or trying to work but barely making ends meet; and the "submerged tenth," who were floundering below the minimum level of socioeconomic viability. This stratification system, embedded in the structure of the industrial city under White supremacy, existed apart from the wider White society and encompassed everyone who exhibited a Black phenotype. No matter how affluent or educated they were, "Philadelphia Negroes" lived in the ghetto. Black professionals served other Blacks.

The immediate legacy of slavery was a White supremacist ideology that defined people of African descent as less than human, innately inferior to the country's White majority. This ideology and the all-encompassing inequalities it justified persisted long after Emancipation. Throughout the Great Migration, African Americans were commonly relegated to the most menial positions.

In Philadelphia, the educated few managed to attain positions as schoolteachers, doctors, lawyers, ministers, and small-business owners, but the vast majority were consigned to a subordinate position through racial exclusion, segregation, and economic subjugation. Generally Blacks could get only the least desirable, lowest-paid jobs, and they were the last hired and first fired (Du Bois [1899] 1996). In public, Blacks were consistently treated as second-class citizens. Blacks who migrated from the South to Philadelphia after the Civil War worked hard to learn marketable skills. Their entry into the trades and niche markets such as catering allowed them to gain a precarious foothold in the local occupational structure. During the late nineteenth and early twentieth centuries, however, recurring waves of European immigration depressed their economic position. New White immigrants consistently leapfrogged over African Americans in the labor market.[3] As the newcomers competed directly with the growing Black population, their Whiteness trumped their foreignness, and they parlayed that racial advantage into a better social and economic position than was available to Blacks (Du Bois 1899; Lieberson 1981; Davis and Haller 1998). While some Black men got jobs as laborers, most Black women were confined to domestic service, and both were vulnerable to unemployment. For a long time these arrangements undergirded, supported, and elaborated the powerful caste-like system of racial exclusion, resulting in ever more profound inequality. With World War I, however, the combination of economic expansion and immigration restriction generated demand that could be met only by Black labor.

During World War II, there was enough work for everyone, including Blacks. By the 1950s, few Whites competed with Blacks for jobs, and White working-class Philadelphians seldom lived in the same neighborhoods as Black Philadelphians. As the racial composition of neighborhoods changed when Whites moved to the suburbs and were replaced by poor Black families, the city became even more segregated.

The influx of southern migrants into Philadelphia that accelerated during the two world wars and continued through the 1950s led to rapid growth in the Black working-class population. Typically, after a few venturesome souls had established a local beachhead, relatives and friends joined them in urban ghettos or Black "areas of first settlement" in Philadelphia. The men secured relatively well-paid, low-skill factory jobs. With the support of the neighborhood, local Black institutions, and the church, including the lively "storefront" churches newcomers established in the city, migrants were able to improve their own and their children's life chances. Whole extended families moved north, and a new generation came to maturity in postwar Philadelphia.

These socioeconomic developments in themselves did little to dismantle or even unsettle the caste-like system of race relations existing in Philadelphia and other northern cities. It was the critical mass of Black people moving into these new areas that invigorated the ghetto both socially and economically. Suddenly unburdened of the most repressive strictures of racial caste, Blacks began to develop a new sense of self and social orientation as they envisioned racial equality.

For the first time, many Black people saw themselves on equal footing with Whites, working among them, even living in "their" neighborhoods—if only for the short time it took for the Whites to flee. Though they were still separate and unequal, this situation was very different from what they'd left behind. Now they could compare themselves with Whites, measuring themselves against what the "White man" had and raising questions about the disparities they observed. Their new socioeconomic condition raised many African Americans' expectations and led them to develop a greater sense of entitlement—not so much as Blacks but as citizens.

Black people's new more critical and assertive perception of self in relation to the wider system of social stratification (Pettigrew 1980) had far-reaching ramifications. With continuing migration, the fuller participation of Black soldiers in the military, and a rising standard of living for large numbers of Black city dwellers, African Americans increasingly questioned their second-class status. Their leaders turned their attention to challenging the system and petitioning for full inclusion. In this fraught situation, Black Americans raised the issue of what it meant to be a citizen, eligible for all the rights, obligations, and duties that citizens were supposed to enjoy, yet to be denied the ability to exercise those rights in crucial aspects of public life.

Across the United States, these persistent tensions and profound social questions culminated in the modern civil rights movement (Pettigrew 1980; Morris 1984; Williams 1989). Here the concept of American equality was on trial. Sit-ins, demonstrations, and mass boycotts challenging segregation made the situation utterly untenable across the South. With productive competition between leaders such as Whitney Young and the Reverend Martin Luther King Jr. and militants such as Stokely Carmichael (later Kwame Turé), H. Rap Brown (later Jamil Abdullah Al-Amin), and Malcolm X (formerly Malcolm Little, later el-Hajj Malik el-Shabazz), tension arose not only across racial lines but also over the meaning of Black identity. In this tumultuous time, the United States made incremental progress toward full citizenship and greater inclusion of Black Americans.

Eventually these conflicts precipitated civil disorders in many urban centers, including Philadelphia, and inaugurated a new and provocative phase of the movement. Of course not all Blacks rioted or otherwise participated in the civil disturbances of the day. But enough did so to attract the attention of the rest of the country and the world.

After the 1965 Watts uprising, riots became politically and socially contagious, occurring in city after city across the country and culminating in the massive destruction that followed the assassination of Martin Luther King in 1968. Many younger Black people all but gave up on a system that drafted them for patriotic sacrifice during the Vietnam War while simultaneously withholding the privileges of first-class citizenship.

The promised paradise of consumer goods eluded them too, as unemployment and underemployment remained endemic in Black communities. Many people became deeply disturbed and alienated by these contradictions.[4] The civil rights movement had highlighted the disparity between Blacks' and Whites' rights and privileges, but there seemed to be no way to address the most deep-rooted injustices, including police brutality, poverty, and the powerlessness of inner-city residents. Philadelphia experienced demonstrations and riots in some of the most concentrated ghetto areas. In response to these "long, hot summers," the administration of President Lyndon B. Johnson formed the National Advisory Commission on Civil Disorders, known as the Kerner Commission, to study the causes of the civil unrest.

In light of the landmark 1954 Supreme Court decision in *Brown v.*

Board of Education, which, more than a decade earlier, had declared the state-sponsored segregation of schools unconstitutional, the conclusion reached in the commission's report could not have been more alarming: "Our nation is moving toward two societies, one black, one White—separate and unequal" (Kerner Commission 1968). The report interpreted the ghetto uprisings as a response to pervasive exclusion and discrimination rooted in "White racism," a system it likened to South Africa's notorious apartheid. Initial public denials were followed by debate and hand-wringing by public officials, and eventually progressive social legislation was enacted, most notably affirmative action, set-asides, and "fair housing" laws, which effectively ameliorated racial tensions. These policies favored the growth of the Black middle class and enhanced Black citizens' tentative sense of enfranchisement.

These developments had profoundly ambiguous effects on the African American class structure. The federal government, in partnership with major cities, declared a "War on Poverty," in theory to address the economic marginality of urban dwellers. Although some community organizers agitated for the "maximum feasible participation of the poor" in designing anti-poverty programs, social service agencies and economic development corporations enlarged career opportunities for the middle class while doing little to promote employment for the poor—what Daniel Patrick Moynihan (1970) called maximum feasible misunderstanding.

At the same time, American government, business, and academia began reaching out to bring Black people into the White establishment (Zweigenhaft and Domhoff 1991). Business, academic, and political leaders made strenuous efforts to increase the number of visible Blacks in any establishment that was open to the public, giving rise to criticism of "window dressing." These policy initiatives helped increasing numbers of Black people pursue college and professional educations, obtain rewarding employment, and move into the middle class, but they were met by a severe backlash from many Whites who felt their own rights were being undermined by programs designed to extend opportunities to Blacks.

Yet many socially comfortable and politically liberal White people became supporters and mentors to Black people entering their workplaces. Fundamental change was occurring in the Black class structure, a change first formally observed by William Julius Wilson in *The Declining Significance of Race* (1978). For the first time in American history, Wilson argued, class was becoming more important than race in determining the life chances of Black Americans. The caste-like system of race relations according to which the Black community had long been organized was changing as middle-class Black people were finally able to make their way in the wider White society while poor Blacks were increasingly isolated in neighborhoods of concentrated poverty.

With the enactment and enforcement of fair housing legislation, Blacks who now had the resources that homeownership required were able to leave the ghetto and venture into areas formerly reserved for White people. The process transformed neighborhoods in Philadelphia and around the country. Typically, as Black people moved into White areas, racial tensions were heightened, and when the Black presence rose beyond a certain "tipping point," Whites would leave the neighborhood. Areas that formerly had been all White and closed to Blacks gradually changed from White to Black, and they seldom if ever changed back, except in cases of gentrification (Anderson 1990). Those neighborhoods had exhibited some ethnic diversity before Black families arrived, but when the Black middle class began to move in, it was treated as a signal for many ethnic Whites to leave.

For a short time, in response to the interest of prospective Black homeowners, property values in these all-White areas rose, with Black home buyers often paying exorbitant prices. Realtors engaged in "blockbusting," scaring Whites into selling their homes at below-market rates and then reselling them to Blacks at inflated prices. As Black families succeeded Whites, property values plummeted, eventually bringing some neighborhoods within reach of working-class and poor Blacks. A critical mass of such people, typically described as southern migrants with "ignorant country ways," was said to discourage the middle-class

Blacks who had preceded them and to presage their departure. The combination of cultural discomfort and declining property values with the prospect of a better environment elsewhere prompted the middle class to move on, leaving the area to the working class and the poor. In the typical scenario, public services such as garbage collection, housing code enforcement, and schools declined markedly, creating blight and slum conditions and, in effect, replicating the racialized urban ghetto. In contrast to the Black communities of the past, inner-city neighborhoods now had relatively few middle-class residents and became more and more disconnected from the labor market and other institutions of mainstream society.

Over time, class positions became increasingly dependent on achievement and less on ascription. The lighter-skinned descendants of the colortocracy and the darker-skinned descendants of the working class regularly encountered one another on more or less equal terms in American institutions. Businesses, government bureaucracies, and professional employers had little or no stake in the color-caste system; they employed qualified Blacks of all shades, making few distinctions among them. These practices have contributed to a trend toward political and social integration within the Black community, which no longer respects only the dictates of the traditional elite.

As the civil rights movement gathered steam, young people from relatively privileged backgrounds, including those with lighter skin, embraced Black consciousness and joined their darker-skinned peers in criticizing both the exclusionary White system and the elitist old guard of the Black community. At times they became extremely militant, castigating both the wider White society and their elders, often in the same breath.

The changes brought by progressive policies and practices affected not only the wider social system but also the African American class structure. One of the most underappreciated but profound consequences was the destabilization of the former system by which Black society had long been set apart from White society and internally organized based on human capital that was mediated by skin shade.

Affirmative action policies, which were largely indifferent to variations in complexion among Blacks, effectively worked to blur these differences in the Black community by providing qualified darker-skinned people from the old working class with the same opportunities as lighter-skinned members of the old colortocracy (Anderson 2000; Appelrouth and Edles 2008).

A certain egalitarianism was introduced into the emerging Black color-caste and class configuration. Lighter-skinned Blacks' privileged position compared with darker Blacks was diminished. Blacks of all hues began attending formerly White universities, working in formerly White companies and hospitals, and teaching in formerly White schools and colleges. These developments affected historically Black institutions, which in light of such far-reaching changes in the wider society could no longer afford to discriminate so boldly in favor of the colortocracy. The barriers of racial caste gradually gave way to a locally more inclusive atmosphere. Corporations, universities, and government agencies began to usurp control of interracial relations from the colortocracy. Status within the Black community became somewhat less arbitrary as color-caste inequality was undermined.

Today, a century after Du Bois, his typology is still recognizable, even as the overall circumstances of the African American community in Philadelphia have changed dramatically. Those with the resources to move out have breached the ghetto walls. The Black population has not only continued to increase but has also dispersed widely throughout the metropolitan area. Black Philadelphians now live in many formerly White areas throughout the city and region, but their location varies by economic class (Sharkey 2014; Alba, Logan, and Stults 2000).

The old Seventh Ward of Du Bois's day has now been gentrified, but structural poverty has engulfed many Black neighborhoods in South, Southwest, West, and North Philadelphia. The Black middle class can be found in racially mixed Mount Airy, Germantown, Yeadon, West Philadelphia, and parts of North Philadelphia such as West Oak Lane, as well as in neighborhoods bordering areas of concentrated poverty. For the time being, the Black elite resides in predominantly White and affluent areas such as Chestnut Hill, Cheltenham, Society Hill, and parts of Yeadon.

RACIAL INCORPORATION

The peaceful civil rights movement and ensuing disorder was national in scope and brought about institutions' attempts to incorporate Black people. The revelation of the Kerner Commission's 1968 report—that major changes were needed in the relationship between Black people and their government to alleviate the problems of "White racism"—signaled the beginning of what I have described as the "racial incorporation process," a set of measures designed to bring Black people into the system as full citizens with equal rights, protections, and opportunities under the law. Second-class citizenship was to become a thing of the past.

Affirmative action became one tool of racial incorporation. Through this process, the system placed a premium on Black skin and tried to give companies, universities, and government agencies incentives to integrate their workplaces. This created wholesale mobility for Black Americans, energized in large part by a movement to alleviate the discrimination and exclusion that were such an important part of the legacy of slavery and White supremacy—and, more immediately, to "cool out the long, hot summers" besetting the ghettos of the major urban centers of the country. Of all the changes in public policy, "affirmative action" was the most provocative and most consequential.

These policies worked to open up the wider society and reminded White citizens to behave more tolerantly toward Black people. Major universities not only reached out and recruited Black students but also inaugurated Black Studies programs, while both White and Black students called for "relevant" courses. A national conversation on race relations occurred; indeed, White America had little choice but to participate. To be sure, there was pushback from the political Right, but amid the ongoing urban conflagration, a sense of urgency prevailed, and the political momentum remained with the Left. Over the long term, this positive energy for social change morphed into a broad ethos of civic tolerance toward Black people, and ultimately for various others who constituted the growing "diversity" of urban America.

The problem of Black inequality had become apparent to all, and the powers of the day judged that racial inequality had no place in modern-day America. Perhaps the situation was acceptable in the "backward South," but not in the North and East. It was these attitudes about the failings of the American opportunity structure that encouraged numerous privileged White youths to join the civil rights movement and to assist disenfranchised Black people not only to form and reinforce a movement for justice but also to create an America that embodied the ideas America is meant to stand for. With this momentum, racial incorporation became a reality for many Americans. Black people were suddenly showing up and being better received than ever before. Given the cumulative effect of generations of racialized second-class citizenship, underscored and reinforced by ghetto residence, the wider White society—and those identifying with it—often developed and solidified a group position that worked to further exacerbate racial inequality.

As a result of racial incorporation, major changes have occurred in the American occupational structure, with important implications and consequences. Because of these changes, the Black middle class has grown phenomenally. Almost everywhere across the United States, Black people can now be found participating at various levels of society in positions and occupations that would have been unthinkable for their ancestors. People of color are now broadly represented in almost every area of American society.

For Blacks these changes have meant that more and more Black people have been able to access the system and leave the ghetto behind. As mobile Blacks left, the ghetto underwent a radical transformation. Soon, rather than providing a haven that protected Black people from racism, the ghetto became a reservation for the poor and disenfranchised. Within the urban ghetto today, the most disenfranchised Blacks stagger under the burden of persistent urban poverty, which becomes powerfully conflated with race. Thus, despite the remarkable progress, the Black ghetto persists as a testament to lasting racial inequality (see Hinton 2017). Nonetheless, for Black people who have left, it continues to be a reminder of their roots.

• • •

One warm September weekday around 2:00 p.m., in another of Philadelphia's ghetto neighborhoods, I stopped at a corner tavern that served as a hangout for a number of retired Black men. A subset of these men work as gypsy cab drivers. These elderly men receive Social Security, pensions, or veterans' pay. Their driving is usually a side hustle to help them make ends meet, but many of them have financial capital that most people in the ghetto lack. Their family car, a "dream car" they, now in old age, have been able to acquire, is typically a heavy, comfortable one such as an older-model Buick 225, a Ford Crown Victoria, an Oldsmobile 98, or maybe even a Lincoln Town Car. They provide comfortable rides for local people without other transportation. Their customers are often single mothers who don't have a man with a car, and they depend on these gypsy cabs to get to the Safeway grocery store, to a friend's home, or downtown.

At the tavern, these men are free and loose. They have fun hanging out together, with no set schedule. Often they rehash or relive how they started out in Philadelphia, narrating the stories of their lives and the challenges they faced, particularly instances of racial discrimination. From their position of financial stability, they criticize those who live around them, who are often financially challenged. They hold forth on social life, comparing themselves favorably with others they view as less fortunate, and find themselves superior. Typically the tavern buzzes with conversation, occasionally interrupted by women who stop by to ask for a ride. The men may chitchat and engage socially, but it's always with an eye to the general context of the city and its race relations. Their conversation necessarily recounts issues that Black people have faced historically as well as in the present.

I came upon a conversation one day as Fred offered the group his

theory on the difference between the southern White man and the
northern White man.

"*The southern White man lets you know right away if he likes you,*"
said Fred. "*If he likes you, he might invite you to his house for dinner.
He'll say, 'Come to my house and have dinner.' Now, the northern White
man will get in your face and say he's crazy about you. He'll invite you
to his house and serve you dinner, but as soon as you leave, he'll throw
your plate away. He'll throw your glass away. He'll tell his family,
'I don't want that n****r in my house.' He'll say, 'I don't want that
n****r coming over here.' He'll pretend. I don't like people who are
hypocritical. I like people to be real with me.*"

John interrupted Fred with "*When I first came here in 1947, me
and some boys were working up there at Broad and Columbia. There
was a bar on the corner run by an Irishman. And we went in there and
started to buy beer. It was draft beer, ten cents a glass. And as fast as
we'd drink a beer, the man would break the glasses.*"

"*Sho' would,*" said Fred, agreeing with the gist of John's story. It
made sense to him, resonating with his own experience.

John continued, "*That was in 1947, at Broad and Columbia Avenue.
You know the bar at Broad and Race, up the street from Hahnemann
Hospital? When I first came to Philadelphia, I used to work at
Hahnemann Hospital. I was trying to support my family back then.
I had two jobs, and Hahnemann Hospital was my night job. Okay,
there was a bar on that corner. I forget what the name of it was. But
they did identically the same thing. They used to break your glasses.
They'd serve you, but then they'd insult you, so you wouldn't come back.
Soon as you got through drinking, they'd throw the glass away. They'd
throw it in the trash can and break it.*"

"*Now, you know Fisher's Restaurant at Broad and Tioga,*" John went
on. "*Well, you know, my church is right across the street. When I came
here, now I'd been in the food service business for a long time. I served
presidents. I came here [Philadelphia] trying to get a job in food service. I went downtown, had my records, downtown, at Eighteenth and
Market. At that time they were specializing in restaurant employees.*"

"A guy from the employment office called me at home and said, 'John, I got just the job for you.' I said, 'Yeah?' and he said, 'Get down there right away; they need a man of good experience, a man who knows what he's doing, and with your record, I think you'd work out.' Now, I used to work at hotels, Royal Palm Beach, the DeSoto in Savannah, all across the country. I worked the Grand Union in Saratoga. I was all over. And I was first captain in the hotel down in Georgia. This guy knew about my background, and he told me, 'With your background, they need you.' He says, 'Get down there in a hurry.'

"And so I rush down to Fisher's Restaurant. Now this is in the sixties, and I went to Fisher's Restaurant to get the job. And when I walked in there, the [White] man met me at the door. You know, like they used to do in Georgia. That's how they used to do it in the South. He said, 'Can I help you?' I said, 'Yes. My name is John Frazier, and I come to do such-and-such a thing. I was sent here by the employment office, and they said you had a job open for me.' And the man said, 'Wait a minute,' and then he goes back to see about this, to talk to Mr. So-and-So about it.

"Now this is within an hour of the time when the man [at the employment office] called me, and I got down there right away. I rushed downtown. Now, I was living up with my sister in Oak Lane. I didn't take the trolley; I drove down there to save time, to get there in a hurry, within an hour's time. The man at the employment office had me rush down there. Now this job is only for a waiter. So he says to me, 'Wait a minute.' He went to the back, and he came out, and then he says to me, 'Oh, I'm sorry, John, but that job's been taken.' And I say, 'Been taken?!' And the man says, 'That job went yesterday.' And I say, 'What?! Yesterday? They just called me.'

"So when I went back to the employment office the man says, 'Did you get on?' and I said, 'The job was taken yesterday.' And he said, 'That can't be! The job's been taken? That can't be. The man just called me an hour and a half ago. I called you telling you to rush down there.' So he called the man on the phone. This is a White guy too, and they talk. 'Oh, ah, oh, ah. That's bad, I'm sorry to hear that. This guy was qualified. He's overqualified.'" John explained, "Well, when I was at the *restaurant and told the guy what experience I had, the man at the job said, 'With your record, you're too qualified. You don't want to work here.' But I said, 'I'm interested in the job.'*

"Now, getting to the key [point], Blacks used to go in Fisher's."

Fred interrupted, "They still go in there!"

John continued, "They used to go in there and wouldn't get served. You'd go in there and sit down, and they would run you out. You'd go in there and sit, and they'd walk around you.

"Leon Sullivan was my pastor. They came back to his church, right across the street [from Fisher's], and people would tell him what Fisher's was doing. So Leon sent a committee. Leon wasn't no fool, and he didn't take their word that this was happening. He sent a special committee over there one Sunday after church. He said, 'Y'all go over there to Fisher's Restaurant, and we'll see if this is true.'"

Suddenly John was interrupted by somebody who wanted a ride. "How far you got to go?" he asked.

"Chesapeake Place," she answered.

"I never took anybody there," he said, "but I need to get twenty for goin' that far."

Getting back to the conversation, John continued, "So what I was saying, here's what happened. Leon sent a committee there, right? And the committee went in there and sat. They sat and sat and sat for over an hour, and didn't get no service. The next week, Leon sent another committee in. And they went in the next week, and the same thing happened.

"After that, Leon himself went over there. He walked in and sat at a table. He sat there for thirty minutes with his committee, and then a man came up and walked away. Leon told him he wanted to see the manager, and he told the manager, 'Look, I been hearing about this restaurant for a long time. And I've sent two committees over here, and they've been ignored.'

"And Leon said, 'Let me tell you something. I've been here thirty minutes, and nobody gave me a menu or said anything to me. But let me tell you something. You see that church across the street? That's my* *church. That's Zion Baptist Church. If I hear any more complaints with discrimination in this restaurant or being ignored, Sunday morning after church—we're not going to stone your place or break your windows or burn you out, or anything like that—but Sunday morning after church is over (and we've got five thousand members over there), we're going to have five thousand members in this line.' And the manager said, 'Oh, Rev, oh, Rev. We're sorry, we're sorry. We didn't mean that. Somebody must have made a mistake.'*

"That's when Fisher's Restaurant started serving Black people," John said. "That was on Broad Street, and that was in the seventies."

CHAPTER 5

A PORTRAIT
OF THE GHETTO

A prime example of a ghetto is the neighborhood in Philadelphia known as Southwest. For many Philadelphians, the neighborhood is not only a physical space, but also it is a mental construct, a place with a local reputation that fuels stereotypes about the "place where Black people live." Before Black people came, its residents were White Anglo-Saxon Protestants (WASPs), Irish Catholics, and Jews, but now the people inhabiting Southwest are predominantly poor African Americans, with a few Latinos, Asians, and Africans. The neighborhood is just to the southwest of West Philadelphia, near the University of Pennsylvania and across the Forty-Ninth Street bridge, a powerful social border.

On the east side of the bridge and beyond is the University City community. It is racially and economically mixed and, to a degree, gentrified; it's generally assumed that well-to-do Whites are moving in while working-class and poor Black people are "on their way out." It's only a matter of time. Politically the community is moderately progressive. It suffers a significant amount of crime, in part because of the poor and desperate people who live within the University City community and across the bridge into Southwest, where persistent poverty is widespread. The racially mixed community is juxtaposed with urban poverty. It's an uneasy balance, with issues of race, poverty, and crime that are prevalent in similar edge areas around the United States, where well-to-do Whites and Blacks live close to poverty and desperation.

In this edge area, on the streets and in other public spaces, until they get a closer look Whites sometimes confuse their Black middle-class neighbors with the poor Blacks they fear. The political correctness of these progressive-minded Whites often falls by the wayside when their safety and security are on the line. Thus, when they encounter people with Black skin they are generally wary. This behavior often angers middle-class Blacks, but for the most part they understand. However, such situations signal the precariousness of their own social position. Largely a problem of perception anchored in background understandings of race, such interactions between Blacks and Whites in public places are a fault line in America's wider race relations.

Just across the Forty-Ninth Street bridge from University City is a community recreation center where I have carried out fieldwork over many years. "Donny," a leader of the community and one of my informants, introduced me to others in this Southwest ghetto setting. He proudly speaks of what he and other leaders of the area have been able to accomplish for young people of the community, especially in acquiring resources like computers, tutors, and coaches for local athletic teams. Donny is a man on a mission, and his enthusiasm is infectious. He believes he can make a difference by making himself fully available to the young people of the neighborhood, where poverty and alienation are deeply entrenched. He calls these young people his kids and does whatever he can to hook them up with summer jobs and after-school programs. With his influence, he has been able to engage local political leaders with his mission. As a result, the center has recently been taken over by the city and now includes a full-time recreational director with staff.

Donny lives in a middle-class section of the city but devotes his time to this ghetto setting so he can "give something back" to his community. "His community" is the Black community at large; the more immediate area surrounding the center is predominantly Black and poor but includes increasing numbers of African and Asian immigrants, whom Donny embraces as well. In many respects, Donny is a genuine "old head"—an older person who feels a responsibility to the community and its people. He is particularly concerned because he feels many young Black men and women fail to take responsibility for their lives and actions. He understands that many of them have their faults, but he is also acutely aware of the challenges they face in the White spaces of the larger society and the prevalence of malignant prejudice and discrimination toward Black people, particularly on the part of potential employers. His chief aim is to improve young Black men's outlook through guidance and through the recreation center, and he has devoted a great deal of his time and resources to making the center a safe place.

The community center and the surrounding area have been through a lot of changes: as manufacturing declined, the neighborhood itself began to change; some people might attribute this change to the classic invasion and succession model introduced by Park, Burgess, and McKenzie (1925). As Blacks began to move in, Whites gradually moved out and more Blacks began to take their place. The consequences are visible not just demographically but also in terms of institutional engagement with the neighborhood. Today blight is everywhere: the police are rarely seen and drive past rapidly when they do appear, while municipal services from garbage pickup to building code enforcement have become substandard compared with White neighborhoods and the core of the downtown. Together with redlining by banks and insurance companies, these developments have worked over time to seal the neighborhood's fate as a ghetto. Now dilapidated and well-kept houses sit side by side. Spacious but run-down Victorian-era townhouses proliferate, cut up into small apartments called kitchenettes. Also, the fully employed live next door to the unemployed, many of whom have given up trying to find work. There is great demoralization among the residents.

At times the most desperate people prey on those "with something": those with little to their name often envy those who are better off, expressed in teasing fights among the young people in the schools and on the playgrounds. Residents are so impoverished that Longstreth, the local elementary school, qualifies for government-sponsored breakfast and lunch programs.

Dominic Mateo, a White former principal of Longstreth, served for many years not only as the principal of the segregated school but also as an informal neighborhood leader. In addition to his duties as principal, after arriving an hour before school each day, he would make sure his charges got inside the building safely, had their breakfast, and were off to their classes on time. Additionally, he chaperoned dances for teenagers and sponsored exercise classes for mothers in the neighborhood. During my fieldwork at the school one morning, I saw Mr. Mateo break up a fight between two students that had escalated into a family brawl. And on more than one occasion, there have been shootings close to the school.

One morning when I arrived at my field site early, I saw him out on a busy corner directing traffic. Mr. Mateo was a rare principal who saw the students as members of his extended family and their struggles as his struggles. He was a social worker, a teacher, a counselor, and a schoolteacher/principal all rolled into one.

In the local neighborhoods, when a resident buys a new television set or washer and dryer, it means the person "has money." Meanwhile, neighbors watch each other's buying habits, and given the level of poverty and desperation of the community, those with resources become mistrustful and guarded toward their neighbors. They're careful about putting telltale appliance boxes out with the trash because they don't want their neighbors to "know their business." Fear and envy put a considerable strain on social relations in the community.

The better-off people are, of course, those who can count on some kind of regular check. Since this may be a government stipend like a pension or welfare check, retired workers or young mothers are most likely to have such income; either way, the local community sees them as having means. To have means is to have power in interpersonal relations and to command a certain respect. Others look to share their good fortune. Some steal from them, but others become solicitous, ready to defer to those with cash. When they ask for a loan, they don't want to strike out.

Once an area like Southwest becomes predominantly poor—signaled by the concentration of Black people who live there and by low property values—the place becomes accessible to other impoverished groups. The newest immigrants may be Black Africans, Asians, or Hispanics, but they have in common poverty and their working-class status. In the Black community, these immigrants get a mixed reception. On the one hand, because many are also people of color, the Black residents see them as somewhat familiar and may feel an immediate connection with them. On the other hand, because of the community's deep parochialism, the new people are at times considered outsiders who may pose a threat, so strangers must be quickly assessed. In day-to-day interactions in the neighborhood, acceptance is always gradual, and it takes a long time before newcomers are treated as full members of the community.

As they settle in, the new people may take on the views and habits of those who already live there. They begin to assimilate, but not in the manner imagined by many Americans—by totally buying into what might be considered the dominant American culture. The Black and brown immigrants mostly adapt to what they observe in the local community. Both men and women typically have a strong work ethic; they may work as taxi drivers, as kitchen help in Center City restaurants, as hospital staff at University City hospitals, or as parking lot attendants. Their children attend the local elementary school or high school. Left on their own, kids mix with the culturally dominant Black youths and typically mimic them; many favor rap music and "hip" behavior, which are highly visible on the local streets.[1] Some begin to adapt to the ghetto culture, including body language and the street vernacular. Their conversation is often indistinguishable from that of other "ghetto" kids; phenotypically they blend in as non-Whites, although their parents may be Asian or African. They represent a novel form of cultural assimilation.

Typically the recreation center welcomes area residents regardless of ethnicity, but most of the people sitting at the picnic tables are Black Americans. Most of the children playing ball or jumping double Dutch are Black. Smaller children play on the swings, alone or with their mothers or siblings pushing them. Mothers often smoke cigarettes as they sit watching their children. People chat as they share sandwiches, soda, or beer, and sometimes they extend a dinner invitation or plan a get-together.

Unemployed teenage boys hang out on the edges of these social groups. On warm summer days, they sit two or three to a step and while away the afternoon. They may play pickup games of basketball on the playground or just hang out with their "homies." Occasionally a few girls are present.

The smaller children run, play, and laugh; the climbing bars are a big attraction. Their moms occasionally run errands or send an older child to the store for snacks or cigarettes. Some of the children are only two or three years old, and the oldest children often watch over the youngest ones. "Watching over" includes trying to keep them out of the line of fire in the occasional shooting.

When I visited the recreation center playground one day at about 3:00 p.m., things were relatively peaceful. My friend Donny had left for the day. A child of about five walked over to the table where I was sitting. His father was sitting there too, his head down on the table; I suspect he was drunk. "Wake up! Wake up!" the child said. His father responded, "I'm not sleeping," then went right back to sleep.

The playground seems relatively safe during the day because everybody is watching what's going on. As evening approaches, the boys and young men grow boisterous, and some act menacing. At night, since "all cats are gray in the dark" and people can't see everything, only the more secure or courageous remain. The women gradually peel away. The young men begin to shoot craps, talk loudly, and drink beer, and sometimes for fun they shoot their newest guns into the air. When the cops drive through, they look over but seldom stop to check things out or try to maintain order; typically they drive on. At times, and from a distance, the boys mock them. When violence occurs in Philadelphia—someone getting shot, stabbed, or killed—it's very often in Southwest. The area is well known as one of the city's "really bad" neighborhoods, and it often appears that violence is lurking just below the surface of ordinary relations. But to most outsiders, regardless of their color, this is the ghetto.

The setting is socially isolated from the wider White society. It's fully segregated racially, with absolutely no Whites. The only White people you see in the neighborhood are an occasional mail carrier or UPS driver. One of the primary manifestations of this isolation is a certain idleness among those occupying the space, especially among the youths. The young men sit in small groups and shoot craps or play cards for money. Soon someone suggests "getting a taste," and the one designated as the runner goes to the carryout for "the forty," or six-pack of malt liquor. The drinking starts at about 4:00 p.m.

By the end of the day, some are broke, desperately hungry but with no money for a hoagie or a beer. The combination of idleness and desperation helps explain the attraction of the drug trade for many of these youths. It picks up the slack when the regular economy fails the local community, and virtually everyone on the playground knows this connection. Many would prefer to work, but typically the "pee test" or a police record undermines their chances to find a job.

In Southwest, respect for the civil law is typically absent or weak, and for many residents street justice fills the void. The threat of physical retribution is often very close to the surface in everyday life here. People feel they are on their own. When things go amiss, such as when a debt is not paid on time, this is often taken as a personal affront. A person who feels profoundly disrespected may threaten or commit violence to get even, to protect his street credibility, to "get my respect back" or be "treated right." On the street, one's credibility is valuable coin for negotiating safety for oneself, one's loved ones, and one's homies.

The incessant search for street credibility has turned the community against itself. The local homicide rate has recently risen by leaps and bounds: Philadelphia as a whole has one of the highest murder rates in the country, and this community has one of the worst rates in the city. The area's negative reputation worsens with each report of a crime or murder, and all local communities that are predominantly Black gradually take on this reputation regardless of their crime rates. The status of Southwest seems to be indiscriminately applied to all Black communities: "If you've seen one ghetto, you've seen them all." This is the meaning of the iconic ghetto.

Typically for outsiders, the symbolic representative of the ghetto is the Black person, so in this sense every Black person carries the ghetto with him or her. Thus, if the public wants to contain the ghetto, it works to contain the anonymous Black woman or man, impairing the person's ability to find employment and influencing if not determining his or her treatment outside the ghetto, especially by the police.

During my fieldwork, when young Black men robbed and shot up a tavern in a well-to-do White area of the city, one of the old heads of Southwest commented, "There go fifty jobs, just like that." He believed that whenever Black men commit egregious and highly publicized crimes, the whole Black community suffers. Prospective employers use the incident as an excuse not to hire Black youths, never mind that they had nothing to do with the crime (Kirschenman and Neckerman 1991). The old head's point was that this is the way racial prejudice works: "This kind of crime makes us all look bad."

Moreover, the young Black men's idleness in public places reflects hopelessness. When hope for the future is limited, drug use, teen pregnancy, and interpersonal violence may follow, and young people are inclined to take more chances. In the ghetto they say, "Go for what you know" or what satisfies you in the present. "Do it now because in the street anything can happen and you may not see tomorrow, for 'tomorrow ain't promised to you.'" Young people sense threats from many sources, and their challenge is to navigate and negotiate their way through them. The answer for many is to "be cool," adapt, and figure things out (Majors and Billson 1993). This wisdom is handed down from parents to children and from big brothers and sisters to their younger siblings.

KINGSESSING AVENUE

In Southwest Philadelphia, the main drag is Kingsessing Avenue. The street is the community's "business district" and offers local residents everything from restaurants and carryouts to convenience stores, taverns, and delis. On one corner is a barbershop, down the street is a realtor, and a bit farther on is a currency exchange offering various services including cashing checks and renewing driver's licenses and car registrations. Residents sometimes call Kingsessing simply "the block" or "the street"—that street-corner scene where "everyone hangs out or eventually passes by" and where neighborhood folks can catch up on the news. An outsider walking down this street will witness the effects of the area's profound social isolation. Signs of blight are everywhere, including dilapidated buildings and overflowing trash cans on both sides of this main thoroughfare. Police cars, when visible at all, speed through the neighborhood but seldom stop; the police presence is intermittent and usually arbitrary.

In this area, residents know they can't depend on the police, so they feel they must be ready to defend themselves. Many have guns, and people can be counted on to be armed, including senior citizens and teenage males.

The local businesses typically are open during regular business hours, but most stores pull down riot gates in the evening. People stand around in front of the local carryout, the dollar store, or the corner barbershop. In certain drug and grocery stores, a pane of bulletproof Plexiglas separates the customers from the clerk, and the goods sit behind the divider, implying that the store's customers are not to be trusted, as everyone knows. The inhabitants understand that they should take the same precautions with one another as the clerks and store owners do. Realizing they are responsible for their own safety, they also understand the police officer's disengagement, because they know he wants to get home safely. Moreover, they also understand the need for riot gates: without them, break-ins would likely occur incessantly. They also know they shouldn't let down their guard. They must never give the stickup boy the chance to rob them but should let everyone know they are not "the one" to be a victim. Every person is required to be vigilant about their own personal security.

In the convenience stores along Kingsessing, items are typically overpriced and are sometimes sold beyond their expiration dates. Still, for most residents such a store is a meeting place and a hangout. It's also a place for trouble. These businesses form a community where there are always people milling around and hanging out, or a critical mass of "young brothers" ready "to get into something." Not only do people shop, drink, or have meals on this street, but they also "profile," presenting themselves in public and planning what they'll do that night. The "street" or the "block" is understood to be a "staging area," a busy place where "things are popping." It's where you go to see "what's happening," to get the "news." You can get everything and anything here—drugs, alcohol, or sex—it's where "anything can happen." And occasionally it's where people get shot or stabbed, and die. When people greet one another, it's often with "What's happening?" or "What's going on?" People always want to know, and on this street they typically find the answer.

Here people sometimes "show out" or get rowdy. They act out of character or out of "the zone" of normality. A person who might otherwise be "square" can come alive here. The place itself brings out these things, and others want to see that. It's no place for people who aren't street-smart, for the setting is generally regarded as "fast." To operate on these streets, you must know "what time it is" not by the clock, but by a peculiar "social time" that presupposes a deep understanding and cultural knowledge of the next person's proclivities and abilities and of what can happen when. With a supply of such "street knowledge," people get along by understanding their own capabilities. Because they know their limitations and those of others, they are seldom told no: they know what to ask for.

On the street, the experienced or the "hip" are ready to take advantage of the "slow" or "lame" person. To navigate this space, "You must be fast and constantly on your toes"; a common piece of motherly advice to the young is "Be aware, and act like you been around the block." Part of being hip on the ghetto streets is to drink, do drugs, or carry a weapon—ways to almost instantly gain street credibility. In addition, it's important to surround yourself with members of the fast crowd; the boys who are slow want to be with hip boys of the 'hood—the stickup boys who mug people, especially the weak and the slow.

In this section of the city, the wrong look, the wrong word to a stranger can cost a person his life. Recently, at a local convenience store, a young man of sixteen simply looked at a stranger of about twenty-five. The stranger said to the younger man, "What you looking at?" The younger man then said, "What are *you* looking at?" With that the older man finished his business in the store, went outside, and waited for the younger man. When the younger man appeared outside the store, the older man shot him dead, then disappeared into the night. He is now "on the run" from the authorities. With surveillance cameras proliferating in such convenience stores and on the neighborhood streets, there is a chance the assailant will be apprehended and brought to justice, but for many residents this outcome is highly uncertain (see Shaw 2021).

The young girls are almost invariably at risk of being hit on verbally or even sexually assaulted or being seduced to become "drug hos." The young boys, often in financial need, are at risk of having their heads "turned" by drug dealers and being drawn into the drug trade. Drug dealers are on the lookout for young boys, especially those who look needy. Persistent poverty effectively feeds on itself and makes all these young people needy, and thus vulnerable. The drug trade can provide employment and money where the regular economy does not.

In teaching their children to survive the ghetto streets, parents encounter a problem: How much should they teach them about the street? To be naive is to be a likely target. Often the most "decent" parents try to be strict with their kids, warning them repeatedly of the dangers of the corner, but far too often such lessons are to no avail.

A TASTE OF THE 'HOOD

Across town is another large ghetto area—West Oak Lane, located twenty-plus miles northwest of Philadelphia's Center City. Ogontz Avenue is the main drag, the neighborhood's central business district. The UPS driver bolting from his truck to make a delivery, the clerk in the flower shop, the pharmacist behind the drugstore counter, the young women pushing strollers, the tellers counting out money in the bank, and the policemen patrolling in their cars are all Black.

Decades ago the area was middle class and WASP. The Irish working class came next, the Black middle class later, and the Black working class later still. Finally the ghetto poor were added to the mix. At first Black folks arrived gradually, but the trickle became a steady stream, then a flood. As in so many other invasion and succession scenarios, when the Black population reached a tipping point, the area became undesirable to Whites. Soon the local housing market faced a shortage of buyers and stable renters.

As in Southwest, with White home buyers looking elsewhere, housing values plummeted and homes that were once out of reach for Black buyers became affordable. Churches where White Presbyterians had worshipped now accommodated Black Baptist and Pentecostal congregations. Some White homeowners who did not—or could not—sell became landlords; they typically cut up their properties and rented them to Blacks as kitchenettes. Over many decades, not unlike the situation in Southwest and other parts of the city where Black people had succeeded the White populations, municipal administrations were largely indifferent to the needs of the local Black community, and local building codes and city services were typically ignored, whereas White communities could take these services for granted (Hunter 2013). Moreover, insurance companies and banks typically redlined the area, as was the accepted practice in other ghetto areas (Coates 2014). The resulting lower rents and cheaper housing attracted even more poor Black people. Almost overnight the housing clientele, as well as the local businesses, changed from White to Black and from middle class to a mix of working class and poor. Today both the crime rate and the poverty rate are higher than in other parts of the city, patterns that often follow Black residence.

One morning I visited a small carryout place called Breakfast, on Ogontz Avenue. In the middle of a busy block, the storefront is distinguished by a huge, colorful sign emblazoned with the restaurant's name. Everyone in the neighborhood knows about this carryout—a popular place where, for a very reasonable price, one can get a tasty breakfast of scrapple and pancakes, bacon and eggs with hominy grits, or fried fish.

I was there to order takeout breakfasts for myself and two African American friends, which I planned to take back to their house. The space inside felt cramped. Three Black waitresses stood inside a U-shaped counter with their backs to the kitchen. As I took a seat at the counter, one of the waitresses smiled, making immediate eye contact. She eagerly took my order, carefully writing down everything I asked for. It was a long list—my friends and I wanted "the works." A few more customers joined the line as she took my order. That it was already past noon on a weekday didn't seem to matter. This place served breakfast all day, every day.

Business was slow, so the service promised to be quick. Behind the counter, two stout young Black men stood over a hot grill preparing the food. The aroma of frying bacon and pancakes wafted through the air. In the back I spotted a young Asian man. Although he seemed to hang back, not quite out of sight, he kept a careful eye on the door, tracking those who entered and left, and he monitored me. I guessed he was the owner.

As I waited, a middle-aged Asian man carrying a large bag entered the restaurant and sidled up to the counter beside me. The Black waitresses greeted him pleasantly, as though they knew him. He spoke little English, so the women pointed and made faces to communicate with him; mostly he was silent. Shortly, he produced a small cardboard box of DVDs and music CDs, which he passed around to the women. Between customers they began to discuss the videos. He offered to sell them for five or ten dollars, depending on the title; the CDs were priced from a dollar to two or three dollars.

Obviously delighted, the women picked through the videos, ignoring the man. Then, in a bid for their confidence, he offered to play the DVDs on his own Sony player, apparently to demonstrate that they would not find their bootleg bargains either not working or marred by the bobbing heads of theatergoers where the video was illegally recorded. Throughout the interaction, it was clear that the women were familiar with this routine. Within minutes they completed the sales, and the man prepared to leave. But first he turned and offered me his wares. The box included a few titles currently playing at first-run theaters in the malls, but I declined to purchase any. The salesman nodded and waved goodbye to everyone. The man walked out, perhaps on his way to the next sale; maybe he'd return to Breakfast to peddle his merchandise another day. For now the women laughed among themselves, satisfied with their purchases. They planned to watch the movies as soon as they got the chance.

Surprisingly, my bill came to less than twenty dollars, a bargain for a hearty breakfast for three adults. As I prepared to pay, I noticed that the young Asian man in the back was still watching me. Clearly I was of some concern to him.

To place this concern in perspective, it's important to understand that despite the apparent comity in the neighborhood during the day, this "ghetto area" qualifies as a high-crime community. Local "street knowledge" stereotypes Asians here as interlopers or as visitors to be tolerated. It's generally understood that these Asian merchants provide valued commodities such as groceries and cheap prepared foods, as well as employment. At the same time the homeboys, and many of the criminal element, take a peculiar view of them. They see them chiefly as exploiting the community, as having limited moral authority, and therefore as people who can be mistreated with little compunction or few consequences. Thus when a stickup boy becomes desperate enough to "get paid," there's little to constrain him from robbing an Asian merchant at gunpoint. Although one of his own Black people might be off-limits, the Asian merchant is fair game. When it comes to choosing a victim, however, feasibility most often outweighs skin color or national origin.

As I left the establishment, I looked around carefully, watching my own back, but I was met by friendly smiles. I made my way to my car and drove about twenty minutes to my friends' home on a mostly "White" cul-de-sac in the nearby upper-middle-class, racially integrated Philadelphia suburb (my friends were the only Black people on that block). My hosts were delighted with the meal I'd brought. The husband knew about Breakfast from "way back," having discovered it on one of his many forays back into the 'hood, where he grew up, to search for authentic food. Occasionally he visits a place called the Rib Crib, which sells pork ribs with all the fixings—banned among Black middle-class folks trying to maintain healthy diets despite their occasional craving for the "real soul food" I'd been sent to pick up that afternoon.

We ate our takeout meal in their breakfast nook. The housekeeper, a forty-something Black woman, brought us coffee and milk to go with our delicious pancakes; we ate every last bit. We joked that we were splurging. We certainly didn't eat like this all the time: too much fat, sugar, and empty calories. But it was fine to take a holiday from our diets, appreciating that people from the 'hood eat like this all the time.

Although Black people like my friends have left areas like West Oak Lane, they retain many connections to the community. Here and in similar places, they are likely to encounter old friends from the 'hood—people who may resemble them in class status and ties to the old neighborhood, qualities they often miss in their "new" location, though they've lived there more than twenty years. By returning to the old neighborhood, or by enjoying the food and camaraderie available there, they demonstrate to themselves and to one another that, despite the improved circumstances that formal education and professional salaries have brought them, they haven't sold out or forgotten where they come from. It's in this special respect that they embrace, or "show love" for, the 'hood.

CHAPTER 6

THE LOCAL CAR WASH

A Racial Advertisement

Most White people and others who comprise the White space typically refrain from almost any opportunity to socialize with anonymous
Black people. Usually, they just "keep their distance," which means they
have relatively few chances for actual social intercourse with Blacks.
Moreover, many of these people form their own social identities in
distinctive opposition to the Black people they observe, especially those
they "place" in the ghetto.

Most commonly, in "knowing" about Black people, they rely on
stereotypes fueled or even "proven" by their passing observations of
Black people in public, "where the races meet," the "cosmopolitan
canopies" of the city that include local streets, public transportation,
or settings like the Reading Terminal Market, the former "Gallery," or
Rittenhouse Square. Typically, they drive rapidly through ghetto areas
on their way to and from work or their own racially homogeneous
neighborhoods.

In this vein, the Brightway car wash is a setting where the behavior of lower-income Black people is on full public display. It is in

this way that the car wash can be viewed as a "racial advertisement," a place where "Blackness," or the iconic ghetto, may be consumed up close without serious risk to themselves, and may then be generalized.

Thus, not only do White and Black people meet at this establishment to get their cars washed, but also they are able to observe Black people close-up, a view that often serves to confirm or to reinforce their notions of the iconic ghetto, and of Black people more generally. Most of these White people know few Black people socially, and for the most part are satisfied with their level of interaction. In this context, stereotypes flourish and the most compromising and negative images of Black people endure, supporting the Whites' own sense of group position (see Blumer 1958; Bobo 1999; Evans-Pritchard [1940] 1969; Emirbayer and Desmond 2015).

But more than this, the car wash is a place where low-income Black people can eke out a living, albeit in hardscrabble ways that suggest that such employment serves as an interface between street crime and legitimate work. The Brightway is located on a main thoroughfare of Northwest Philadelphia in between a racially mixed middle-class area and the Black ghetto, and not far from a concentration of desperately poor Black people. When I first came across the Brightway, it was drawing some of its clientele and most of its workers from this local community; its workforce consisted largely of middle-aged to older men formerly employed in local manufacturing jobs. Some of these men were retired or supplemented their income by working at other places part-time. Many of the workers had been in trouble with the law or were ex-convicts, and a few were younger men out to pick up a few bucks "at the 'wash." Some of these men were responsible for the petty street crime in the neighborhood, including stick-ups, burglaries, and dealing drugs. Most of the men ostensibly shunned criminal activities, but if they became desperate for money, the local neighborhood's residents were at risk.

Thus, the money the workers earned at this car wash served as a stopgap to street crime, as it could provide them with just enough incentive to avoid criminality. However, if, say, it rained all week and customers stayed away, the men developed an incentive to return to the streets in search of money. Thus, the tension between street crime and legitimate employment ran through the workers' everyday lives.

Its diverse clientele and the apparent ease with which people interacted here piqued my interest. I began simple reconnaissance visits to the Brightway, engaging in a kind of "folk ethnography" (see Anderson 2011). Gradually, I began to engage in a more systematic participant-observation study of the place. Over time, I became increasingly interested in the setting and became a regular customer there. After my car was finished, I would linger and hang around, engaging other customers and some of the workers in conversations in order to learn what I could.

I would pull certain workers aside and speak with them personally about their backgrounds and how they became involved in this line of work. I also interviewed some of the customers in order to gain a sense of how they saw this place. I was straightforward, informing the subjects that I'd like to get to know them better, and that my inquiries might lead to an ethnographic research project. Everyone was surprisingly candid in his or her answers to my queries. The more time I spent with them, the more questions I had. Who were these customers and workers, where did they come from, how steady was this work? What were their previous backgrounds?

It was not uncommon to observe White people watching the goings-on at the car wash with great interest. The place itself was particularly interesting for its mix of ethnocentric and cosmopolitan orientations toward American society, that salient cultural division in our increasingly diverse society. Racial and ethnic tensions, however, characterized on occasion the relationship between the workers and the proprietor.

AN HONEST HUSTLE

On sunny days, and especially weekends, the car wash was busy. In the long white one-story building, car after car moved along through its wash tunnel. Individual vacuum cleaner stalls lined the side of the building, where after or before the wash, customers detailed their own cars personally, taking as much time as they wanted. A few other businesses, including a service station and a convenience store, were located nearby. The workers went there constantly for cigarettes, soft drinks, and Philadelphia's famous individually wrapped Tastykakes. The work atmosphere was loose. The workers decided how to structure their time. They weren't typically required to have credentials or résumés. Almost anyone could simply show up and work, trading his labor for "ready money," observing the establishment's implicit promise of a day's work for a day's pay. In the parlance of the street, they engaged in an "honest hustle." Most car washes around the city employ workers more formally, often at minimum wage, but at this particular one only a few people were actually hired. Most of the men (and, on occasion, women) worked as freelancers, essentially self-employed—working for themselves and informally negotiating their wages in the form of tips, not with the employer but directly with the clientele.

Once a car stopped at the entrance to the wash tunnel, a formally hired clerk for the business appeared and began to sell the job, negotiating the price from a menu of choices. The customer selected the extent of the job and paid the money up front. The driver then remained inside the car, as two other salaried employees, one on either side of the vehicle, began to prep it. As the driver remained behind the wheel, the men went about their work, scrubbing the sides of the car and soaping it up, including the windows, sidewalls, and hubcaps; shortly, the car was soaked with a soap-and-water spray to loosen the road dirt.

Then the mechanized chains hooked underneath began to move the car along between the large brushes on either side. The car was then sprayed with warm water followed by waxy polish if the driver had opted for it. Shortly thereafter, hot air was blown all over the car to pre-dry it before it made its way through the 'wash to the end. At this point, the driver was prompted to start the engine and drive the car out the front of the car wash.

When the car exited the wash tunnel, a dryer might cry out, "My customer," indicating to all that he had an established relationship with this person. Or alternatively, he simply wanted to claim a prospective customer for himself. The others usually deferred, and a complex system of taking turns ensued. The negotiations were not always orderly; at times, confusion and misunderstandings led to disagreements and even fights.

Usually each man worked solo, so he could claim the tip all to himself. But if things got especially busy, he might accept the help of another dryer. With rags in hand, the individual worker or the small team dried each car down and applied the extra elbow grease in hopes of a good tip. They took control of the car and began the job. They dried the outside and cleaned the inside, wiping the windows. If the customer was deemed to be worth it, the dryer detailed the chrome hubcaps and then painted the tires with Armor All to turn them shiny black again.

All the while, the dryer made small talk with the customer and tried to communicate that he was working for tips. The most effective way to do this was by working hard on the customer's automobile, for which he expected a large tip. If the customer failed to get the message, the dryer might be more direct.

This performance was watched and recorded not simply by those actively involved but by onlookers, who then learned the score: that these men work for tips. Among the most attentive were the newest customers, their small children, and the occasional passersby who took in the blow-by-blow of the performance, which was played out repeatedly all day long, as one car followed the next car in line, one car after another, after another.

Near the drying area was a large cart containing towels and cleaning supplies, which the establishment provided at no cost to the men. But, in an effort to be effective entrepreneurs, workers often customized their operations. They were in the market for their own special supplies of Armor All for tires, or extra Windex for windows and interiors. To meet this need, "traveling salesmen" made their rounds through ghetto neighborhoods hawking stolen, and sometimes unopened, boxes of cleaning supplies. Workers might walk around the car wash with their private supplies hanging from their belts and lend them to close buddies in need.

On Saturdays in April, the car wash could become especially busy because nice weather was in the offing, and local Black people like their "rides" clean for Sunday church services. The thinking goes that a 'wash can do wonders for the most nondescript jalopy that has been in need of such TLC all winter. When it was sunny and warm, folks were drawn to the car wash; the weather promised the start of the season when things are more easygoing, people are carefree, and life seems good.

One such Saturday, I observed a young Laotian man, nicknamed Chico, drive up in his new white Nissan car, with his stereo system turned up, emphasizing the bass. After Chico's 'wash, he pulled his car over to the side of the building. There, among so many other young men, he began to "detail" his ride. For him—because he had the money—this meant engaging a few of the young men to perform some service. Others looked on attentively as they went to work. Chico was a no-nonsense young man. He kept an unsmiling, stern look on his face. He was a handsome young man with a striking cornrow hairdo, braided with numerous tracks across the top of his head. Dressed in tan Timberland boots, baggy pants, a gold necklace and chains, he was cool and calm as the young men worked on his car. He just stood back and watched, inspecting the show as it progressed. Through his body language and speech, he presented himself as an authentic homeboy from the 'hood—and he communicated that he was no one to mess with. This man was a spectacle, adding to the intrigue of the car wash; while he was not Black, he publicly exhibited the signs of ghetto culture to onlookers.

Carefully, and apparently well aware of his performance, he scoped the scene and "profiled," watching those watching him. His furtive glances made for a number of possibilities—such as that when drug dealers are out and about, they must watch their backs. On the streets, they know their lives are always at risk—from other drug dealers or from the police.

As this action continued, Chico proceeded to play his music loudly. Rap music blared from his custom speakers and the beat was infectious, and as the young Black men worked, their heads bobbed along; they clearly enjoyed these sounds. They worked happily, apparently gaining great satisfaction just by having the chance to be so close to this ride—touching it and caressing it as they applied their rags along the car's sleek lines. The workers sopped up the small beads of water from the windshield and from the hood of the car. Simply to perform this service seemed to be a reward in and of itself, the expected pay simply an added bonus.

Clearly, the young Laotian man was proud of his car, which symbolized what he had been able to achieve in his young life in America and in Philadelphia. While it was not clear that he was in reality a drug dealer or simply a drug dealer "wannabe," he clearly could pass for one. This was a confusion he seemed to encourage. The main thing is that the public, particularly those of the car wash and passersby, were inclined to see him this way. In a sense, he and his car inspired the young men to work hard and, maybe, to be like him.

One of the first workers at Brightway whom I met and came to know was "Wesley," who worked as one of the dryers. I had observed Wesley at the car wash on a number of visits, and "knew" him from these occasions, and he told me he "knew" me as well, that he had noticed me. Wesley was particularly observant of strangers. On a number of occasions, he had dried and wiped down my car, an older blue Ford Explorer. And while he performed these tasks, I struck up conversations with him and anyone else within earshot.

Wesley was about six feet tall, thin, and brown-skinned, and was about thirty-five years old. He typically dressed in worn jeans and a light army jacket, as the weather dictated. He styled his hair in dreadlocks, and with his athletic build, he moved about quickly, his shoulder-length locks dangling down; he was a distinctive figure. I was immediately impressed by the attention he gave to my car. He was careful about his work and gave me what I considered to be the "full treatment," spending what seemed like an inordinate amount of time wiping down each and every crevice of my car, inside and out. To show my gratitude, I felt obligated to tip him well, and did.

Like some of the other dryers I'd observed, Wesley's interactions with customers often included an unequivocal indication that his compensation was primarily based on tips. This message was an announcement of sorts, and often stated loudly enough for others within hearing distance. It was a critical piece of information that Wesley and others there wanted the clientele to know. He simply needed to get paid for his work, and with this little nudge, customers would often comply. Wesley and the other men effectively negotiated their wages, with Chico, with me, and with everyone else.

In time, Wesley introduced me to other men of the car wash, and from these introductions, I spread out and met other workers there. I soon felt comfortable enough to ask them personal questions. Some of the men lived with a wife, or an uncle or aunt, and a few lived with their grown children. Others lived alone; two or three of the men were homeless, in and out of the local shelter, and living from hand to mouth. Additionally, some of the older men were drawing military disability, pensions of some sort, or Social Security. As I came to know these men, they were forthcoming with their own stories or stories about their friends.

Whenever I visited the car wash, I'd look out for Wesley, to engage him more. Or if he was not around just then, I would talk to someone else I knew. In time, I became Wesley's regular customer. As he worked on my car, we became closer, and I'd engage him in small talk about almost anything—the weather, local politics, his family, his background, and about the workings of the car wash itself, including his place there, and his relationship with the other men, and their relationship with the proprietor, "Mr. Kim Chou." I was very curious, and Wesley would indulge me. He provided me with information, while expecting me to be a good customer. I complied, and on this basis we built our relationship.

In time, I learned that Wesley grew up in the local neighborhood, and that he'd been a high school basketball player, who, in his own words, had a "mean jump shot." Wesley had been drawn to the streets and had failed to graduate from high school. He also has a criminal record. He is the father of a young daughter, Lucy, for whom he cares deeply.

When Lucy was born, Maxine, her mother, simply gave her up to Wesley and told him, "You raise this child! You the daddy, so you raise her. She's yours!" With this, Lucy's mother all but departed Wesley's life. As Wesley told it, she was on drugs, so this was "for the good." But over the years, their relationship was intermittent, on and off. Lucy was seven when I met Wesley, and he had been deeply involved in her care "ever since she came into this world." Wesley lived alone with the little girl, but he had help from his mom and sister, whom he saw regularly and who from time to time would watch Lucy.

During this time, Wesley had played the role of Mr. Mom. He often shopped for food and prepared meals for Lucy and himself. Each day, he made a point to leave the car wash early enough to pick her up from school on time, and when needed, he braided her hair. Around the car wash, his story was well known, and the other men "understood" and respected him for being the little girl's "mommy and her daddy." He had to take time off from work to perform his caretaking role, but a flexible schedule was one advantage of working for tips at the car wash.

After I got to know Wesley better, he shared with me that he was an ex-convict. He did time for armed robbery in Pennsylvania's Graterford Prison, which has a storied place in the imaginations of many young Black men of the local neighborhood, some of whom have been in and out of Graterford, or have family members—including cousins, fathers, uncles, and brothers—who have spent time "in the joint." I found out from Wesley that he was not alone in having such a biography; many other young men who worked at the 'wash had done prison time. Indeed, there are many "graduates" of Graterford residing throughout inner-city Philadelphia and in the local neighborhood of the car wash as well.

As it is such a common story around the car wash, many of the workers there treated this history not so much as a stigma but as a source of pride. Ex-convict status is often viewed as a badge of esteem, for if one has been to prison, others assume that such a person—particularly because he survived prison life—must be pretty remarkable and tough, and must know how to take care of himself on the streets.

Over time, I learned that most of these men who work at the 'wash prided themselves as being veterans of the streets, or coming from the "school of hard knocks," and also that prison time was an important part of their biographies. In fact, every man I talked to seemed to have a story of hard times and disadvantage, and the back of the car wash was where they commonly shared them.

Although Wesley had sold drugs and knew the streets very well, he now wanted to cope with life by working for a living, as "decent" people do; he said he wanted to set an example for Lucy, who meant the world to him. But even so, when money was scarce, he had to exercise a great deal of self-restraint to keep from going back to the street.

Despite his aspiration to live decently, Wesley, like many men at the car wash, felt alienated from American mainstream society. He had little respect for the police or the justice system; whenever he had encountered them, he was always on the losing end; on occasion, he ranted about the police. Strikingly, the car wash men shared a philosophy about the wider system, about "the White man," and about conventional society. For struggling young men like Wesley, the system was a monolithic, arbitrary power structure that meant them no good.

In this mentality, "we don't trust them [the police] and they don't trust us." This ideology neutralizes any claim conventional society might have on those who see themselves as victims of the system. While they don't always voice it, they share a belief that racial inequality is a cause of their poverty. Recitations of firsthand knowledge of this circumstance continually undermine their connections with the wider society.

The widespread sense in the local Black community that it is all but impossible to get ahead by accommodating the system, and that the system itself is not only alien but also antagonistic to the aspirations of poor Black people, seriously weakens the constraints that would prevent these men from taking recourse to antisocial enterprises. Thus, while the inner city is victimized by such crime, the residents often understand how the wider society's racism is powerfully complicit in their travail at the hands of the street-oriented neighbors. As Ray Charles once said, hard times can make a good man go wrong.[1] Wesley told me that he was not going to be a criminal if he could help it. He had "been through that," and now that he was older and wiser, he saw a way that he could manage. But he acknowledged that if times got tough, it was hard to say what he might do.

"THE THUG LIFE"

The car wash workforce included younger men between eighteen and twenty-one years old. These young men generally had a history of contact with the criminal justice system. During the time I was studying the car wash, the young men loved Tupac, Biggie Smalls, NWA, and the other alienated rappers of that time. One youth said about Tupac, "That's my n****r."[2] Compared to the older men, the younger ones were more transient: here at the 'wash today, gone tomorrow. They might be around for two or three days, or maybe a week, but then they were off to find somewhere else to hustle. They became easily discouraged by the lack of opportunity.

During my fieldwork, I invited a small group of the young men to lunch for an interview. Promptly at 2:00 p.m. one Friday in June, I pulled up in my Explorer, and they piled in. In just a few minutes, one of the young men plugged his own device into my radio and commandeered my console. Moments later, we were riding down the thruway to the beat of loud rap music. At periodic traffic lights, we attracted the attention of other motorists. The young boys seemed in their element.

Soon we arrived at a restaurant that was part of a downtown hotel. I parked and took out my steering wheel lock, but before I could attach it, Tony, one of the young men, shook his head and said, "That ain't gon' help you." "Oh, no?" I responded. "If somebody wants your car, they'll have it in five minutes," he replied. Then Mike, another young man essentially agreed with Tony. "Naw, man, ain't gon't take 'em that long." The two young men argued and compared techniques for stealing cars. I attached the lock anyway, fed the meter, and the four of us walked across the street to the restaurant.

Inside, the maître d' seated us around a four-top table. Once seated, I had to encourage them to order. Finally, Tony ordered onion rings and a Coke, while Mike ordered a hamburger and fries. I ordered a salad, which to them was quite "square," but soon we had a table full of "bad food," and the boys feasted. As they ate, they shared stories about their lives.

Of these four young freelancers whom I later interviewed extensively, and got to know fairly well, one had been in jail, where he got everything he wanted because he knew to run it, or so he told me. The father of another of the young men was an admitted car thief. One day this young kid followed his father on an errand, discovered what the father did, and asked him, "Show me this stuff, Dad." So his father taught him how to steal cars. Another boy declared with tears in his eyes that his father was "nothin' but a sperm donor. Never with me when I needed him. Never took me to Little League. I hate 'im." He and his father would fight on occasion. One of these youths said to me about himself and his friends, "We know guys who carjack people and put them in the trunks of their own cars. We don't do that, but we know guys who do that. We're not like that."

But neither were these young men the sort of people who work a regular job. For the time being, at the 'wash, they had a great deal of freedom. They floated in and out, forming a loose-knit community, as they dreamed and looked for a job, a job that never seemed to materialize.

People who had regular employment elsewhere came to the car wash on occasion to supplement their income. For instance, a man named T.J. worked at the car wash on occasional Saturdays "to pick up some change." But he also had a job as a manager at a local McDonald's. His wife would join him at the 'wash and was one of the few women who worked there sporadically; on a good Saturday, she could make up to $90. They worked as a team of freelancers. The stability provided by the husband's regular job made them stand out as an exception in the world of the car wash. It separated them from the attitudes and pressures that make so-called social "respectability" out of reach for most of the informal workforce here.

As I roamed the premises and became more invested in studying its life, I got to know the various workers in their own element— their backstage, the part of the 'wash where the goings-on were not so apparent to the clientele who glimpsed certain happenings only in passing. Located off to the side in the back of the establishment were a number of makeshift seats of crates, a couple of old chairs, and a table, where the men occasionally took time out to play cards and to shoot craps on the ground; they engaged in other forms of gambling, too, betting on penny tosses against the side wall.

Here, they partied and had fun with one another, smoking marijuana and drinking liquor, especially when business was slow. Then, when things suddenly got busy, they could not always end their preoccupations so abruptly, and so on occasion the needs of the clientele became secondary, losing out in competition with the goings-on in the back of the 'wash.

There was always a certain amount of tension backstage, as competitions and jealousies emerged. On occasion, the men played games of personal attribution with one another, teasing those who seemed to deserve it, highlighting shortcomings with pointed jokes and references—at times, just to the edge of anger. Over the course of the day, the men had their little ructions, their occasional arguments, fights, and altercations, but these matters were soon settled, giving way to a return to normalcy.

Clearly, the 'wash represented more than a workplace; rather, it was also a second home for some, a setting for close-knit friends, whose dues were paid by one another's presence and the degrees of involvement they showed one another. Over time, I became a participant in some of these activities and was able to engage in participant-observation among the men in their backstage activities. This put me on "their side" vis-à-vis the Brightway's owner, Kim Chou, who, unlike the workforce, was not there to fraternize or gamble.

MR. KIM CHOU

Since its beginning, Brightway has been through a succession of owners—and identities. The workers served as the institutional memory of the setting, and in remembering, they embellished the history, telling it the way they thought or surmised it was. As their collective story went, at one time the Brightway was part of a national chain that went bankrupt, and then it became the property of a small group of local White businessmen. It became something of a troubled business, unable to turn a sustainable profit. Enter Mr. "Kim Chou," a short, bespectacled, fifty-year-old Korean immigrant, who arrived in Philadelphia some fifteen years before I studied the car wash, and became the proprietor of Brightway. It was rumored among the men that he acquired this business along with several other businesses in New Jersey and Delaware.

Mr. Chou moved about the Brightway attending to the various housekeeping duties. The men observed him policing the area, picking up loose trash and towels on the floor; on occasion, he would even sweep the premises. Such physical labor, some of the men believed, was unbecoming of a boss.

Mr. Chou managed his workers by cultivating certain ones, treating them as "trusties," or special workers on whom he could depend. He extended to them certain privileges and shows of trust, such as handling money or driving his car to run an errand for him. The trusties were often but not always on a formal payroll.

At times, Mr. Chou tried to joke with his workers, superficially blurring their differences, but everyone realized that he was closer with those he regarded as trustworthy, and distant from those who essentially bore watching. He navigated the premises like a busy bee, his brow furrowed, as he concentrated on managing his business. This gave him a perpetually troubled look.

On occasion, his workers would challenge him, as most of them were "down" with the "code of the street," and interpreted his look of worry and his attempts at being friendly as weakness, and not the show of strength they respect. Some of the workers referred to him derisively, behind his back, as "the Chinaman"; to most of the workers, anyone with Asian features was Chinese.

Mr. Chou kept three or four employees on a regular payroll: a clerk or cashier, who made sales and took in the money; a man who vacuumed and soaped up the wheels and otherwise prepared the cars as they began their trek through the wash tunnel; and a man who drove the cars out after they had been washed. These three or four men were the skeleton force on which Mr. Chou relied. Mr. Chou appeared to turn a profit, and presumably was able to do so by not paying wages to any of the men but these three. He himself divided the workers into a loose status dichotomy.

TRUSTIES AND FREELANCERS

Generally, the trusties at Brightway were at "the end of the line." In so many respects, this was in fact what the car wash represented to them, the end of the line. Many of them had an assortment of pressing health issues, including alcoholism; these were men who had seen better days, and their lives were pretty much behind them. The trusties were known for "loving the oil," as people say, or the booze. In some ways, they resembled the men I wrote about in *A Place on the Corner*.[3] Some love to "get a taste," and some of them were working for that taste. But without these men, a true skeleton force, Mr. Chou would have had trouble running the place. Because a man could sometimes make more money as a freelancer than as a trusty, the ranks of the trusties were fluid, with workers moving back and forth, or in and out, as they saw opportunities; these men had incentive to try their luck elsewhere.

Naturally, the situation was unstable, and sometimes there was trouble. Once the owner asked Vincent, one of the trusties, to do for $10 a detailing job that would cost the client $69, and Vincent refused because he couldn't see the "Chinaman" reaping all the profit. Provoked by this open defiance, the boss got angry and hit him. Vincent then threw a brick that missed the boss but smashed the window of his Lexus. This was a spectacle of violence on full display to the public. Things eventually settled down, of course. Vincent even continued to work there.

Charley was also a trusty. His wife, Annie, drew Social Security, and this kept a roof over his head, but the car wash allowed him to earn enough money to buy liquor and, equally important, to socialize with the congenial group of other trusties, in a setting where he felt he belonged.

Vincent had been a trusty, but had now fallen on hard times—he came to the car wash daily, but he was such an alcoholic that he sometimes wandered about the North Philadelphia streets looking for booze.

Another older man, Anthony, became the clerk for Mr. Chou for a period; he was entrusted with working as the cashier. He was an honest man who engaged in no criminal activity and was completely trustworthy, but his employment opportunities were limited because he was Jamaican and lacked a green card.

RESERVE ARMY OF THE UNEMPLOYED

For decades in Philadelphia, a large number of Black men have been jobless. Chief among their problems is their limited human capital as well as the persistent racial discrimination they face. For at least the past half century, the city has been undergoing a profound change from its old manufacturing economy to a service one, in the context of an increasingly globalized national economy. What were formerly local manufacturing jobs have been shipped away, to non-metropolitan America and to developing countries, where people work for a fraction of the wages such jobs used to pay in Philadelphia. Low-paying service jobs do exist, but many of these are located far away from the neighborhoods in which Black people live.

At the same time, because of the stereotypical violent crime and

poverty that has over the past several decades been so strongly associated with the inner-city Black community, prospective employers
are often wary of Black job applicants. If a Black worker has been in
trouble with the law, or has a record, he has great difficulty impressing
anyone, particularly a prospective employer who has so many others to
choose from. This was the economic and social situation for so many
of the Black men who wound up at the car wash.

They gravitated to this place, where credentials, including recommendations and work history, were not required. Many worked here
until they could find something better, or until they began to simply
drift about as discouraged workers. Some worked here sporadically,
or in spells, or when they "felt like it." The most desperate—those
without viable credentials that would allow them to obtain decent
employment elsewhere—lingered for long spells. They were loath to
fill out application forms, finding such "papers" intimidating. The red
tape they had endured in life usually led to few rewards, whether they
were seeking unemployment benefits or workers' compensation.

All this paperwork represented only a chance to get paid, and—like
the lottery—seldom panned out. Their past experience with the formal
agencies of social control, especially the criminal justice system, made
them wary about becoming ensnared in the morass of bureaucracy that
may only lead to trouble. For these and other reasons, they tended to
be proprietary about their personal information, and felt that in the
wrong hands, it could further complicate their lives.

Brightway was a place where an inner-city Black man could get a
job by simply showing up, and where he could get paid in ready money
on the spot. The workers tended to be easygoing about allowing new
people to join them and work alongside them. They simply had to
show up, grab a towel, and dry cars.

The car wash, with its lack of constraints, constituted a quasi-
community centered on being free rather than bound to labor. Freedom
was an important value for the workers here: they came as they wanted
and went as they pleased and felt themselves be their own bosses. In
this sense, the car wash was similar to the street corner, and the fact

that one could make money out of it without the risk of prison was something of a bonus.

Many of these men had a present-time orientation and a habit of instant gratification. They had learned that if you wait, things don't go your way, or that "tomorrow ain't promised to you." They had witnessed too much disappointment, seen too many friends and loved ones get sick and die, not on their own terms. Their plans had too often been short-circuited, so they had a profound distrust of promises. Many had repeatedly been told "no" by those in power.

Frequent rejections of their job applications by authority figures who distrusted them had circumscribed their lives. But at the car wash, a worker could show up with empty pockets and leave no longer broke that day. In addition, the car wash mediated against much that was negative in their lives. The chance to touch nice cars, even to drive them for a moment, could in itself be a thrill. These perks kept the men interested in working here. Even the car wash, however, proved to be unpromised to them.

One warm Monday in July, the men approached the 'wash around 9:00 a.m., as they usually did. But this day was different. Wesley and the others who approached with him that morning, Vincent and Sebastian, were shocked by what they saw—the customers were being attended to by a phalanx of Africans new to this country.

"What you all doing, man?" asked Sebastian, half asking and half stating, but through it all demanding an answer. The Africans just looked at them.

"What's going on?" Wesley asked, demanding an explanation. The Africans remained silent.

Eventually, a tall, thin, dark-skinned African appeared; apparently he was the new manager. "What can I do for you?" he asked.

"We work here," Wesley said.

"Not anymore," said the new African manager. "You don't work here anymore."

"Where the Chinaman at?" asked Sebastian, looking around for Kim.

"He gone," replied the African. "He sold the business."

"He what?!" said Vincent.

"He no longer the owner. He sold the business. You can't work here anymore," stated the African, firmly.

"What you mean?!" said Vincent, defiantly.

Vincent, Sebastian, and Wesley just looked at each other, as if they'd received a collective kick in the gut. They didn't know what to do, and for now just milled about the perimeter of the building.

Others of the old workforce began to trickle in. I arrived a few minutes after the confrontation and received the news. It was if someone had just pulled the rug out from under us. It was awkward. And, finally, the question was repeated, "Where's the Chinaman?"

But he really was nowhere to be found. He had sold Brightway to a Dutch company, we came to learn. The Dutch company had brought in the new crew of Africans. They hailed from Somalia and other parts of East Africa. Now there was an African "Boss," or manager, set to run the place to his liking.

The group in the old workforce slowly became demoralized. And then anger emerged. Vincent wanted to find the Chinaman and, he said, "do something to him" for letting them down. This was where they worked and played, where they could count on a certain level of sociability and good times. The 'wash was like their clubhouse, and now they didn't know what to do.

After about an hour and a half of milling about and cursing the Chinaman, and, increasingly, the Africans, the group began to disperse. A few of the men went to the nearby park abutting German Avenue near Chelten; others went over to Wesley's, and a few of us, including Vincent and Sebastian and me, went to McDonald's and had breakfast. On the way, we discussed what had just happened, but especially the Africans and the Chinaman. After placing our orders for hotcakes, we found a table and began to eat.

Between bites, Vincent blurted out, "Damn Africans! Who they think they are? Come over here and gon' take over. I never did like 'em. They my color, now, but they not my kind. They some stuck-up people, and when you pass 'em on the street, they think they too good to speak. Some ugly people, too! Don't like their women, either."

Sebastian then chimed in, "Yeah, didn't like that big guy's attitude. Acted like he owned the place. That's where we work."

"No, that's where we USED to work," corrected Leroy.

The conversation continued in this vein. The men continued to say disparaging things about Kim and the Africans. The general feeling was that Kim had let down the car wash workers by selling them out, and that he had never meant the men any good. The men vented by relating story after story about Kim that supported an increasingly negative picture of their former boss. And the emerging picture of the Africans was just as unflattering. Finally, we collected ourselves and left, unsure just what would happen to the group of men who formerly worked at the 'wash.

Much later in the summer, I ran across Vincent in a parking lot and found him looking rather disheveled. We were standing near a carryout at 11:00 in the morning, which suggested to me that he had already been drinking at that early hour. He expressed his anger at "the Chinaman" for selling the place without telling anyone. Vincent was still so angry, he said again that he wanted to "do something to the Chinaman." He felt that the owner "really messed with us" and misused them.

Vincent had worked at Brightway for fifteen years, he told me. Without the 'wash to go to, he is on the streets a lot of the time. He roams his North Philadelphia neighborhood looking for his friends, looking for a drink. Luckily he has a wife with some kind of income who gives him a place to stay. But he has no money of his own, including no unemployment compensation, since Kim Chou didn't pay into that. So Vincent has to hustle, but at fifty-five he's too old to hustle the way he used to.

After some time had passed, I returned to the car wash and saw that the Africans appeared to be adapting rather well to it. They were busy servicing cars the way the old workforce had done previously. But

I learned that under the new ownership the workers did not negotiate directly with the customers—they were now formally employed and negotiated directly with their boss.

More time passed and then I reached out to invite Vincent for lunch. We dined on hamburgers, and he opened up to me, reporting on what had become of his former coworkers. The story he told was disheartening, for a few of the men had quite predictably gone back to the streets, to drugs, to alcohol, and a few had landed in jail. Vincent ran down the list of men by their names—Johnson, Herbert, George, and Tom. Now the workers at Brightway have names like Moussa, Marwan, and Tki. These men are being paid the minimum wage and know that this is a "bad job," but are striving for something better.

Because of their precarious immigrant status, the Africans are more likely than members of the previous workforce to be law-abiding. They are bilingual and can switch back and forth from tribal language to English with facility. As international labor migrants, they are on the make, looking to move up and into better opportunities.

Of course, the change in the car wash was a real loss for Vincent, Sebastian, and the others. Now, if they try to go back, Vincent says that the foreigners tell them to get off the lot. This makes them angry. Invoking the civil rights movement, they say the Africans are unaware of how much they are benefiting from "the struggles of Black people." And, too, the new Africans associate American Blacks with the under-class; the group of African Americans that is doing well seems to be invisible to them.

For a long time in this country, being Black meant generally being of the same kind. Historically there has been a strong kinship within half of this binary system of race; Black people, when push came to shove, were racial brothers and sisters. But with surges in immigration of people of color, there have emerged major divisions among Americans of color. Such divisions complicate the historically caste-like situation of American Blacks. This ongoing process highlights the "ethnification of race" in America.

This ethnographic account of the car wash points to the increasing diversity of the city as well as toward a more general consideration of the contours of ethnic competition among different Americans of color for place and position. Drawing as it does from a pool of distressed workers, it suggests one model for a process of change in American Blacks' own racial identity as they compete for place and position (unsuccessfully in this case) with others of their color but not of their kind.

The modern civil rights movement that resulted in the still-ongoing incorporation of Blacks as full American citizens altered the racial landscape in one way, giving rise to a new Black middle class. More recently, the influx of great numbers of immigrants of color from many different lands has altered the racial landscape further still, effectively disaggregating skin color from ethnicity. One can perhaps see on the horizon, be it near or distant, a time when social "place" and Black skin color are two aspects of identity less paired, one to the other.

The current historically high levels of immigration—especially Black people from the Caribbean, Latin America, and Africa, as well as people of color from India and Asia—expose Americans to broader and more varied experiences with non-Whiteness. By the same token, as the new immigrants of color move into the urban mix, and the suburbs as well, they stake their claims on neighborhoods and in workplaces, giving a kind of wake-up call to America's most vulnerable: workers like those at the Brightway who might not conceive of themselves as victims of anything so grand-sounding as "globalization" but who happen, nevertheless, to be. And in settings like the car wash, Black people continue to be the subject of passing observation by everyone—Whites, immigrants, and even middle-class Blacks—who wants to distance themselves from the ghetto.

CHAPTER 7

THE STREET HUSTLE

Making Ends Meet

At a local carryout in the West Philadelphia 'hood one night, I sat around a table casually drinking forties with a group of young Black men. We experienced a certain camaraderie that night, our conversation skipping from one topic to another, until the subject of jobs came up—then, one of them asked abruptly but rhetorically, "Tell me, Dr. Anderson, why is it so hard for me to get a job but so easy to sell drugs?"

I found this question intriguing, for it illustrates the seemingly intractable predicament in which so many young Black men of inner-city communities so often find themselves: despised, distrusted, and rejected by the larger White society, and especially by prospective White employers, many of them become deeply alienated and are unable to make a living through legitimate means. Out of deep frustration, they may find themselves drawn to the underground economy that promises "fast money" just to make ends meet—hustling to survive financially day to day.

Despite remarkable social progress since the racial incorporation of the 1970s, 1980s, and 1990s, the Black ghetto persists as a bastion of inequality. Within the inner cities, the most disenfranchised Black people groan under the burden of persistent urban poverty, which has morphed from a problem of the least industrious few to a problem based on structural inequality. If at one point people of the larger society could easily blame the victims for their failure to work and make a decent living, today the opportunity structure is hugely different.

STRUCTURAL INEQUALITY

As the United States and other Western industrial countries have moved from manufacturing to high technology and service industries, great numbers of working people—White and Latino as well as Black— have difficulty making an effective transition to the emerging forms of economic organization. For most unemployed and underemployed Americans, the problem is their profound lack of the human capital necessary to make this transition. In other words, to make a decent living in the emerging economy, prospective workers require education, skills, and other resources that are necessary for finding a place in the new socioeconomic organization.

But those of the Black community often have an additional burden. Like many other Americans, Blacks often lack the human capital to effectively make this transition. But more than this, they need the prospective workplace to be receptive to people who look like them. This problem is complicated by the persistence of racial discrimination and social exclusion, which is rooted in the nation's racial history.

The Black ghetto's status as an icon has been spawned, developed, and shaped by successive numbers of Whites who have developed a peculiarly adversarial relationship with the urban ghetto, and the people they assume live there. Today, not only are these Whites and their progeny competitors in urban spaces—people who historically have been among those who fled when Black people moved into their communities (White flight)—but they constitute an adversarial work- force that is absolutely not interested in hiring and promoting Blacks, whom so many of them now associate with the iconic ghetto. Hence, despite the incorporation of vast numbers of Black people into the

American occupational structure, many others have been left by the wayside, victims mired in today's structural poverty.

The civil rights movement and the urban riots that followed occurred at a time when the American economy was expanding: the moment was optimal for upward mobility and racial incorporation (Marglin and Schur 1992). Now, as opportunities evaporate, the ghetto poor are left to work in what remains of the manufacturing industry or in low-wage service jobs, positions that usually pay too little to live on. Moreover, the neighborhoods where they live are stigmatized; in the minds of many, to be Black is to be from the ghetto, a place stereotyped as a den of iniquity where poverty, crime, drugs, and violence proliferate. And to be "from the ghetto," signaled by Black skin, is to be burdened with a deficit of credibility, especially in the White spaces of the larger society where Blacks compete with others for place and position. Since Blacks are so burdened, they are profoundly disadvantaged in this job market.

Additionally, to live in the ghetto is to be heavily policed, though the police are highly selective in enforcing the law; typically they pick the "low-hanging fruit," which reduces their physical risk but counts as performing their duties. Thus the ghetto school and the less dangerous areas of the neighborhood draw their persistent attention. Here young boys and girls await, to be arrested for smoking weed or whatever. At the inner-city ghetto school, an argument or a simple fistfight becomes an opportunity for police intervention, giving the young people a record of "contact with the police." This record puts them at a profound disadvantage in the emerging service industry and often results in serial unemployment or malignant joblessness (see Pager 2009). Great numbers of the ghetto's most desperate citizens cannot adjust to this profound transformation. Many live paycheck to paycheck, bartering or borrowing from one another to make ends meet. When they can't do this, many try to survive any way they can.

Black people living in the urban ghetto are among the weakest elements of the urban economy and are increasingly impoverished, overwhelmed, and frustrated. On the one hand, they identify strongly as American citizens and generally feel entitled to better opportunities than they see before them. At the same time, they witness the influx of new immigrants, many of them people of color, who constantly seem to leapfrog over them for opportunities in the labor force; historically, European immigrants did the same, mainly because they had the advantage of White skin in a White supremacist–dominated society (Higham 2002; Davis and Haller 1998; Asbury [1927] 2008; Du Bois [1899] 1996).

Poor Blacks generally lack the human capital necessary to rise above their circumstances; their situation is not fully within their control. The modern workplace is increasingly high-tech, and many of the manufacturing jobs their parents and grandparents relied on have moved to the Third World. In desperation, the residents of ghetto communities do whatever they can to meet the exigencies of daily existence. The most alienated resort to the underground economy of hustling, drug dealing, or some other criminal activity. And although the wider society, increasingly socially conservative, is prepared to "blame the victim" for the conditions of these communities, their "self-destruction" is in reality the result of global and structural economic forces.

THE THREE PRONGS

The inner-city economy at "ground zero," the most economically distressed part of the city, rests on three prongs: low-wage, casual jobs that offer little continuity of employment and few if any benefits; welfare payments, including Temporary Assistance for Needy Families (TANF), food stamps, and other government transfer programs; and the informal economy, which encompasses legal activities carried on outside the marketplace, such as bartering labor and goods among friends and relatives; quasi-legal activities such as small businesses operated out of the home, below the radar of regulation; and illegal activities such as drug dealing, prostitution, and street crime (Anderson 1999). Through a process of push and pull, these prongs work to circulate capital throughout the impoverished ghetto community.

The poorest and most desperate Black people rely for subsistence on anything they can, and often on all three ways of gaining income (Valentine 1980; Stack 1997; McLeod 1995; Anderson 1999). For example, welfare payments and earnings from employment not only supplement one another but provide capital and consumers for informal businesses such as braiding hair, hand washing cars, or minding children. Within the community, money circulates, moving from person to person. But if any one of the three elements of the ghetto economy is unproductive and fails to deliver financial resources, people are pressed to rely on the remaining two. Members of families, households, and neighborhoods engage in nonmarket exchanges—bartering, borrowing and lending, and, in the process, transferring and transforming these resources. As local residents obtain money from one or more of these sources, it circulates throughout the inner-city community. With the recent drastic reductions in welfare payments and the latest contractions in job opportunities for less-educated workers, many inner-city residents increasingly rely on this informal economy, but without the benefit of the civil law.

When disagreements occur, debts go unresolved and unpaid. As tensions mount, the more desperate some people become, and the more this local economy becomes characterized by retributive violence, including "payback" and revenge. During especially hard times, rates of violence and homicide are likely to escalate.

For too many young Black men in areas of concentrated poverty, daily life consists of simply meeting the challenge of staying alive. To avoid being killed as they navigate within the disenfranchised community, they acquire a persona with a street-toughened edge. This image becomes generalized, supporting the negative stereotype that has become a master status of the Black man throughout the larger society and, more specifically, the iconic ghetto (Hughes 1945; Anderson 1990, 2012a,b,c). Employers often reject young Black male applicants based on this image, further undermining their prospects for legitimate employment (Kirschenman and Neckerman 1991). Joblessness then has deeper ramifications that feed on themselves, leading many young men to rationalize their involvement in the illegal, and often violent, underground economy (Anderson 1990, 1999; Venkatesh 2009).

At the same time that elected leaders have made major reductions in the social safety net, including welfare and other supports, poor people must compete ever more fiercely for low-paid jobs and scarce resources with new immigrants to the United States as well as indirectly with poor working people around the globe. Thus globalization has completed what suburbanization and deindustrialization began. When corporations send their manufacturing operations to other places that offer plenty of low-wage labor — now including China and India as well as the US South and West, Mexico, and the Asian Pacific region — even more jobs leave Philadelphia and other industrial centers, creating a powerful employment vacuum: work disappears (Wilson 1996).

Inner-city Black men have many competitors for the relatively few jobs that do exist. Black women may have an advantage in customer service positions; immigrants may get a foothold in key employment niches. For the truly disadvantaged, especially high school dropouts or men with criminal records, jobs are even more difficult to obtain (Pager 2003a,b, 2007a,b). President Bill Clinton's promise to "end welfare as we know it" coincided with a brief period of unusual expansion in the labor market, fueling the illusion that most people would be able to move from welfare to work, but the recessions that followed have deepened the effects of these structural shifts, and joblessness and distress are now widespread (Edelman 1997).

As the industrial base of the American economy changes from manufacturing to service and high technology within an increasingly global economy, dislocation spreads and workers with limited marketable skills bear the brunt of it, facing persistent joblessness. Great numbers of people find it harder and harder to adjust to these changes. Moreover, the service jobs that do become available often don't pay a living wage. The resulting poverty is best described as "structural." As the wider economy fails these citizens, they cope the best way they know how, relying on whatever forms of capital they can summon. As they go about meeting the demands of making a living, or of simple survival, their coping strategies, legal and illegal, are often dramatized in the public media, which is inclined to showcase the most sensational and negative images of the community, effectively racializing their efforts to cope with economic distress.

Black ghetto residents not only face long-standing prejudice but develop a peculiar negative capital, or even find their individual stigma exacerbated. As they compete with others who do not have the disadvantage of being associated with the iconic ghetto, gainful employment becomes further out of their reach. People living in the inner city who do manage to find a job despite all the obstacles are the working poor. They toil as night watchmen, janitors, office cleaners, street sweepers, dishwashers, construction laborers, car washers, landscapers, fast-food workers, nurses' aides, office assistants, and domestic workers. Most of these jobs pay little and provide few if any benefits.

These ghetto residents are often the first casualties of economic downturns such as the Great Recession of 2008–9 and the pandemic of 2020, encouraging their participation in the informal economy. Despite the fluctuating national employment rate, conditions in many inner-city Black neighborhoods generally fail to improve, with the impact felt most acutely by uneducated young Black men (Mincy 2006). And a great many people who do find employment remain impoverished even while working. Thus the "neighborhood effects" of concentrated poverty described by William Julius Wilson (1987, 1996) become ever more salient, exacerbating local problems.

In the inner-city ghetto community, money earned is quickly spent, and many people walk the streets almost broke. One common scenario begins with a man receiving a paycheck from a legitimate employer. Since he, like many inner-city residents, may not have a bank account, he likely cashes his paycheck at a local currency exchange, which charges an exorbitant fee. Often he goes from the currency exchange to the corner tavern for "a taste," a drink of liquor with friends. Typically the man has accumulated debts to associates on the corner that he must repay when he sees them or answer to the lender. His debts have accumulated in part because he earns too little to cover all his expenses between paychecks; to make ends meet, he must often borrow from friends.

The week before payday, men can be heard soliciting others to "let me hold ten [borrow ten dollars] until Friday." When payday comes, if the debt isn't repaid, quarrels leading to outright violence may ensue over the money owed. When a debtor is seen using money for something other than repaying his debt, the lender can feel disrespected, or "dissed." He may then need to "set the debtor straight," to communicate his feelings of disrespect. And if the debt is not repaid promptly enough, the lender is not likely to extend credit again (see Wherry, Seefelt, and Alvarez 2019).

The third element of the ghetto economy, the irregular component, includes business ventures that fall close to the blurry line between legality and criminality. For example, a party host might sell dinner platters for six or seven dollars. People routinely gamble on card games; a minimum stake of twenty or thirty dollars a person may be required, and the game goes on all evening, with players joining in and dropping out. People organize other forms of gambling in their homes, in the back rooms of barbershops and bars, or on the street.

Among the most desperate ghetto residents, illegal activities include dogfights, cockfights, dice games, robbery, burglary, fencing stolen goods, dealing drugs, and loan sharking. On the legal side are various interpersonal accommodations such as the barter system—exchanging goods and services. For example, people may repair a neighbor's car on the weekend, help paint someone's steps, perform a plumbing job, or style someone's hair but take no money for any of this work; rather, they wait to be paid back with a favor in the future (Anderson 1999). Mothers routinely trade child care in the same manner. Legal gambling—the state lottery—is also highly popular.

Marginal forms of work merge into the informal economy: freelancers may work on their own, doing odd jobs or engaging in petty entrepreneurship as street vendors, or they may work for someone else, perhaps at a local car wash. This sector of the economy, where relations are informal and characterized by age-related peer groups, family relationships, and personal connections, resembles the marginal urban economies in developing or underdeveloped nations.

Low-level forms of crime have taken up some of the slack left by the termination of government transfer payments and the contraction of wage earning from legitimate jobs. Illegal activities supply some income to the neighborhood. With such pressures, men can now be overheard in barbershops and bars saying such things as "I'm gon' get mine somehow" and "Somebody's gon' pay me." Men who appear to be peaceful do at times act out these allusions to street crime. It is hard to quantify such impressionistic evidence, but an observer gains a clear sense of the high level of frustration in the community.

Although many people manage to adjust, others develop short fuses and are easily aroused to anger. The Korean grocers who have opened stores in otherwise all-Black neighborhoods often bear the brunt of this frustration. Not only are they of a different ethnic group and national origin but they appear to be making money off the Black community. To be sure, many Korean proprietors are solicitous of local people and employ them in visible positions, but enmity can build, and occasionally this tension mounts to the point that a clerk is killed in a robbery of the family's businesses (Lee 2002). There is an observable connection between frustration levels and the number of robberies and assaults occurring on the streets. When frustration levels are high, the potential for violence rises.

Informal social transactions become an increasingly common way to survive. But these exchanges are typically made without the benefit of civil law. In the local community, the civil law and its agents have only limited credibility. Street justice fills this void, becoming an important principle of local status relations, and reputation or street credibility becomes all the more important, serving as a form of social coin. But "street cred" must be nurtured, husbanded, and replenished from time to time. It is replenished most effectively not by talk and recriminations but by actual deeds, which must be performed repeatedly to earn the desired result: respect. Certain inner-city residents are always looking for opportunities to develop, and have others validate, their street credibility. The constant need to address shows of disrespect creates a stimulus for interpersonal violence (Anderson 1999).

The peculiar forms of social capital and regulation that develop in the isolated inner-city community—street justice and street credibility—not only sustain the drug trade but exacerbate its violence and extend its reach. Living in areas of concentrated poverty in which hustling and crime flourish, poor inner-city males see possibilities for making money just outside their door. Drugs appear to be omnipresent as the illegal enterprise moves in where the wider economy has failed local residents. Young men, who cannot avoid confronting the drug network, often seize the economic opportunities it presents and the remunerative street crime that accompanies it.

Although the dominant society fears the violence of alienated young people, the inner-city neighborhood itself suffers the greatest harm at their hands. In response to persistent structural poverty, failures of public policy, and intensifying joblessness, the irregular economy expands, and its fallout is violent crime perpetrated primarily by desperate young males and increasingly females (Jones 2004; Ness 2004). Many alienated and otherwise idle youths enter the drug trade voluntarily, motivated by a street culture that emphasizes material objects, such as brand-name sneakers, gold chains, and leather jackets, which function as signs of status and may help a man win young women's attention and prestige among his peers. For many of these young people, selling drugs is a strong bid for financial success.

In Philadelphia, the drug trade is organized hierarchically, as "top dogs," "middle dogs," and "low dogs" (Anderson 1990), similar to a pyramid scheme. The top dogs seem to make the most money, operating as drug kingpins, but to local residents they are mostly invisible, known largely in the abstract or as urban legends. As aging baby daddies, homeboys, brothers, cousins, nephews, and sons, the middle dogs are more visible and often have an everyday presence in the community. Ranging in age from twenty-five to thirty-five, they visit the local street-corner carryouts, clubs, barbershops, and car washes and drive around the neighborhood in Lexus, Mercedes, or BMW sedans, their flashy "rides" attesting to their financial success and drawing the admiration of youthful wannabes. On their rounds they "do their business," but they are also on the lookout, or even outright hunt, for young recruits to the trade. Their most likely prospects are financially strapped young boys in need of self-esteem. Typically these boys lack a "decent" and strong father figure or other male presence in their lives, but the draw of the street is so powerful that even boys from intact families can be taken in.

On spotting vulnerable boys, sometimes as young as thirteen or fourteen, the middle dogs seek to cultivate them and turn them into "low dogs." By showing them attention, the middle dogs subtly or overtly court them, perhaps letting them "hold" (borrow) a few dollars or doing them other small financial favors. The task for a boy may be as simple as serving as a lookout. Each task completed forges a bond between the young boy and the middle dog, and mutual confidence grows. As their relationship develops, the middle dogs "let" the boys do them larger favors, with completed tasks earning them more trust. Eager to please, the young boys want to "step up to the plate" and prove that any degree of faith shown by the middle dog, which may well be confused with respect, was justified and not misplaced—to show that he is "ready." In time these little favors turn into "odd jobs" and other tasks for which the boy may be paid, encouraging his dependence and bonding him to the middle dog. Benefiting from the occasional largesse of the middle dog, the young boy may at times use his credit and build up a debt that becomes harder and harder to repay. As the young boy becomes increasingly dependent on this relationship, his street credibility is ever more strongly tied to his job performance as evaluated by the middle dog. This hierarchical relationship has elements of coercion as well as seduction, given the differences in age and power between the two. A young boy who is directly approached by an older man to work for him may take the offer as a threat; discovering that the man is a real dealer, he may feel intimidated and believe it is too risky not to work for the man—that if he refuses his life may be in danger.

But with the promise of "living large," getting ready money and enhanced street credibility, why not? To seal the deal and initiate him into the drug trade, the middle dog may offer the young boy a "package" to hold or even assign him a corner to stand on and sell drugs. Deeply flattered, but also anxious, the young boy may find it easier to comply than to refuse. The stage is now set for him to become a full-fledged low dog in the local drug trade. Consummating his new status, he stands on the corner day and night, typically making drug transactions and handling large sums of cash. In the neighborhood and on the streets, the boy is now "clocking," which means that the middle dog has "fronted" him drugs to sell, often on consignment. But it also means he has taken on the burden of a drug bill, a promissory note that must be repaid, either in money or by the return of the unsold product. If the youth cannot meet his account, his life may be on the line. These debts can easily grow to unwieldy proportions, since "interest" rates of fifty cents on the dollar are not uncommon. If the boy borrows money from a dealer and fails to repay it within the time allotted, a middle dog may allow him to work it off in the trade. Failure to collect on a debt jeopardizes the middle dog's street cred, leading him to exact payment through physical harm or even assassination (Anderson 1999).

Making matters worse, endemic poverty has encouraged the emergence of "stickup boys" who roam the ghetto streets looking for money or drugs and robbing the low dogs who stand on the corner selling drugs. If a boy is robbed and cannot account for his drugs by producing the right amount of cash, his middle dog may tell him: "If you don't pay up, you have twenty-four hours to live." To come up with the money on short notice, the boy may well resort to robbery himself or commit other forms of street crime. Before scores are settled, several people may die. With the erosion of civil law, street justice becomes one of the few ways of mediating disputes, and street credibility becomes the coin for both expressive and instrumental reasons.

For his own security, the young boy becomes highly motivated to get a gun, which he sees as standing between him and his own death. He must be prepared to defend what's his, be it money, drugs, or street credibility. From his experience of the streets, he knows that his very life depends on having respect on the street. A gun provides instant street cred, and guns are readily available; young boys beg, borrow, rent, and steal them. Once he has a weapon, the boy often carries it. When he doesn't, he sometimes adopts elaborate ruses to present himself as "strapped," including a hunched or labored gait that, for those who are streetwise, sends the unmistakable message "I'm packing." Through the multifarious drug transactions that "go down" on the corner, the young boy becomes entangled in a web of social and financial relations that are regulated not by civil law but by the code of the street (Anderson 1999). Arguments can arise almost anywhere at any time, and the boy must be prepared to deal with them, so he carries his "piece" to the multiplex, to Mickey D's, to his girlfriend's house, sometimes even to school—or to any "staging area" where trouble might arise and beefs might be settled.

This almost insatiable need for street credibility, reinforced by a code of silence that prohibits and punishes "snitching," contributes powerfully to the high urban murder rate. A root cause is persistent urban poverty, which sometimes leaves no clear way to acquire money other than this criminal, violent dimension of the underground economy.

As we see, young Black men face extreme disadvantages just by living in areas of concentrated urban poverty. Yet most families in inner-city communities—even those who are most impoverished— hold "decent" or mainstream values although they are under extreme pressure in the neighborhood. When venturing outside their homes, they must deal with the "street element," and to do so many will present themselves as "street" or at least as capable of "getting ignorant" if they need to. Culturally, they understand that shows of decency are taken as signs of weakness and will not "get you much on the street." Many parents try to socialize their children to have decent values, while understanding that the open display of these values can be dangerous by calling the children's street credibility into question. Thus youths from decent families of the ghetto must learn to code-switch, and they often develop an exquisite ability to tell "what time it is" and behave accordingly.

Meanwhile, the neighborhood peer group smokes marijuana

"blunts," experimenting with mind-dulling drugs. By the time these young Black males get out of school and approach the job market, many of them cannot pass the background check or the drug test. The employer then has a ready excuse not to hire dark-skinned young men, typically discriminating in favor of immigrants or young people from the suburbs.

The life course of the young Black male in the inner city is shaped by the concentration of poverty in an isolated, segregated community. In this racially circumscribed environment, his contacts with the wider society are limited and he has little exposure to role models not in his situation. Instead, the Black youth naturally identifies with others who are similarly situated; they likely become his most important reference group. This restricted experience and perspective shape his orientation and, ultimately, his outlook on life, its possibilities and limitations. In the company of peers, he strives to fit in. To be sure, a large part of his worldview is a function of the real world in which he must survive and function every day. Typically his home life is female-centric; he lives with his mother and perhaps his grandmother or an aunt, but not with his father. The men in his life are his brothers and cousins, and occasionally an uncle or a grandfather. Seldom does he have the positive and direct influence of a father who lives nearby and stays in touch. When a father figure is present, he is rarely a positive role model. This lack is largely a function, both directly and indirectly, of the absence of family-sustaining jobs and opportunity that would inspire and reinforce a positive view of the future. Because of this, young Black males in the ghetto more often than not grow up without a strong sense of connection to mainstream society and the wider culture.

The persistent issue for people is not having enough money. The whole community is in the pit of poverty, and it seems there is never enough for anyone. Residents need money for the bare necessities of everyday life, to be sure, but for many it also becomes important to acquire the trinkets that are so important for enhancing social identity: the gold bracelet or neck chain, the iPhone, the jacket, and the sneakers. The oversized white T-shirt worn over pants that hang well below the waist is part of the urban uniform that makes one presentable, and at only a few dollars, it is relatively inexpensive. The local youth culture is highly competitive, pervaded by envy; young people often feel an intense need to show they are "better than" the next person. Dress becomes a visible sign of belonging and status. By the same token, wearing worn-out clothes or going about unkempt has major social costs, so material things define status in the local culture.

Many young men get spending money from their mothers or uncles, or they borrow from one another; a few have part-time jobs. But if respectable money is not forthcoming, a certain urgency makes these boys vulnerable to the street ethic of chasing "fast" money. When some become ensnared in the fast life, their example beckons to others. A boy can become increasingly alienated; often shortsighted and confused, he is "out there" doing what he feels he must to survive. Survival is a matter not only of subsistence, however, but also of status. So powerful are these "needs" that they "justify" a range of unsavory activities from sticking someone up or snatching a pocketbook to "picking up a package." Street hustling can become a way of life, but there are consequences when things go awry—as they almost always do eventually. Violence culminating in jail or death is the common result. Young Black people at ground zero know the fatal consequences of resorting to these expedients, but they seldom see any alternative. Like soldiers in a war zone, they become preoccupied with simply staying alive, and they adopt the attitudes and postures that survival on the streets requires. It is with this orientation that the maturing inner-city male approaches the world of the ghetto, including the institutions there that connect with the wider society: schools, churches, stores, the police, the criminal justice system (Hinton, Henderson, and Reed 2018).

We now know that one in three Black men ages twenty to thirty is in the hands of the criminal justice system—in jail, on probation, or awaiting adjudication. Although poverty and the desperation it breeds in Black communities are certainly at least partly at fault for this shocking statistic, no less a contributing factor is the severe scrutiny that the criminal justice system inflicts on Black people (see Tonry 2010;

Pager 2009; Goffman 2014). Particularly outside their communities, Blacks are too often penalized for things that in others might not even be noticed. Yet in distressed areas, Black people continue trying to come to terms with their world—to seek wholeness in the light of so much misery and destitution. That, to say the least, is a challenge. The life of a young inner-city Black person is all but guaranteed to be deeply alienating.

This is not to say that "nobody makes it out." Of course, some young people do advance, "make it out," but the odds are against them. Much depends on luck, hard work, and connections. The fortunate few who do succeed tend to have effective role models—often coaches, teachers, or parents—who provide them with direction and help them to cope, giving them a piece of the human capital they need to succeed.

CHAPTER 8

POLICING THE ICON

The larger White society typically conceives of neighborhoods where Black people are concentrated as "bad" or "dangerous" and strongly associates them with persistent poverty and street crime. Typically these areas are hyper-policed, apparently not so much for the benefit of the Black residents as to prevent crime from spilling over into adjacent White neighborhoods. Areas deep within these neighborhoods may hardly be policed at all, leaving these residents to feel that they are on their own—until there is a shooting, at which point the police come fully armed and in force. As residents, they are encouraged to take matters of personal defense into their own hands; thus, they arm and prepare themselves and their families for trouble.

For public safety and security, many feel the need to cultivate street credibility—"street cred"—which promises certain retribution for transgressions against them, their loved ones, and their close friends. Elsewhere I have described this as a "code of the street" (Anderson 1999), a set of prescriptions and proscriptions of behavior that when followed maintains a certain order in the local community. When things go amiss, violence occurs, alerting not only the local neighborhood but sometimes the city at large. As these violations of the code occur, the "bad" reputation of the troubled neighborhoods only worsens, further stigmatizing not only the iconic ghetto, but Black people more generally.

Hence, when Blacks "stray" into homogeneously White areas, the people there often become defensive. And anonymous Blacks there are often assumed to be "from the ghetto," up to no good, and crime-prone. As icons or symbolic representatives of the ghetto, they are surveilled and followed. When the police are summoned, the Black person may be stopped and frisked, sometimes getting injured or killed in the process. The anonymous Black person often is approached with suspicion and effectively criminalized on sight not only by bystanders and passersby but most consequentially by the police. When they arrive, typically they approach the Black person as a "criminal" and aggressively arrest him. If he demands that his rights as a law-abiding citizen be respected, they may accuse him of resisting arrest, manhandle him, physically assault him, and too often take him away to be jailed.

Most Black residents are convinced that Whites are not treated the way they are. They know that when a Black person is violated or harmed, little will be done to rectify the situation or solve the crime. And they know that if a Black person is suspected of committing a crime against a White person, there will be hell to pay. So ghetto residents generally distrust the police. Practically speaking, this means that, to be safe in the community, residents figure out they must take responsibility for their own security. What is assumed to keep one safe is the effective promise of personal retribution or certain vengeance, or "payback," if one is violated. This dynamic of aggressive self-protection is one of the primary causes of the high rates of violence and homicide in inner-city communities, especially among youths. Young people wage campaigns for respect within as well as outside of the schools, occasionally giving rise to physical conflict.

Moreover, desperate poverty fuels intense competition for honor and respect (Anderson 1999; Horowitz 1983). Many young people jealously guard the respect they achieve in the eyes of their friends, while others act out of envy. Impoverished in a world of plenty, young people commonly flaunt material things that signify their status and success. At the same time, those who "have something" remain desperate for money. Luxury consumer goods circulate as people hock them for cash.

Older and more conventional role models have become less and less attractive because, given the severe and persistent contraction in the local labor market, the younger generation cannot follow in their elders' footsteps. It's demoralizing. To succeed socially and financially, some young people decide they must try for the big score—too often, hustling, drug dealing, and stealing seem to be their best bet. But to follow through they must find others who will watch their backs. Often this means joining a group that defends the neighborhood. The authorities often refer to these groups as gangs, but most consist simply of "homies," friends whose main responsibility is to take up for local people against outsiders or members of other groups who try to exploit them (Hagedorn 2017). Local folks are allowed to exploit other local folks, but outsiders must "keep their hands off what's ours." Youth groups, male and female alike, are extremely proprietary and constantly repel competitors with threats, actual violence, and "payback."

For young people, this means being prepared to meet challenges with counteractions. When they are hit or otherwise violated, they may hit back. An important part of the code is to manifest street credibility and not allow others to take advantage or "chump" you—to let the next person know you are "about serious business" and aren't to be trifled with. The message that you are not a pushover must be loud and clear, for street credibility is high maintenance: it can't be established once and for all but must be constantly negotiated.

Crime has a special place in the predominantly White areas that border the city's impoverished Black ghettos. The issue here is often as much race relations as it is crime itself. In particular, the conflation of race with status and with criminal proclivity shapes the way race is lived and plays out in the daily life of these communities and beyond. When Blacks appear on the streets of the homogeneously White community, ordinary residents take notice of the "outsiders," and many see them as profoundly threatening. Who are these people? What's their business here? Blacks must be explained. People in middle-class areas may have a hard time distinguishing ordinary, law-abiding Black citizens from the desperate few who might feel compelled to commit robbery. Such assessments may define the state of the relations between Blacks and the White community, which can become peculiarly unified against them.

Over time the Black community has been subjected to containment efforts by the wider, predominantly White society, notably by the police, who often work informally to maintain boundaries between Black and White neighborhoods. For instance, in the racially mixed Philadelphia neighborhood of Powelton Village late one evening, a White couple drove across the well-known boundary of Spring Garden Street into a Black and impoverished "high-crime" area of Mantua in West Philadelphia. After a short while, a police car pulled them over. The White officer inquired, "Are you lost? This is a Black area." The implication was that a White middle-class couple has no business driving the streets of the ghetto, and those who do are likely to be up to no good—perhaps looking to buy drugs. Martin, the man, answered, "No, we know where we are. We're visiting a friend." The policeman seemed dumbfounded but let them go on their way. In Philadelphia and other major cities, it's well known that suburban Whites often venture into the ghetto to "score" hard drugs, so White people moving about the ghetto are almost immediately assumed to be out of place, perhaps out for a drug run.

To the extent that crime is "contained" in poor inner-city neighborhoods, it may not bother the White community much; typically the wider society easily rejects any responsibility for Black sections of the city (Sharkey 2014). Yet the crime that occurs in areas of concentrated urban poverty does sometimes spill over into the predominantly White, more affluent neighborhoods beyond. Alarms go off when White people are mugged, raped, or killed. Calls for action are made and heeded. The police respond, and when they do they tend to be polite and respectful to the Whites who summoned them, in contrast to the rude treatment Black respondents say they often receive in the adjacent Black community. The issue here is in large part differential policing by race. Black communities are assumed to be "bad" and dangerous and are generally less highly valued in the minds of police officers and the public at large. It may be that the police do in fact behave one way in middle-class White neighborhoods and quite another way in ghetto neighborhoods. The level of regard the police feel for these communities varies widely. In their mind, the two hold starkly different degrees of moral authority.

When the police respond to a summons from the Black community, they are inclined to engage in a kind of urban theater, presenting themselves as "rough, tough, and ready," prepared to meet any perceived threats or challenges to their authority. When they arrive they are seen as having a chip on their shoulder; often they try to "go for bad," as residents say, daring anyone to knock it off. Thus they often abuse the residents who called for help in the first place. The police are known to talk loudly and use foul language as a tactic to put everyone on notice.

Although this appears to be a front, a presentation of self for the benefit of the residents, such performances resonate, and reports quickly spread throughout the local community. Through these theatrics, police gain and reinforce a reputation of being tough, and through such intimidation they count on restraining those inclined to commit violent crimes. Ghetto residents often see through this act and understand the nature of it, since it mimics the "code" in certain respects. At the same time, understandably, the police want to return to their own homes in one piece. This has given rise to what Blacks in the ghetto call "trigger-happy" policing—police often shoot first and ask questions later. When such practices are accepted or formulated into policy, more Black people die.

THE LAW

For many Americans, including some middle-class Blacks, a Black man on a dead-end street at night is a frightening image. The conception of Black males as dangerous or threatening is reinforced by local news reports, particularly when a Black man's picture is plastered across the evening news as having committed a heinous crime, be it a drug-related murder or a robbery of a business in which local people are killed—especially when the victims are White. Such criminal behavior is strongly associated with the ghetto community; it's common enough to seem expected.

Violent crimes are most often committed by Black males against other Black males or their associates (Nada 2021; Philadelphia Comptroller 2021). If he is Black, the victim is implicitly blamed for the crime. Thus the brief coverage these stories receive in the local media sends a message that not only are such crimes to be expected but they are of little significance and can to some extent be tolerated. Black people in particular take away a special message: that they are second-class citizens and their value as a people is limited. They become even more alienated from and distrustful of White people, particularly those who treat the pattern as insignificant—business as usual.

The public has come to understand that if a crime is committed against people of "the mainstream"—White people—the press will show more concern and the event will command greater prominence, including community outrage. Thus the local media provide a glimpse into the racial order of the city and, indeed, of society at large. Often, community residents understand that news of a Black person's death historically has been buried in the back pages of the newspaper or otherwise minimized. This discrepancy of coverage has serious implications for the iconic ghetto and what it suggests to local citizens. It encourages the stereotypes that shape the iconic ghetto and the wider White society's view of Blacks as a people apart, as somehow lower than all others. Among the most marginalized Whites and other groups, this view reinforces the importance of distancing themselves from those of an even lower status—the ghetto poor. And in subtle but important ways it empowers and fuels the long-standing racial principle of White over Black.

Selective scrutiny based on skin color largely accounts for why so many Blacks—but relatively few Whites—are behind bars or otherwise in trouble with the law. Since the days of slavery, Black men have been sought as fugitives by White authorities, even when the crime was slaves' "stealing" themselves. Today mass incarceration affects the Black inner-city ghetto more directly than any other community (Alexander 2010; Eason 2017). The iconic ghetto is deeply implicated in this connection and at least in part responsible for it. Authorities of the wider system spend a good deal of time and resources policing the ghetto, where crime is considered rampant.

Part of the problem is rooted in slavery and the institutionalized segregation that so often defined Black people as outside the law, thereby criminalizing much of the ordinary behavior engaged in by Blacks—particularly young males. For example, many towns once had laws against too many Black people gathering in one place. Others stated that Blacks had to be out of town by sundown or they'd be arrested. Many Black men thus developed a relationship with the police or with the bounty hunter. Great numbers of Black men through time have been relegated to being "on the run," consciously trying to stay out of the authorities' way, or at least one step ahead. And to the authorities—including many police officers and judges—young Black men have been suspect until they could prove their innocence.

• • •

On the streets of West Philadelphia one night, as I was driving to a friend's home, I saw an unmarked police car roll up on the sidewalk to corner a young Black man. As I watched, two White policemen got out and started to frisk the eighteen-year-old. "Put your hands out. I'll blow your fucking head off!" I heard one officer yell. The young man seemed terrified but kept his composure. I saw him shrug but cooperate.

He seemed to know the drill, as the police checked his identification and questioned him rudely. The police officers then dumped his backpack out onto the pavement. After about twenty minutes, they released him.

When the policemen left, I interviewed the young man, who by then was shaking like a leaf. I tried to calm him down and asked if he knew why the police had stopped him. "I don't know. I was just coming home from basketball practice. They were probably looking for drugs." Then

the shaken young man sighed and said, "It's the routine," implying that
he and his friends are commonly subjected to such random police stops.

· · ·

Black men have carried the burden of criminality since the fugitive
slave laws, creating a virtual outlaw class of people who are often one
step away from being "locked up." To carry such a burden day in and
day out is to experience institutionalized alienation.

The icon has become so powerful and well established that whole
Black communities, and any Black individual, can be linked with crime
occurring there; in time the negative iconography has come to constitute a large part of what it means to be Black, particularly in the minds
of those charged with law enforcement and social control. A familiar
example is the "stop and frisk" laws that are commonly applied against
young Black males, regardless of their social class and where they live.

This state of affairs has contributed to an adversarial relationship
between Blacks and the police, or even the civil law. Since the days of
slavery, Blacks have realized that there are two systems of law: one for
Whites and one for Blacks. When the police are called by Black people,
they typically arrive "too late, or in some cases not at all, or when they
do show up they abuse the people who called them in the first place," as
residents report. Implicit in this double standard is the understanding
that Black people will be punished more severely for crimes against
Whites than for similar crimes perpetrated against Blacks.

Equally important, Black people of impoverished communities
have learned that once a crime has been committed, the authorities
are more likely to seek justice if Whites are victimized than when the
victim is Black. On the streets of the Black ghetto, Black people who
are known to have killed other Blacks sometimes appear to "get away
with murder." In these circumstances, respect for the civil law erodes.
And members of the Black ghetto community come to understand that
they can't rely on the protection of civil law, which includes a fear of
providing information to the police.[1] Instead, the "code of the street,"

a kind of vigilante justice, has evolved to keep would-be perpetrators in check, which then fuels the local homicide rate, as the failure or inability of the police to serve and protect Black people reverberates through the community.

At the same time, since Blacks are more likely to be scrutinized by the police, it's important to remember that the economy leaves a significant number of young Blacks with severely limited options for making a living. Hence, a large proportion of Black men "live on the edge," engaging in petty crime or tolerating it in their midst simply to survive.[2] In addition to self-defense and economic survival, a third explanation for such behavior is the legacy of slavery itself. Some Black men today justify their alienation as well as crime, particularly against the wider society, as a form of reparations—an opportunity to "get paid back" for all the years of unpaid slave labor their ancestors performed. Thus many are none too enthusiastic about upholding the law in every little detail, particularly when it appears to work against them and their community.

THE COPS

When a Black male is stopped and frisked, it sends a message to him and to law-abiding White citizens alike: the problem is contained, controlled. If the Black male resists or complains, the situation escalates, giving the officers cause to Taser or manhandle and handcuff him. Once this process starts, the usual conclusion is that the man goes down: to jail, to a hospital, or to the morgue. The police are usually judged to be the good guys even when they violate the Black man's rights or shoot him dead; they seldom have to account for their actions.

George, a middle-aged Black man, shares one such experience from his youth:

When I was just a senior in college, I was dating my wife, who worked at a hospital there in the neighborhood. I was picking her up after work. So, I was sitting outside in my car, and it was a nice car—in fact, it was a brand-new car. So, the sharp new Chevy, all cleaned up, and I'm sitting out in my car waiting for her to finish work, to come out and join me.

Police car, police wagon—"paddy wagon," here in Philadelphia is what we would call the wagon—pulls up, and the two White officers tell me to get out of my car, and they put me in the back of their van. No explanation, just "Get out of your car," have me get out of my car, put me in the back of a van. And they drove me to the corner—literally to the corner of the block. And inside the van they had another Black kid, who worked at the hospital as a dishwasher.

So, they pull us up to the corner of the block, and they open the van and a woman, who looks out, says, "No, neither one of them."

And so then they tell me that I could get out. And by that time I'm in college, I know a little bit more about my rights, and I've become a little bit more aware of how police in Philadelphia approach Black people, and how they were always militaristic and didactic, and oftentimes ended in physical disputes, so I asked, "What did you stop me for?"

And there's a White guy, I mean, you know, redneck-looking White guy, you know—short, squat, thick-necked White guy, looked like he may have had a high school education, not very much more. He says, "Well, there's a woman that called from the hospital that said there's some people outside in the parking lot looking around people's cars, messing around people's cars."

"So, you stopped me because I was Black?"

And the guy looked at me with rage and anger in his face, but not anger like he wanted to fight—it was like indignation, you know. "She said there was a Negro male! I stopped you because the description was a Negro male!"

I said, "So, you just picked up every Black male that you saw, without any questions, and arrest them? I mean, you know, you detained them?"

"Well, yeah. A Negro male, that's what she said."

That was the moment where I truly understood that in Philadelphia, in that city, and the neighborhood especially what being Black really meant. It meant that if you were Black, and something happened, and the description was "Well, they were Black," that it doesn't matter what car you drive, or how you were dressed, or what your social background was, they would pick you up!

• • •

The intensified police presence in poor Black communities fosters this negative association in residents from a young age. Poor Black children see police officers walk the hallways of their schools as though they were in prison. When Black boys are involved in a fight or a disruption, instead of being sent to the principal's office, they're often handcuffed on the spot (see Riddle and Sinclair 2019). Experience teaches Black men that police officers exist not to protect them but to criminalize and humiliate them. Few Black boys get through adolescence without a story of police harassment, and with age their stories proliferate.

I've often visited schools in Philadelphia, such as Simon Gratz, Germantown High, or West Philadelphia High—Black schools that used to be White schools. Typically these schools have a police desk at one of the main doors, a couple of officers, an instructor, and a Black man or two from the community hired to act as role models for the children. This arrangement underscores the active involvement of men to provide "strong" role models and to invoke discipline, presumably to discourage the students, especially the boys, from going astray, but it actually alienates them. When they make a mistake or become involved in what may be a minor altercation, instead of being dealt with by the school officials, they may be escorted to a waiting police van and taken to jail for booking.

During my field research, I found that some cops, Black and White alike, are friendly and do try to build relationships with students, but the process is arbitrary, and many young people still wind up with a criminal record, which makes obtaining employment all the more difficult down the line (Pager 2009). The policemen and the Black "role models" seem to have all the power and can invoke and negotiate for "the law" at any moment. In trying to establish themselves with the young people, and with one another, some police officers overdo it. This is a part of the school-to-prison pipeline operating before your eyes.[3]

The next stop on this pipeline is city hall. I've been astounded time and again by the spectacle of Black and Latino (but primarily Black) people coming through, charged with anything from traffic tickets to "petty" crime—a parade of young Black men in handcuffs with White deputies on each side, leading them through the marble hallways into the courtroom, where they meet their public defenders and the judge (Kohler-Hausmann 2019). After a short time the youths are led back out on their way to jail. In the front of the courtroom, there's usually a group of White police officers, with perhaps one or two Black officers, doing court duty. The hallways and the courtrooms look "color coded," since White citizens are seldom treated this way (Anderson 1999).[4]

Whether his crime is real or imagined, aggressive police tactics can turn any Black male into an object of suspicion and skeptical scrutiny, opening him to further harassment. Black men engaged in innocuous activities—walking home from the corner store, examining a BB gun on sale at Walmart, or leaving a bachelor party—become targeted as criminals by authorities who appear to relish such encounters.

"Howard," a sixty-one-year-old Black man living in a middle-class yet segregated section of Philadelphia, talks about what he's had to do to avoid being harassed by the police:

I must say, I've never had a negative experience with the police. I think that's because of the way I carry myself. I've had experiences with the police, and whenever I get stopped for a traffic violation, the cop pulls me over, and the blue lights come on, my heart starts racing because I don't know what's going to happen to me, what's going to happen next. Pressure goes up, I get very nervous. But I think about something I learned from my parents. They taught me how to carry myself around police, and the message I learned was to be cooperative, to always be polite: "Yes sir, no sir," and all the while I'm doing this I'm very nervous because I don't trust the police.

I'm one of the few who haven't had a bad experience, but 90 percent of the Black people in this area have had a bad experience with the cops. I think it's just my parents, the way I was raised. I always knew how to carry myself.

THE TALK

With each negative encounter, local Black men build up antagonism toward law enforcement. They develop defenses and toughen up to protect their pride and perceived respectability. With this built-up hostility, interactions over minor offenses—like suspicion of selling loose cigarettes—quickly become emotionally charged.[5]

Typically the ranks of the police include some of the most racially insensitive people in our society. They are often drawn from local blue-collar neighborhoods filled with people who may see themselves and their communities as in fierce competition with Blacks for place and position—and as losing ground. Many Black police officers I've interviewed have expressed this, and some have felt the wrath of their White colleagues. In such circumstances the Black police officers' role has become extremely difficult; because of their skin color, many have been mistaken for criminals or suspects, and some have been shot by their fellow officers. The police campaign to be tough on crime has brought countless Black deaths owing to over-policing of the Black community.

The recent urban racial turmoil, particularly the Black Lives Matter demonstrations in the summer of 2020 after the killing of George Floyd, reflects the explosive release of a pent-up resentment of this police campaign by Black people and many of their brown and White allies. The motives of some of these allies, particularly those who destroy property, are questionable. They might well take part only to discredit the peaceful demonstrations by well-meaning Blacks. To combat this danger, Black parents often sit their teenage sons and daughters down for a ritual talk that goes something like this: "If a policeman stops you out on the street, be polite. Don't talk back. Say 'Yes sir, no sir, Officer. What seems to be the trouble?' Don't make any sudden moves. If you're driving, don't reach for the glove compartment. If he asks to see your identification, reach for it very carefully; he'll be watching your every move. Let the policeman take the lead. Listen to him. Do as he says. Defer to him. And as soon as you're able, call me."

When the police mistreat Black people, arrest them without cause, shoot them, or kill them while making an arrest, as happened to George Floyd in Minneapolis, such incidents become spectacles that may touch off protests around the world. But even more important, they indicate and publicize the lowly place of Black citizens in American society and culture, especially the role of the iconic ghetto in defining Blacks as a separate, lower caste, undermining their moral authority in the minds of their fellow citizens.

Moreover, many Whites have not adjusted to the idea that Black people now occupy more positions of privilege, power, and prestige—or just appear in places where they were historically unwelcome. When they see Blacks in such places, many Whites, though not all, unconsciously or explicitly want to banish them to the iconic ghetto—to the stereotypical space where they think all Black people belong, a segregated space for second-class citizens. Not courageous enough to attempt this feat alone, many of these self-appointed color-line monitors seek help wherever it can be found—such as from the police. The Black "interlopers" may simply want to visit their condominium's swimming pool, something Whites typically do without a second thought, or take a nap in the common room of their student dorm, make a purchase in an upscale store, drive a "nice" car, or visit a Starbucks. Shawn's experience with the police is important, and all too common for young Black men.

"Shawn," a law student in Washington, DC, grew up in inner-city Philadelphia, but he was able to attend private schools, where he did very well. Then he went on to college and to a prestigious law school. He and the handful of other Black law students were the only non-White residents of the affluent neighborhood near the law school.

One evening after classes, Shawn was waiting for a bus to go home.

Although his apartment was only a ten-minute walk away, he had stopped at the local grocery store and had groceries and books to carry, so he decided to take the bus that stopped just across the street from the law school. As he waited, Shawn was talking to his girlfriend on the phone when he noticed a police car drive slowly by. It drove by again, then circled the block a third time. On the fourth pass, the officer pulled up behind Shawn and sat for about three minutes, with the car's floodlight shining on the bus shelter where Shawn sat.

Then Shawn was startled to hear a blow horn order him to put his hands out where they could be seen and to turn slowly toward the light. As Shawn did so, with his phone still in his hand, he saw that an officer had stepped out of the cruiser and was reaching for his gun. Another law student, a White woman Shawn didn't know, who had also been waiting for the bus, called out that Shawn was only holding a cell phone. The officer yelled for Shawn to drop the phone, which he did, then told him to put his hands against the wall and not move. The officer immediately handcuffed and frisked him.

Shawn asked what was happening and explained that he was a student at the law school just across the street, waiting for the bus to go home. The officer ignored his explanation. By this time seven other police cars had arrived and blocked off the street. At the same time, a crowd of students and professors from Shawn's law school began to form across the street, but no one made a move to assist him. He felt humiliated.

The police cursed at him and ordered him to cooperate. Although he did so, they repeatedly kicked at his ankles, forcing his legs farther and farther apart until he was spread-eagled. They kept pushing his face against the wall or down toward his chest, telling him to keep his head down and stop resisting. He was frisked two more times and his wallet was taken. His textbooks and laptop were dumped out on the sidewalk; his grocery bags were emptied as well. He was restrained by three officers, who held his handcuffed hands along with the slack from his shirt and pants to prevent him from running away. They questioned him rudely, showing no respect for him as a law-abiding citizen.

When Shawn again asked what was going on, he was told he fit the description of someone involved in a shooting a few blocks away. Just then a police radio crackled, "Black male, five feet eight inches, blue button-down shirt, khaki dress pants, brown dress shoes." The description fit Shawn exactly. Hearing himself described over the radio, he was sure he was going to jail.

After Shawn had been forced to stand straddled, physically restrained, and handcuffed in front of his peers and professors for ten minutes, another radio bulletin informed the officers that the suspect had been apprehended. The policemen removed Shawn's handcuffs and told him to sit down. The officers who were standing around got back in their vehicles and drove off while the officer who made the initial stop took down Shawn's information for the police report. As the officer filled out the form, he tried to make small talk with Shawn, who felt humiliated and was still afraid, but mostly angry at being disrespected and at the clear racial profiling that had just taken place.

During the commotion, a group of White neighbors had congregated on a corner behind the police barricade. As the officer took down Shawn's information, a neighbor came up to the officer and, in front of Shawn, asked if that was "the guy." The officer said no, it turned out to be someone else. The neighbor, whispering within Shawn's hearing, offered to follow Shawn home to make sure. The officer said that wouldn't be necessary.

Shawn later heard on the local news that the actual suspect was the shooting victim's college roommate, who had been playing with a gun when it accidentally discharged. He was a White male. That was when Shawn realized it was his neighbors who had called the cops and provided his description. They had heard there'd been a shooting, and when they saw Shawn, who had been living in the neighborhood for three years, standing on the corner at night, they called the police, concluding that this Black man must be the suspect. These were the

neighbors who had stared at him every day yet avoided eye contact
as he passed them on the sidewalk on his way to and from law school.
(Adapted from Anderson 2011, 249–52.)

• • •

The tensions between the "iconic ghetto" and the "White space" are reflected in the many social struggles taking place between Blacks and lower-order Whites in the public arenas of everyday life. These powerful and persistent perceptual categories held by Whites and Blacks shape this struggle and are shaped by it; they operate in tandem, defining Blacks and Whites for each other in the abstract. Too often they see each other as mortal enemies, but Whites are most often armed with both the moral authority and the powerful weapons that typically shape and define this situation.

CHAPTER 9

THE HIDDEN INJURIES OF RACE AND CLASS

The social classes within the African American community today are qualitatively different from those of Du Bois's time, but we can still discern the four basic layers he discussed in *The Philadelphia Negro*. Du Bois argued that the problems of Black Philadelphians stemmed largely from their past servitude, which hindered them as they tried to negotiate an effective place in a highly competitive industrial urban setting where the legacy of White supremacy was strong and their competitors were favored because of their White skin. Moreover, the European immigrants tended to be more able because of their experience of freedom, which gave them a powerful advantage over recently freed slaves. Given this edge, they benefited from the prejudice of White employers who sought them out to the exclusion of Blacks. To White employers, White skin was a sign of a good worker, while Black skin meant a poor one. In many work settings, once the White workers were there in force, they collaborated against Blacks, often closing the workplace to Black workers. They sometimes threatened to quit if Blacks were hired.

This negative reputation preceded Blacks in many instances, setting in motion a self-fulfilling prophecy. Du Bois saw, too, that White supremacy similarly undercut Black entrepreneurship. Through his research on the history of Black business in Philadelphia, he discovered that at times middle-class Blacks were doing fairly well. There were Black doctors, lawyers, businessmen, and caterers. In fact, in the mid-nineteenth century, Blacks dominated the catering business. Many barbers were Black too, cutting White people's hair.

But he also saw that from time to time as Black people began to achieve middle-class status, a fresh wave of immigrants from Europe would arrive to undermine the position of the emerging Black middle class. This eventually happened to the Black catering business: its members lost their dominant position to caterers with White skin, who had an advantage because Whites preferred dealing with Whites, their place of origin notwithstanding. This scenario had devastating effects on Negro Philadelphians. Their families, their community, their churches, and their very identity suffered. What was socially disorganized remained so or became worse.

Du Bois distinguished four grades as making up the class structure of the Negro community. Grade I comprised the talented and well-to-do. Grade II comprised laborers who worked hard and were decent and law-abiding. Grade III comprised the working poor, who were barely making ends meet. And Grade IV was the "submerged tenth" of the Philadelphia Negro population. As Du Bois noted, this stratification was extremely volatile and precarious, primarily because of the interaction of racism and economics at the time (Anderson 1996).

For Du Bois, racism and political-economic forces strongly affected all four segments of the class structure. Today, although African Americans have been incorporated at all levels of mainstream society, the Black community continues to be socially organized around issues of racial oppression and calls for political unity to combat it, among other issues of daily life and neighborly relations.

THE ELITE

Presently the new Philadelphia Black elite emerges from a wide variety of backgrounds. Some are the typically dark-skinned sons and daughters of the old industrial working class, while others emerge directly from the old colortocracy, the light-complexioned progeny of slave masters and slaves, often the professional class that was traditionally educated in Black colleges and practiced medicine or law or ran businesses that served the segregated Black community. Often but not always indifferent to earlier cultural rules regarding color caste, darker- and lighter-skinned Blacks in this class commonly socialize with and marry one another or choose White, Latino, or Asian American spouses. In describing the operation of this color-caste system within the Black community at Barack Obama's inauguration, Rev. Joseph E. Lowery succinctly stated the principle: "If you're light, you're all right; if you're brown, stick around; if you're black, get back."

Although the cultural nationalism movement of the 1960s and 1970s undermined a lot of this thinking, color-caste prejudices linger in the everyday affairs of Black people, and their effects can still be discerned within the Black community's neighborhoods, local businesses, and social clubs. In the interest of unity against White racism, these caste lines are often downplayed, ignored, or even denied outright. Typically the Black people who embrace these principles keep a low profile, but occasionally mix with outsiders (see Frazier [1957] 1962; Graham 1999; Lacy 2007; Robinson 2011; Pattillo-McCoy 2013).

• • •

During the Christmas season one year, my wife and I were invited to a party at the home of a member of Philadelphia's Black elite. We arrived promptly at 7:00 p.m. at the entrance of his gated community and gave the security guard our names and our host's name.

After scrutinizing us, the guard waved us in. We parked near the house, rang the bell, and greeted my friend, who introduced us to his wife and some other guests.

As we made our way through the expansive kitchen to the living room, where about fifteen to twenty other elegantly dressed guests were seated, the host made a few more introductions, telling us the names of other guests. Although he was gracious, he clearly had his hands full that evening. Still, he made sure to cite not only the guests' names but also their pedigrees and their businesses or professions in some detail.

The large white Christmas tree was adorned with gold balls and tiny lights. The couches and easy chairs were also white, as was the carpet. Yet our brave host served red wine! The guests sat around the Christmas tree and made small talk. Everyone at the party was Black, some of the city's most prominent citizens. Although I knew a few of them, most I'd known only through the news. There were entertainers, business executives, local journalists, medical doctors, and attorneys, all successful in their fields.

The music of early Miles Davis softly filled the air, followed by Dizzy Gillespie, Sarah Vaughan, Count Basie, and Ella Fitzgerald. It was a lovely party, including a few guests from Washington, DC, and New York City.

• • •

The Black elite is often connected with the White elite nationally and internationally, and increasingly enjoy a common social history. Many attended the same prep schools as their White counterparts and then elite colleges and universities. As early beneficiaries of affirmative action and other equal-opportunity policies, many are now highly accomplished, and a few are very wealthy. Relative to the masses of Blacks, their lighter skin and their class demeanor matches that of their White counterparts, though many are concerned to maintain a low profile. Some even quietly pass for White. In the old days, those who were discovered to be Black according to the "one-drop rule" were typically ostracized from White communities. Such discoveries might bring expulsion from positions where they'd been assumed to be White (Graham 1999).

Refined and elegant in self-presentation, the Black elite understands the White elite's mores and values and embody them to a substantial extent. At the same time, these Blacks typically remain acutely conscious of their distinctive identity and adopt a complex and often dualistic approach to social life. They tend to socialize with a wide range of people, including Whites of equal status, while most worship in all-Black congregations.

Those who pass for White, if discovered, may use their Black identity as simply a part of their ethnic makeup, as other ethnic groups increasingly do. They often belong to predominantly White social clubs, and most live in upscale, mostly White neighborhoods. Few if any of their neighbors know they are Black until their relatives and friends start showing up (Graham 1999).

Members of the Black elite often live in two worlds, in a liminal existence. They connect socially with both Whites and Blacks of their own social standing, but also with middle-class and working-class Blacks, with whom they are comfortable and feel kinship, meeting them at the barbershop, church, or social club or in long-standing friendship groups. Though they operate comfortably in both social worlds, the two circles rarely overlap. Their experience brings to mind an affective accommodation to the cultural twoness noted by Du Bois ([1903] 1995).

THE MIDDLE CLASS

The racial incorporation process spurred a substantial increase in the size of the Black middle class, and many members have moved from the Black ghetto to the suburbs, where they often experience segregation again as the Whites they join flee the neighborhoods they have breached or may shun them in public.

Black people now work in a wider range of occupations than ever—not simply in menial jobs but in a variety of professional positions where they rarely appeared before, including as doctors, lawyers, professors, corporate executives, and elected officials, and many of them are highly successful (Lacy 2007; Landry 1988; Pattillo-McCoy 2013; Robinson 2010; Wilson 1978).

Many of these Blacks now live in solidly middle-class residential areas that once were not open to them but are now mostly Black because of White flight (Alba, Logan, and Stults 2000; Sharkey 2014). Others live in "nice" homes and apartments in some of the city's most exclusive neighborhoods, and their children attend formerly all-White schools (Logan and Zhang 2010).

During their leisure time, these Blacks may join White friends or others for tennis or golf; some attend predominantly White churches and belong to country clubs, where their families may be among the few Black members. They send their children to exclusive private schools or to Catholic schools and encourage them to study languages, literature, and music while gently warning them not to forget where they came from and urging them to hold on to their Blackness.

However, their children sometimes become intimately involved in diversified play and social groups that totally belie their parents' experiences with the nation's racially segregated past, which the younger people are sometimes fundamentally unaware of and may be unable to relate to. Sometimes the parents have a rude awakening about racial realities when their thirteen- or fourteen-year-olds are abruptly excluded from birthday parties or social events, especially when children reach dating age. The White friends they played with when they were younger may now cut them off; in this way they learn their place as Black people in what is essentially White space.

Sometimes this awakening can happen even earlier, as the following story illustrates:

"Malik" was a dark-skinned five-year-old attending a prestigious Philadelphia school. He was the only Black child in a class of about fifteen White children and two Asian children.

One of the regular parts of class was "circle time," in which the students would stand in a circle and hold hands. One day, during circle time, they eagerly took everyone's hand except for Malik's. That evening, around the dinner table with his parents, Malik recounted his experience. He said, "During circle time, none of the children would hold my hand."

"Why not?" his mom asked.

"They said my hand was yucky."

• • •

As this new Black middle class becomes better established, its members become more and more accomplished. But to many White people, those in the Black middle class are indistinguishable in phenotype and skin color from the Black people of the local ghetto, and for this reason they are occasionally profiled, being defined and treated as outcasts. Such treatment not only disturbs them greatly but also encourages them to be highly selective in their associations with White people and wary of the White spaces they control and dominate.

Some of these women and men drive expensive Range Rovers or Mercedes-Benz and Lexus sedans, but when driving through White neighborhoods, they attract special scrutiny; on occasion they are stopped and questioned by the police, who then may "discover" charges on which to detain them. If they question the police or make a false move, they may be assaulted on the spot or killed while being hauled off to jail. In these instances the police are typically unrestrained and largely unaccountable; after murdering numerous Black people, police officers are very rarely held accountable. Compared with White people, these Blacks know they have limited moral authority, so they navigate civil society with care, especially in predominantly White areas, where they are often unwelcome and are highly vulnerable to the arbitrary transgressions of the White people there, especially those in authority.

On occasion these middle-class Black people, like their elite counterparts, dine at some of the city's finest restaurants and shop at high-end stores like Brooks Brothers, Chanel, and Neiman Marcus. Members of this class occasionally mix business with pleasure, casually doing deals with one another and with their White counterparts in settings that are exclusive because of the expense. Highly status conscious, these Blacks pay close attention to the figures they present at work, at play, and at home, in predominantly White or in racially mixed settings (Lacy 2007; Pattillo-McCoy 2013; Robinson 2010). They often, but not always, appear distinctive and well-dressed, wearing expensive designer clothes. But particularly when they dress more casually, they may be challenged in restaurants, in their cars, in their office buildings, on the golf course, or in a fancy hotel lobby, and may even be arrested for "breaking into" their own homes (see Ogletree 2010).

Although they are increasingly present in the consciousness of the larger society, members of the Black middle class can be rendered almost invisible by the image of the iconic ghetto. Police officers, taxi drivers, small-business owners, and other members of the general public often treat their Blackness as a "master status" that supersedes their identity as ordinary law-abiding and competent citizens. Depending on the immediate situation, this treatment may be temporary or persistent while powerfully underlining the inherent ambiguity in their public status (Anderson 1990; Becker 1973; Hughes 1945).

Whether they hail from the ghetto or the middle-class suburbs, most critically they exist "while Black" in virtually everything they do in public. Their Black skin marks them as being "from the ghetto" even when they aren't. While operating in the White space, they are often in social, if not physical, jeopardy. Thus they are often burdened with a special penalty—a Black tax—for the putative transgression of acting in ordinary ways in public and being Black at the same time.

Members of this group are typically only a generation or so removed from the ghetto, and many have poorer relatives who actually reside there. While their lives are markedly different from those of their ghetto-dwelling kinfolk, they typically enact professional roles with limited credibility. In predominantly White spaces, their status is almost always provisional and subject to negotiation (Goffman 1963;

Jaynes 2004; Anderson 2011). As a relatively privileged class of Black people generally, they walk through the world in a somewhat peripheral status, if not a peculiar invisibility; they operate on the margins between the ghetto and the wider White society and are mostly unseen by the larger populace (see Cose 1993).

Like the elite, the new Black middle class is primarily a product of the nation's affirmative action and equal-opportunity programs, though many like to deny they are beneficiaries of such "help," claiming they were meritorious in their own right and are fully deserving of the positions they hold. This class is strongly supported by liberal society's egalitarian ethos of tolerance for diversity and racial incorporation, without which their numbers would be diminished.

The presence and advancement of members of this class in many organizations strongly reflects the support and mentoring of liberal Whites as well as of relatively secure Black people (Anderson 1999), but they are also attractive prospects because of the very remarkable recent growth in human capital among African Americans (see Darity 1982; Coleman 1988; Loury 1976).

The children of the Black middle class, particularly those attending private and suburban schools, increasingly assume mainstream cultural orientations; many advance to elite colleges and universities. However, some seek out historically Black institutions for a distinctively Black social and academic experience, in part because they learn to value the Black cultural orientation and the social sustenance such institutions provide. Generally their close friendship groups, anchored in urban cosmopolitan neighborhoods or racially mixed suburbs, at least while they are fairly young, encompass a range of ethnicities.

As they get older, they are sometimes surprised and challenged by the change in their White friends' acceptance of them; as mentioned above, this usually occurs when they begin dating and experience some rejection from their peers. It's often at this moment that they and their parents realize they might have missed a culturally important "Black" upbringing. Often their parents are perplexed by such developments and may feel contrite. Yet as they mature, these young people sometimes become the essential cultural brokers among the increasingly diverse elements of the metropolitan area. As part of this growing middle class, the parents of these young people may continue to face racially based challenges in the workplace and sometimes complain to their Black friends that they have a hard time fitting in at work, especially when they find themselves excluded from dinner parties and learn that their White colleagues, some of whom are not as "connected," have been included. In time, they may become demoralized, and ultimately seek out other Blacks for support and sociability, while holding on to relatively cosmopolitan ideals.

While some members of this new Black middle class testify to being well received in civil society, many others report the occasional direct insult and other acts of acute disrespect, which they deeply resent (Cose 1993; Anderson 2011). Moreover, in public places such as restaurants they may become especially sensitive to slights that they "could not ignore and had to answer." And often they answer in kind. These experiences contribute to ambivalence about the broader society; many Black people in particular wonder whether most Whites generally hold ordinary Blacks in contempt, and they struggle with social and political alienation. Feeling they are not completely welcome in predominantly White settings, they retain some measure of insularity.

Unlike their White counterparts of various ethnicities, members of this group only rarely go to symphony concerts, museums, theater performances, or upscale restaurants or, in Philadelphia, visit Longwood Gardens, a popular arboretum, or attend Phillies baseball games. In particular, if the performers on the stage or athletes on the field are entirely or predominantly White, middle-class Blacks get the social signal that these places are not for them. Strikingly, these Black people hope to see themselves represented in the concert hall or on a theater stage in ways their more assimilated White ethnic counterparts might take for granted. And Black performers, sensing this, sometimes try to actively "represent" their people.

The members of this class often have experienced recent upward mobility and typically come from "decent" working-class families of the iconic ghetto. Brought up with financial stability and strong family- and community-oriented values, they were poised and ready to take advantage of the opportunities offered by desegregation and affirmative action. Earning from $59,000 (the average for American families) to upward of $140,000 a year (attainable by two-earner families), many work in corporations, educational or health care institutions, and government or social service agencies. Some upwardly mobile employees began in clerical positions or as middle managers or systems engineers; others started small businesses and became successful entrepreneurs. Professionals such as teachers and social workers may attain senior administrative positions.

As accomplished and talented as they are, many of them rightly believe that without equal-opportunity programs and the egalitarian ethos that inspired them, there would be far fewer of them in their workplace, and they tend to be concerned about possible budget cutbacks. When they look around their workplaces, they often see a paucity of Black people and immediately understand why: the organization has never seriously attempted to recruit, retain, and promote Black employees or has recently turned its back on affirmative action and equal opportunity.

Members of the Black middle class tend to be somewhat ambivalent about assimilation. Many rose in the system largely because of organized efforts to promote racial incorporation. But that goal, along with the concomitant goal of full cultural assimilation with Whites, is often widely questioned, if not discredited outright. Many middle-class African Americans, wary about giving up their Blackness for dubious racial inclusion, reject assimilation as impossible or misdirected. For some the term itself is provocative or even offensive.

Meanwhile the elite and the striving, upwardly mobile set tend to be "open" to "all kinds of people," their racially particularistic upbringing notwithstanding. Ironically, this group is already largely assimilated, particularly with regard to family names, religion, language, lifestyle, and core cultural values. Still, their socioeconomic position is weaker than that of middle-class Whites because their mobility is relatively precarious and has not been fully supported by the wider political-economic system; they are still working to establish their position. Additionally, African Americans tend not to inherit as much wealth as White Americans (Oliver and Shapiro 1995; Conley 1999; Pfeffer and Killewald 2019).

Well-educated and often holding well-paid jobs, members of the Black middle class have increasingly chosen to live away from the ghetto in racially mixed communities, though some remain in their old inner-city neighborhoods. For some Black newcomers, interracial encounters in racially mixed residential communities become tests of whether Whites will run true to the stereotype and behave badly toward them. From this defensive posture, incidents that may have amounted to simple negligence or color-blind incivility often become racialized in their minds. As the store of racially offensive incidents grows in public and private memories, many find themselves unable to put aside the country's troubled racial past, and they worry about its returning in some malignant form. The media reminds them incessantly of police mistreatment and White insensitivity, eroding their expectations of fair treatment.

Sometimes society reinforces these diminished expectations. When the police shoot an unarmed Black person, when an Eric Garland or a Breonna Taylor is killed by White police officers who are later acquitted of using excessive force, when institutionalized discrimination is exposed, middle-class Black people are reminded of their precarious position. These inescapable incidents rivet the community's attention on race and encourage Blacks to develop strong and particularistic bonds with all other African Americans, across class lines. The communal memory thus can become a polarizing force in local and national Black communities.

In response to both personal insults and racial injuries, middle-class Blacks sometimes gravitate toward all-Black communities, all but giving up on the wider system. As with Du Bois's concept of twoness, they adopt a double life, working in the White community and socializing in the Black community. They may live in racially mixed middle-class neighborhoods, but they return to the ghetto to get a haircut, get their hair done, and attend church services, weddings, or funerals (Du Bois ([1903] 1995). Older members of this group are keenly aware that younger Blacks may take for granted much of the social progress achieved on their watch or by the previous generation. Working downtown or in the suburbs, eating lunch with diverse co-workers, and earning a respectable income, these young people are a part of the new social reality.

This is a group on the move as they build collectively on stores of human and social capital (Coleman 1988; Darity 1982; Loury 2012). On weeknights the most ambitious may take foreign-language classes or attend evening courses for university degrees, advancement at work, or self-improvement. Some take voice lessons or play with classical-music ensembles in recitals for predominantly White audiences. Their children may take flute or piano or singing lessons from ethnically and nationally diverse teachers. Incidents of discrimination continue to unnerve them, undermining feelings of comity and goodwill that they believe should prevail in their lives. But most of the time they adopt a positive attitude and press on.

While many avoid looking back, some members of the new Black middle class are ambivalent about their success. Having rapidly risen in socioeconomic status, they may feel guilty about leaving others behind; many feel obligated to reach back and offer help but don't know exactly how. At times this impulse is expressed in calls for race unity and activism. In many cases it takes more personal forms. Relatives and childhood friends with whom they maintain close relationships often lack the resources to address the problems of the ghetto. For successful Blacks, getting a call in the middle of the night because a member of their extended family needs money for legal or medical problems is not uncommon. Despite their hard-earned ascendance, members of this group are not so far removed from the ghetto socially.

THE GHETTO WORKING CLASS

Although almost everyone in poor inner-city neighborhoods is struggling financially and therefore feels a certain distance from the rest of

America, the decent family and the street family represent two poles of value orientation, two contrasting conceptual categories.[1] The labels "decent" and "street," which the residents themselves use, amount to judgments that confer status on local residents. The labeling is often the result of a social contest among individuals and families of the neighborhood. Individuals of the two orientations often coexist in the same extended family. Decent residents judge themselves to be so while judging others to be of the street, and street individuals often present themselves as decent, distinct from others. In addition, there is quite a bit of circumstantial behavior—one person may at different times act as both decent and street. Although these designations result from so much social jockeying, there are concrete features that define each conceptual category. Meanwhile the police, the store clerk, the taxi driver, and others who meet the public for a living tend to lump together people "from the ghetto" and make few distinctions.

Generally, "decent" families tend to accept mainstream values and try to instill them in their children. Whether married couples with children or single-parent (usually female) households, they are generally "working poor" and thus better off financially than their street-oriented neighbors. They value hard work and self-reliance and are willing to sacrifice for their children. Because they have some faith in mainstream society, they harbor hopes for a better future for their offspring, if not for themselves. Many of them go to church and take a strong interest in their children's schooling. Rather than dwelling on the real hardships and inequities facing them, many such decent people, particularly the increasing number of grandmothers raising grandchildren, see their difficulties as a test from God and derive great support from their faith and from the church community. Extremely aware of the problematic and often dangerous environment they live in, decent parents tend to be strict in their child rearing, encouraging children to respect authority and walk a straight moral line. They are almost obsessively concerned about trouble of any kind and remind their kids to look out for people and situations that might lead to it. At the same time, they are polite and considerate of others and teach their children to be the same way. At home, at work, and in church, they strive hard to maintain a positive mental attitude and a spirit of cooperation.

"Street" parents, in contrast, often lack consideration for other people and have a superficial sense of family and community. Though they may love their kids, many of them cannot cope with the physical and emotional demands of parenthood and find it difficult to reconcile their own needs with those of their children. These families, who are more fully invested in the code of the street than the decent people are, may aggressively socialize their children to this norm. They believe in the code and judge themselves and others according to its values.

In fact, the great majority of families in the inner-city community try to approximate the decent-family model, but there are many others who clearly represent their worst fears. Not only are their financial resources extremely limited, but they may misuse what little they have. The lives of the street-oriented are often disorganized. In the most desperate circumstances, people frequently have a limited understanding of priorities and consequences, so frustrations mount over bills, food, and at times drink, cigarettes, and drugs. Some tend toward self-destructive behavior; many street-oriented women are addicted to opioids, alcoholic, or involved in complicated relationships with men who abuse them.

In addition, the seeming intractability of their situation, caused in large part by the lack of well-paid jobs and the persistence of racial discrimination, has engendered deep-seated bitterness and anger in many of the poorest and most desperate Blacks, especially young people. The need both to exercise some control and to lash out at somebody is often reflected in the adults' relations with their children. At the least, the frustrations of persistent poverty shorten their fuses, contributing to a lack of patience with anyone, child or adult, who irritates them.

In these circumstances, a woman—or a man, although men are less consistently present in kids' lives—can be quite aggressive with children, yelling at them and striking them for the least infraction. Often little if any serious explanation follows the punishment. This teaches children a particular lesson. They learn that to solve any kind of interpersonal problem, you must resort to violence. The young mother often craves peace and quiet and at least the appearance of calm, respectful children, but at times she will be very punitive in trying to get them. Thus she may be quick to beat her children, especially if they defy her rules, not because she hates them but because this is the only way she knows to control them. Most street-oriented women love their children dearly, but many subscribe to the notion that there is a "devil in the boy" that must be beaten out of him or that "fast girls need to be whupped." Thus much of what social authorities see as bordering on child abuse seems to these mothers like acceptable parental punishment.

Many street-oriented women are sporadic mothers whose children learn to fend for themselves when necessary, foraging for food and money any way they can get it. The children are sometimes employed by drug dealers or become addicted themselves. These children of the street, growing up with little supervision, are said to "come up hard." They often learn to fight at an early age, sometimes modeling themselves on the short-tempered adults around them. The street-oriented home may be fraught with anger, arguments, physical aggression, and even mayhem. The children watch these goings-on, learning the lesson that might makes right. They quickly learn to hit those who cross them, and the dog-eat-dog mentality prevails.

To survive, to protect yourself, you must marshal inner resources and be ready to deal with adversity hands-on. In these circumstances, physical prowess takes on great significance. In some of the most desperate cases, a street-oriented mother may simply leave her young children alone while she goes out. The most irresponsible women can be found at local bars and drug dens, getting high and socializing with other adults. Sometimes a troubled woman will leave very young children alone for days at a time. Reports of drug addicts abandoning their children have become common in drug-infested inner-city communities. Neighbors or relatives discover the children, often hungry and distraught over their mother's absence. After repeated absences, a friend or relative, most often a grandmother, will often step in to care for them, sometimes petitioning the authorities to send her, as the children's guardian, the mother's welfare check. By this time the children may well have learned the first lesson of the streets: that survival itself, let alone respect, can't be taken for granted; you have to fight for your place in the world.

Guns and drugs proliferate in the local community, and residents suffer collateral damage from the violence that follows. The civic authorities, represented by the local police, apparently abdicate their responsibilities as high rates of homicide and violence are tolerated and publicized. Many people in such communities become resigned to being on their own and cope any way they can. Street justice, manifested in the code of the street, trumps the eroded respect for civil law. Street credibility becomes extremely valuable coin that promises security but in fact exacerbates violence and homicide rates on the inner-city streets (Anderson 1999; Goffman 2014).

Meanwhile a significant but undetermined number of people in the larger society, particularly many of those who live in the White spaces, look on with disgust, pity, judgment, and fear. Their visions and assessments often ignore the impact of structural poverty and racism on the inner-city ghetto and its people, and many of them are inclined to blame the residents themselves for "living that way." In their eyes, the ghetto poor are pariahs, more likely to victimize others than to be victimized themselves (Wacquant 2007). Members of privileged society see many images of the Black ghetto from the nightly news reports of rampant Black-on-Black crime and at times from observing Black people in public. Here the ghetto becomes intensely iconic, a distressed place where Blacks have been relegated to live apart from the larger society. This perspective, this White frame, encourages a universally low opinion of Blacks as a racial category (Feagin 2006; Massey and Denton 1998). Thus not only does the physical ghetto persist, but it has become a highly negative symbol in American society and culture, serving as a touchstone for prejudice, a profound source of stereotypes, and a rationalization for discriminating against Black people in general.

This racial spectacle supports and underscores the provisional character of the Black middle class, an association heightened by their assumed connection to the urban underclass. The underclass in America today is mainly young and Black, but it includes Hispanics and other people of color who also live in the ghetto. The underclass no longer defies its racial segregation but bases parts of its expressive identity on its alienation and thrives on distinctiveness (Auletta 1982; Wilson 1978, 1996).

This identity is developed and promoted by popular culture, and some who are not alienated in the same way begin to find its norms and aims attractive. White teenagers and new immigrant youths take on an orientation whose more authentic representatives are alienated young Black men. This racialized image becomes a "master status," affecting the perception and position of all Blacks in the wider community. Through the master status of Blackness, the iconic Negro identity, all Black people are evaluated with respect to how closely they approximate the urban underclass (Hughes 1945; Becker 1973; Anderson 1978, 1999). Middle-class Black people are beset with contradictions and dilemmas of status and often must distinguish themselves from the urban underclass in order to be tolerated in civil society, or at least to not be unduly scrutinized by the Whites they work and play with. Even so, they continue to be profiled in White spaces owing to the stereotypes of the iconic ghetto.

In the toxic environment of the ghetto, young men live as though a direct pipeline leads from desperation to prison or the cemetery. Yet entrepreneurs—both on the street and in the popular culture— glamorize this lifestyle, packaging and selling it to the wider society. This image should be opposed to the roles and aspirations of the Black middle class. If the inner-city community glorifies violence and unwed pregnancy, the middle class glorifies family life, Standard English, higher education, financial success, and abiding by the rules of conventional society.

These upwardly mobile people espouse aspirations and behavior that the street element associates with "acting White" and selling out. But because middle-class Blacks are often not far removed from the inner city and White society often resists their presence, they have to make their peace with the ghetto. They maintain connections with their inner-city kin and temper their embrace of the dominant culture's values.

Most do not buy into White-identified interests; rather, they inflect their tastes with Black culture, preferring jazz and blues, for example. The young and mobile neither completely disconnect from the ghetto nor completely embrace the dominant society. Even those who assimilate exist in a no-man's-land between the ghetto and White society. They are forever trying to give back to those they left behind, or at least they give lip service to that notion; putting it into practice is painfully difficult. Within the Black class structure, a certain fluidity enables Black people to feel a connection with those at the lower reaches of society. But if there is a connection, there is also a threat, a social risk of contagion (cf. Matza 1969); this makes middle-class Blacks fear that, their achieved status notwithstanding, they may be dragged down by public association with less fortunate ghetto residents.

Because of Philadelphia's history of racial segregation, the working class and the underclass tend to be interspersed in inner-city neighborhoods. This residential pattern means that both are exposed, though in differing degrees, to the "neighborhood effects" of concentrated urban poverty (Wilson 1987). The 'hood is home to diverse elements, which often are not distinguished by people unfamiliar with the inner city.

A Philadelphia couple I'll call the Harrises were members of the post–World War II Black working class. Now retired, living on Social Security and pensions from lifelong steady jobs, they have tried, not always successfully, to distance themselves from the problems of the inner-city neighborhood, including crime, violence, and the desperation of so many suffering people.

After working a lifetime to pay for a home that is now engulfed in a destitute community, they can't move away. They try to get along with their neighbors and make the best of a difficult situation. One strategy is to "see but don't see," as they try to mind their own business in public. Another is to limit their activities and shut themselves in after dark. They bond most closely with those they have the most in common with—other retired people who held factory jobs and bought homes in the neighborhood. They engage in community life, trading favors and friendship and looking out for one another.

Some of their counterparts are raising grandchildren, their adult children having been lost to the streets or to prison. Among their working-class neighbors are men and women employed as convenience store cashiers, night watchmen, janitors or office cleaners, nurses' aides, day care center staffers, kitchen assistants, construction laborers, mass-transit workers, and taxi drivers. But Mr. and Mrs. Harris also share the streets and local stores with drug dealers, drug addicts, ex-convicts, and hustlers, many of them armed. They are surrounded by people who are barely coping with persistent poverty or have been entirely submerged by the personal problems it generates.

The Harrises are disdainful of the single mother next door, who seems "ignorant" and "irresponsible," in good times shifting from one bad job to another and in hard times not working at all, and raising too many children without a father. They criticize her for leaving her younger children unsupervised to "tear up the house" and allowing her older children to "run on the streets." They worry about the young men who hang out on the corner and the young women who have their babies. They are afraid of walking past cash-hungry predators and frightened by the sound of random gunfire after dark. The drug trade besieges their neighborhood. The authorities know what is going on but do nothing about it.

Mr. and Mrs. Harris feel threatened and alienated, but there's little they can do. In their frustration they sit and wait, wishing they could move but unable to sell their house for enough to buy into a better neighborhood. Those able to afford it have gradually moved away, leaving behind an ever-greater concentration of the desperately poor. The Harrises try to negotiate with those who remain, tolerating whatever does not directly affect their own safety, hoping they won't be ganged up on and robbed or assaulted.

There are also many decent people of working age in the ghetto, but they can't achieve the financial stability the Harrises found at their age, so they remain marginal. Although they hold jobs, they are employed at the lowest levels of the service economy. Their work is insecure, pays little, seldom provides benefits such as health insurance, and offers no avenues toward promotion.

Generally, people struggle to make do with what they have. When periods of economic expansion enable more Black people to find jobs, prosperity or even stability still remains out of reach. When recessions follow, the Black working class is thrown back into the vast pool of the unemployed. Few can accumulate enough resources to withstand a crisis. The basic structural shifts and brief speculative booms that have brought a tentative prosperity to Black middle-class families have not materially improved the conditions of inner-city neighborhoods. Too many people, even though working, remain impoverished, alienated, and socially challenged. The obstacle that looms largest, particularly for inner-city youths, is the very limited opportunity for gainful employment (Anderson 1990, 1999).

Roughly corresponding to Du Bois's "submerged tenth," the ghetto underclass swallows up the casualties of the contemporary American economic system (Auletta 1982; Wilson 1978, 1987). Their forebears, like Mr. and Mrs. Harris, labored in factories, private homes, and service-oriented businesses and institutions. These jobs demanded hard work and commitment, but there were few obstacles to entry once racial barriers were broken.

Today many young adults in the ghetto lack the skills and education, or human capital, required to compete in a postindustrial society. Entry-level jobs in the expanding sectors of the US economy, including high technology and health care, are open only to high school and college graduates and often require specialized training. Few employers offer career ladders in the workplace, especially for those without a college education. Not only does the path to academic achievement and occupational mobility lead right out of the 'hood, escaping the 'hood is often a condition for success.

Where so many people are underemployed or jobless, the underground economy of drugs and crime flourishes. In circumstances of profound hopelessness, some seek to escape their problems through alcohol or drugs. In addition to serving as a last resort for the desperate, the drug trade holds a certain fascination for young people and offers a strong temptation even to children growing up in "decent" families.

"Wesley," as an exemplar of this underclass, is the antithesis of Mr. Harris. Currently working part-time at a car wash, he has a checkered past that includes robbery, selling drugs, hustling, and doing time in Graterford Prison. Seven years ago, Maxine, who was then on welfare, had his baby, and he is now raising his daughter with the help of his mother and sister, whom he lives with. He tries to take care of his daughter, but his economic position is marginal at best. He works solely for tips, so if it rains all week he makes no money.

In hard times Wesley is tempted to revert to robbery and to preying on the Harrises of the neighborhood. Indeed, although he and Maxine may be trying to approximate Mr. and Mrs. Harris's values, they do so poorly. Without much contact with mainstream institutions, they don't know how to behave in a socially acceptable manner. Yet it's their confused version of the old working-class life that now dominates the neighborhood.

The Harrises look down on people like Wesley and Maxine, whom they readily label "street," considering them ignorant, loud, boisterous, and lacking decorum. Most of the street-oriented tend to be demoralized, jobless, and even homeless; however they may act in public, theirs is not a carefree existence.

An outside observer might persuasively argue that the institutions of the wider society have failed these people. Yet their working-class neighbors readily hold them responsible for their own failures. This stance allows those who are better off to maintain faith in the wider society, especially in the work ethic, while morally legitimizing their own superior position in the Black community's system of social stratification. So they treat members of the underclass as convenient objects of scorn, fear, and embarrassment. The street-oriented thus serve as a social yardstick that allows those seeking to be regarded as decent to compare themselves favorably with others in the community (Anderson 1990, 1999).

Out of concern for their community and social environment as well as for their families and loved ones, many working-class residents become anxious about the effects that economic downturns will have on the neighborhood, worrying about what the absence of income to their impoverished neighbors will mean for their own safety, security, and general quality of life.

The inner city is home to a wide variety of people, but the street element often controls its public spaces, particularly at night, and their alienated, vividly expressive, and at times aggressive cultural style shapes the ghetto image. Outsiders too easily associate all its residents with crime as well as poverty. Nevertheless, most inner-city residents embody decency and, despite their precarious living standards or their outright poverty, enact their own version of the most honorable ethics of the broader society—a reality too often missed by outsiders, both Black and White.

Although the working class and the underclass differ from their counterparts in Du Bois's time, deindustrialization is leaving the ghetto in an economic vacuum that is rapidly filled by the underground economy. Without the prospect of finding a steady job once they outgrow their youthful hustling, some men remain stuck in a perpetual adolescence, at times preying on people who are marginally better off. As a result, the problems of the ghetto are likely to become even more acute over time.

At the other end of the Black social structure, the class categories are dramatically different from those Du Bois described. The elite and the middle class have been transformed from a colortocracy, made up of an elite class of lighter-skinned Black people descended from slaves and slave owners, to a more egalitarian group. Despite ambivalence and continued instances of racism, these African Americans are now acknowledged to be full citizens. Yet the legacy of exclusion and discrimination based on race continues to haunt Black people at all levels of the class structure.

CHAPTER 10

THE "TOKEN," THE "TOM," AND "THE HNIC"

The ghetto has a significant meaning for the mobility of Black people in American society. In this pluralistic, multiracial, and multicultural society, the Black person is fundamentally different: the Black person stands out and most often carries a history of racial injury. On an individual level, this injury is often like an open wound that is easily exacerbated by the rumble of everyday ethnic politics in America's urban centers. Thus, Black people are especially sensitive to racial matters, and prepared to scrutinize ordinary relations to address a problem of racial inequality and arbitrary treatment. Moreover, this historical injury has made Black people especially vulnerable to modern adversaries who can exploit the age-old enmity toward Blacks to better their own position. Black people carry the burden of Black skin and a special relationship to the iconic American ghetto. They alone can claim ancestors who lived through the degradation of American slavery and, later, Jim Crow segregation. And they alone can claim six generations of American forebears, all of whom were assumed to be at the bottom of American society.

Yet the modern-day Black person is often conveniently thought of as an "ordinary" person lacking such a peculiar history or racial burden. Black people are reminded day in and day out that America is an egalitarian society, where the color of one's skin matters less than the content of one's character. According to this trope, the Black person has a fair chance in the sweepstakes of everyday life in America. But nothing could be further from the truth. To the extent that skin color is added into the social equation, the Black person is often held back and disadvantaged through a competitive context in which the primary factor is Black skin color and its association with the iconic ghetto. The most powerful manifestation of this is the "deficit of credibility," the "master status" that supersedes whatever other status one may seek. This deficit is consequential in the affairs of everyday life. Strikingly, the deficit differs from stigma because the deficit is not necessarily permanent but malleable and flexible, able to be improved upon. Black people are charged with working to disabuse others of their presumed negative status. They must distance themselves from that ghetto and, by implication, from other ghetto Black people in order to be taken seriously as a middle-class person, one eligible for the full rights, obligations, and duties that accrue to Americans by virtue of citizenship (Goffman 1963; Loury 2002).

Today, great numbers of Black people are visibly employed in a variety of organizations, and the collective impact of this presence on race relations is immense. The symbolism of Black people working and living alongside their White counterparts in major social positions remains powerful. Many of these people, having emerged from the urban ghettos, now participate in the American occupational structure in ways their forebears could never have imagined. Along with this mobility, as a group, Black people have experienced considerable cultural assimilation, though they don't always like to acknowledge this; and many experience a degree of dissonance as they embrace a society that for so long has oppressed them and their kind. Black people continue to endure a significant racial stigma that is rooted in the racial caste system of the Jim Crow era of segregation (Cox 1948;

Loury 2002; Wilkerson 2020). Today, this legacy is underscored by the iconic status of the ghetto, itself an artifact of segregation. The "social place" of Black people in the American racial hierarchy is powerfully reinforced by the presence of this icon in American cities, large and small alike.

THE WORKPLACE

In the aftermath of the civil rights movement, the workplace and the organizations that Black people joined—businesses, schools, and government agencies—served as primary vehicles by which racial incorporation occurred, ultimately resulting in full citizenship for Black people. But as Black people were incorporated into the middle class through affirmative action and "set-asides," many White Americans became disturbed, thinking that their own rights and privileges were somehow diminished. In a sense, the status or the progress of Black people in society has always served as a benchmark for the status of others in competition with them for place and position. Others often used such comparisons to determine how relatively well-off they were. Many became upset with what they saw and worked to distinguish themselves from Black people, at times causing more discrimination. These people sensed that Black people's advancement threatened to replace or even subjugate them in the putative racial order. They often had assumed that their own position was superior to that of Black people.

In these circumstances, White people—ethnic and working-class Whites in particular—often felt it necessary to put Black people back "in their place" as second-class citizens (Anderson 2016). This unease in the system, related to the ability of Black people to petition quite successfully for their collective mobility, has inspired identity politics where Whites and members of other ethnic groups more actively compete for place and position with Black people—while continuing to see the apparent victories of Black people as affecting their own well-being. This dynamic has prevented Black people and ethnic White people from joining forces and coming together. Often, only a certain tolerance, or even a segregated civility, prevails in Black-White relations (May 2014).

When Black people began to move into White spaces, they tried to make sense of the situation conceptually. They often divided their workplace colleagues into the categories of friends and foes. Since both types were White people, it was hard to know the difference. The friends were White people who reached out and helped, even though they didn't need to do so.

Typically, the relationship between a White friend and a Black colleague was a complicated one, because the friend had to make himself known to the Black person, yet also maintain credibility among racist White coworkers. It was a peculiar kind of dance for the friend. Sometimes the friend would connect with the Black person outside of work, at home or at a bar, where they would talk and share stories, connect and bond. However, when that friend was back at work, he might show a different side, and this behavior made the Black person question the friend's sincerity. There was a phrase that Black people developed in response to this phenomenon. Black employees might conclude—perhaps prematurely—that this was "just a racist White boy." They had faith in this person but then felt let down, and now assumed that this supposed "friend" was just like all of the other racist White people. Soon after, though, the coworker might prove to be a friend again. There were patterns of inconsistency shown by these White friends, and these relationships were negotiated up and down. Sometimes the Black employee would excuse the person and take leave of the notion of "just a racist White boy" yet remain guarded. Since Blacks assumed initially that all Whites were foes, friends had to prove that they were on Black people's side.

Ethnically speaking, a lot of these friends were Jewish, especially German Jews, because their own history of discrimination helped them understand the plight of Black people in ways that WASPs and others could not. In fact, many of these Jews in the 1940s, '50s, and '60s provided financial support to organizations like the NAACP and the Urban League, as well as other Black causes, and they knew Black leaders. The dominant ethos of the friends was to include those who had been excluded on the basis of race because that exclusion went against values of equal opportunity, egalitarianism, universalism, and fair play.

Today, however, we find widespread indifference to racial inequality and a strong narrative of "blame the victim." The messages of the civil rights movement are not easily absorbed, and the population of Whites who feel an urgent need to make the system right has dwindled in number and influence. As White people find themselves unable to live as well as their parents did, we see fewer "friends" concerned about leveling the playing field and find more foes of Black mobility. I daresay the latter group saw Donald Trump as the candidate who would keep Black people in their proper place.

White people, especially those in precarious economic positions, continue to express residual anger and resentment about the presence of Black people in places they want to claim for themselves. At the same time, as part of the organizational culture, the White people who predominate in these settings are encouraged to accept and tolerate "diversity," including Black colleagues; and in order to avoid sanctions, many White employees and supervisors are motivated to show a "good faith" effort to attract and retain Black employees in their organizations.

To be sure, many workplaces are more than willing to comply with fair employment practices, but others do so only if under duress. In these circumstances, many may simply tolerate the presence of Black people, often not wanting to know them and wishing the workplace could somehow be free of them. They may express such feelings indirectly; they don't always approach the Black person with open displays of malice. Rather, under the cloak of "standards" and "work performance reviews," they may even convince themselves they are doing "the right thing." Instead of providing a supportive environment, the workplace at times devolves into one hostile to Black people, and over time it remains a predominantly White space.

"Lola," a retired Black woman, describes her experience at her former workplace:

When I started to realize it was problematic or cold was in my first performance review. When I went in, to my surprise, it didn't seem to be about my performance—it was about whispery things people had said about me. One of my colleagues had said that I didn't give good customer service. I said, "What's that supposed to mean?" Well, it was her perception that there was something she wanted me to do and I hadn't done it. Maybe that's true, but what does that have to do with the quality of my work? Why didn't she come to me?

This was the signal that this was a highly political place—ingrown, backbiting, people with allegiances, et cetera. Once again, I'm the new kid on the block, the only African American senior communications officer. There were other Black employees I knew who left my workplace altogether. One woman was hounded out.

The real bottom line is that if you study hard, work hard, get a good education, get some good experience, you expect and seek the opportunity to perform at your greatest potential, achieve your goals, the most you can achieve, and it's just so demoralizing for people of color who are educated and eager to contribute to run into stone walls of "We really don't want you here, we don't like you, you can't be part of our club." To me that's a shame for the people who are shunned, but also a loss for organizations.

Diversity falls flat because they aren't really trying. There's a lot of evidence of this in what has come out of the minorities who work in Silicon Valley about how they're not promoted, not included, not listened to. In Hollywood, Black people often propose an idea and it's ignored, then the White people propose the same idea and it's accepted. It's like having glasses that screen out the color—they can't see you and they're threatened by you.

Such treatment of Black employees is at times a function of Whites' sense of their own group position, as they feel threatened by the incursion of Black coworkers. They may see the Black person before them simply as a product of the ghetto, even though he or she may never have lived there—but this distinction matters little. Often, their actions are indirect, and in the presence of the Black coworker, they present themselves as civil and cordial. And for the most part, they may try to "get along." What is not said, or not acknowledged, is that the spectacle of the "racial other"—the Black person's very presence—personifies the source of the evaluator's personal distress. And when the Black coworker performs exceptionally well on some task, such racist people may simply be incredulous in light of their initial assumption of a deficit in the Black person.

To repeat, many White people can be very receptive to Black co-workers, but coexisting with such "decent" White employees are those who see the Black person as a menace. The problem is distinguishing which is which, and who is who. Moreover, Black employees understand that a "friend" at work one day can turn into a foe the next. This realization gives the Black person pause. Accordingly, work relationships tend to be somewhat fragile and superficial. Hence, some Black people approach the workplace as something of a minefield, stepping lightly and watching their backs, and when the workday is through, they quickly depart, seeking downtime and, for the time being, wanting no further involvement with their White colleagues and "work friends."

Marcia's experience is germane:

My first job out of college was my dream job, everything I thought I wanted. Except when I went there, I was the only Black person, definitely the only Black engineer. I remember thinking, "Oh, this is interesting." Like, going from Philadelphia to New York City and almost having like a Friends *experience where it's like, inside this office, you almost would think that Black people don't exist.*

The VP who hired me was ecstatic about me. But the other VP, who I actually ended up working under, was not. He didn't like the fact that I was even there. He would actually not talk to me directly, which was weird, as a young person, to say, "Why is this grown-up avoiding a conversation with me?"

I stayed there for three years, and when the firm got acquired, it had downsizing associated with that. And I remember going to my mentor and saying, "Hey, can you look at my profit rates and see if I'm profitable, and if I'm at risk of being, like, laid off or whatever?"

And my mentor was like, "Oh, you're good, you're doing great, your percentages are nice." And a few days after having that conversation with my mentor, I got called to the room to get laid off. And I remember thinking, "I'm the first person in this office to get laid off. That's interesting."

• • •

Black employees may be regarded as tokens, symbolic representatives of the iconic ghetto, considered by their White counterparts to occupy sinecures that render them politically weak. Each day, the token is tested, and any attempts to demonstrate power are summarily rejected or blocked. Hence, the Black employee, actual professional title notwithstanding, is usually shown to be a politically weak actor who is effectively marginalized within the organization. By nature, these employees command limited moral authority and may be disparaged behind their backs. Complaints about such treatment do little good, since they tend to underscore the employee's actual relationship to the organization. Moments of acute disrespect often come as a surprise, if not a shock. When such incidents occur, they are rapidly shared with virtually every Black person of the organization. In large part, these episodes of disrespect are a demonstration of the history of racism in America and point to the perceived weakness of the Black person's position within the organization. For such treatment and disrespect, there are few reliable or effective sanctions, and many non-Blacks whose own positions are precarious may show little sympathy for Black coworkers' experiences.

A peculiar kind of surveillance is often being conducted on the Black person in the workplace. People often measure their own situation in relation to the Black coworker, gathering information about salaries, lifestyles, and personal proclivities, which may in other circumstances become weaponized. Ultimately, no matter how meritorious Black people may be, the iconic ghetto serves as a powerful reference point reinforcing suspicions that they do not truly deserve their position. These suspicions particularly often imply that even if someone does not hail from the ghetto, it is a good bet that they are more familiar with it, either through recent residence or because their relatives and ancestors have lived there. All this history, especially the most unflattering interpretation of it, works to undermine the Black person's claim to moral authority.

In the interest of civility and political correctness, many White employees in such settings are sophisticated enough to know to be on the lookout for racially arbitrary incidents and to be careful when dealing with Black coworkers; meanwhile, others may be utterly unsophisticated and behave crudely with regard to racial matters. In workplace common areas, White and Black employees alike may treat unfamiliar Black people as suspicious. However, this pervasive suspicion makes Black people often question the sincerity of White people in regard to themselves. The risk of betting seriously on the "true" friendship of a White person often appears too great, and many interracial relationships are destined to remain superficial and fragile.

Recognizing this problem, White and Black people are likely to keep their cross-racial friendships on a short tether, characterized by social gloss. Many Whites may be hesitant or reticent because they are uncomfortable being so close to Blacks. Realizing that the Black person may not welcome their overtures, they hang back, feeling constrained and able to go only so far in terms of racial acceptance. At the same time, many other White employees are adamantly opposed to even considering Black coworkers as their equals. To further complicate matters, Black people are sometimes inclined to "play" their White folks—that is, to "play along just to get along." Blacks may act in accordance with others' expectations rather than their own volition, assuming a "moderate," "conservative," or "liberal" stance just to obtain the rewards promised to them for behaving this way.

These tensions in Black-White relations raise questions about employer-employee relationships. Black workers, like anyone in a subordinate position, must carefully study their superiors, figuring out the limits of the relationship and the kind of people they are working for. An employee's livelihood may hang in the balance; thus, Black workers must negotiate with their superiors, seeking their approval at every turn. And here, Black employees may apply a certain amount of gloss to deflect scrutiny to allow themselves to pass inspection and obtain what they need. Black people are often quite aware of the game they must play to get ahead, or just to survive, and some will present a front ranging from the obsequious to the formally distant. In cosmopolitan work settings, one of the conditions of acceptance may be that Black employees are joked about or referred to good-naturedly as hailing originally "from the Black ghetto." Accordingly, on occasion they may play the stereotypical parts, knowing better but still tolerating their White peers' errors and misstatements about race (for instance, "John, don't go ghetto on us now"). Many Black people are reluctant to play such games, largely because such play is reminiscent of the Uncle Tom role, about which most Blacks express a certain dissonance, if not outright disdain.

A retired Black professor who grew up in the Black ghetto, "Marcel Davis," related:

The White man puts the brothers in the corner. They [White people] ain't got no faith in you. Tokenize yo' ass in a minute.

White man ain't gon' give you no respect. Better watch yo'self 'round him, the White man. Black man ain't got no standing in the White man's world. Yo' stuff is like so much tissue paper, you're weak. You there at the pleasure of the White man.

They [White people] trying to marginalize you from the get-go. They say, "Oh, we like Black people," but, man, they stop you from the get-go. Where's your Black worker? Oh, he's over there in the corner (out of sight). The boss man says, "Hey, John, come on out here. John, say hi to everybody." John is for show. "Okay, John. Get yo' ass back in the corner."

*And John, he go right along with it. 'Cause he getting paid. And if he acts up, some White lady might slap him upside his head. If he acts up. Ha-ha. "What's wrong with you, John. What you mean, we don't treat you fair. N****r, quit, go back in yo' corner." John then slinks back into the corner.*

Shit, we laugh at this shit. But it is universal. Black people have the inside knowledge, of what it still means to be Black in America. N****r ain't shit. N****r gon' be n****r all his life. So quite naturally, when moving through the White space, you look around for other Black people. You look for friends. But most of the other Black people do not have your back, because they are trying to make their own deals with the man, trying to get over. The individual Black person always walks on thin ice.

A complex set of attitudes subtly and effectively defines the Black person as an outsider, a status and identity that become clarified through the everyday give-and-take of the workplace. This issue arises gradually and unpredictably during deceptively simple but necessary interactions and minor conflicts. Trivial events become fraught with meaning and significance, implying that the Black person always deserves less social consideration. In many of these cases, the racist act is done by a lower-level employee, one who is less guarded about keeping up appearances relative to the racial order. From the standpoint of working-class White ethnic people, often from a blue-collar neighborhood, the iconic ghetto has much salience and meaning. In time employees may be corrected, or even sanctioned, by their manager. These confrontations reveal the ethnic in the worker, but it is important to note that a person can be "ethnic" without being ethnocentric; the employee's actions may be spontaneous and to some extent beyond their control.

Here, the message commonly given (and taken for granted) is that the setting in which these employees operate is undeniably a "White space." Through these workers' attitudes and subtle actions, they help to define and protect this space. From their perspective, the main requirement for being defined and treated as a full person is being White. If confronted or queried about this fact, White employees will deny this, mainly because such assertions may prove embarrassing, or even actionable, so they cannot let them go unchallenged; yet these White workers may admit among themselves that such racist assertions are true.

As another Black professor, Dr. Charles Crawford, commented:

The weirdest time for the Black professor is the start of the semester, when students come to your first class. From your name on the faculty roster they think you are a White professor, that you are a White man. I mean, most of us have these English surnames, and they don't know we're Black. But when they come to the first class, they see you, a Black man, and [they] can't believe it. Sometimes you can see the disappointment on their faces, but they don't turn around and leave; they stick it out, maybe to be amused. Now, this first class will have about thirty-five students, most of them [are] White kids. I mean, there will be two or three Black kids and maybe one Asian. It is a nice fall day, and the students are back at school. They're like eager beavers.

They're so attentive, hanging on my every word. They inspire me to perform, to give them an enthusiastic lecture— I mean, I am going to town, making this connection, that connection, even being a little elliptical. . . . I mean, these students will sit through the whole class and act so attentive, so involved. Then at the next class meeting, a week later, only six or seven students show up. And of that number, three or four are athletes and maybe two or three are Black.

The university is clearly a White space in which the Black professor has very little credibility. It's demoralizing, but this happens at the start of every semester. Now, most Black professors won't admit this, because they don't want to admit how we're really treated as Black professors. It's embarrassing, the way they treat us. They don't really respect us—in fact, they disrespect us. And it can make us feel like we're tokens.

These realities become apparent as the local division of labor works itself out. Most workers are White, which carries an implication that a mostly White workplace is not only normal, but also right and proper as well as legitimate. Of course, this racial makeup is not always established out of malice; rather, it just happened, so no one White person is to blame. And the few Black employees at the workplace simply tolerate the situation, for they do not want to "rock the boat" and "cause trouble at work." Reticent to a fault, they almost never raise such issues with their superiors. To do so might encourage scrutiny by their higher-ups; they are more comfortable lying low, and generally do so.

TOKENISM

The racial incorporation that unfolded in response to the civil rights movement allowed a relatively large proportion of Black people to escape the ghetto and move into the middle class. Educational opportunities for all Black Americans expanded dramatically. Fair housing legislation enabled affluent Black families to relocate to the suburbs, as their White counterparts had done before them. Fair employment practices and laws expanded the range of occupations open to Black job seekers, with affirmative action programs being the most consequential. The primary rationale for these new employment policies was that the underrepresentation of Black Americans in professional and managerial positions was due chiefly to pervasive and entrenched patterns of racial discrimination; the integration of neighborhoods, schools, and workplaces was supposed to overcome the legacies of the past and ensure more equal opportunities in the future (Wilson 1978; Anderson 2018; Hinton 2021).

As shifts in public policy and the globalizing economy effectively drew some Black Americans into the system while consigning others to an "underclass," a premium rather than a penalty was placed on Black skin color, and its possessors could receive serious consideration for a job. The process contributed to a proliferation of "tokens"—symbolic representatives of the Black community—who now began to assume positions in business, academia, and government. Initially, what could be called "petty affirmative action" was employed, a series of simple steps that allowed those in powerful positions to use token Black employees to demonstrate that they were not discriminatory or racist (Katznelson 2006; Dobbin and Kalev 2017).

Petty affirmative action eventually morphed into a more institutionalized form administered under the watchful eyes of government agencies concerned with making up for past discrimination. Implicit in these actions or remedies was always the background assumption that inequality was the result of past discriminatory behavior, and that if such practices could just be eliminated, Black people would rapidly reach parity with their White counterparts. What was not acknowledged was that White-skin privilege and the racialized system of social stratification provide whole sets of opportunities that are denied to Black people, including personal and professional networks, respect, and moral authority, all of which are critical to success (McIntosh 1989). Without access to the connections and credibility such elements offer, Black people cannot be fully incorporated into the middle class, regardless of their talents and training. The failure to appreciate this fact at the time of its design led to affirmative action being effectively set up to self-destruct. In time, the proliferation of tokens would create a visible-enough Black presence for affirmative action to no longer be desirable or politically defensible as a social policy, for Blacks or for Whites.

At the time, it seemed that racial barriers to employment were falling everywhere. As Black people appeared and prospered in major social positions, accusations that the "racist" system was the source of inequality became less insistent, with the blame implicitly shifting onto the victim (McWhorter 2000). This change in perspective had profound implications, finding its way into public debates over the political viability as well as the legitimacy of affirmative action itself. With the proliferation of tokens, defenders of the system could point to and celebrate the success stories and lay the burden of proof—or the blame—on those who did not rise. In these circumstances, it became increasingly difficult to attribute inequality to arbitrary racial considerations and seemed more reasonable to scrutinize individual Black people and attribute their lowly positions in the system to their own shortcomings. In other words, it became more difficult to blame the system for the lack of Black presence and much easier to "blame the victim."

In 1983, Philadelphia elected its first African American mayor,

W. Wilson Goode, an event that would have astounded W. E. B. Du Bois. During the Goode administration, Philadelphia had Black leadership on the city council and the school board and important, albeit token, Black representation in the business, education, and legal establishments. These developments represented significant progress and offered real hope to ordinary Philadelphians, particularly for Black Americans and other minority groups. Yet these striking political developments failed to alter the fundamental economic condition of most Black citizens. Philadelphia suffered from active disinvestment by major corporations and by the federal government (Adams et al. 2008). Substantial numbers of jobs left the city not only for the Third World and other regions of the United States but also for suburbs such as King of Prussia. "Satellite cities," with their vast industrial parks, compete effectively with Philadelphia, drawing residents and jobs, undermining the city's tax base, and creating a "spatial mismatch" between available jobs and Black workers, who remain concentrated in the inner city and unable to commute to workplaces beyond the reach of mass transit. At the same time, local corporations continue to downsize.

These vanishing job opportunities have made the Black middle class increasingly nervous, impoverished the Black working class, and stranded the Black poor in devastated neighborhoods. The city's financial difficulties contributed to a decline in city services that directly affected the quality of life, reducing the city's desirability for potential residents as well as businesses. The city has been subjected to a kind of social strip-mining, as its human assets have been removed and its economic foundations destroyed, leaving a wasteland of derelict buildings, discarded institutions, and disregarded residents.

Here, as across the nation, the social programs that once aided so many and gave residents hope for the future have had their funding slashed, and many have subsequently been abolished. The public schools that serve the Black poor and working class have been allowed to deteriorate to the point that they fail to educate children for the demands of today's society and economy (Cucchiara 2013). Widespread joblessness and the lack of a social safety net make it difficult to form stable families; many children grow up without effective parenting.[1]

EMPLOYABILITY

The iconic ghetto, or the public image of the ghetto, has special implications and consequences for the ghetto poor. Compared with the Black middle class, the ghetto poor face an extra measure of discrimination and stigma—from which they have great difficulty recovering. Although members of the Black middle class often experience contradictions and dilemmas of status, they are likely to have the social and human capital to shake off the indignities associated with their color caste. Although challenged at times, they tend to have the credentials, the contacts, and often the verbal skills to combat the racism they experience.

In contrast, the icon of the ghetto places the Black poor at a profound disadvantage when they apply for jobs in the emerging service economy, in which "soft skills" are increasingly important. The characteristics that Black youth may display—including language, style, and demeanor—preclude their employment. Work experience is often a prerequisite for getting a decent job, even for high school graduates, and this first stepping-stone is unattainable. Young Black people have limited capital, both social and human, to negotiate their way in the world, particularly as they approach various urban institutions, including the law, prison, job opportunities, and health issues.

But most important, they are in competition with others who use their association with the ghetto against them. Hence, in even the most menial jobs and positions, Black people are rejected or locked out. And a decent job is even harder to come by. Residents of the ghetto internalize these messages, which, together with the real-life conditions in the ghetto, essentially conspire to keep Black people poor. The challenges they face include lack of achievement and motivation, poor schools, alienation from mainstream society, and ghetto culture itself. But these shortcomings have to be viewed as a response to the structural conditions of their lives, and not the other way around, as many conservative commentators would like to believe.

Black skin is certainly a barrier, but it is not just skin color and the image of the iconic ghetto that holds Black people back. It is also the whole host of cultural adjustments that people make in order to survive in the 'hood—whether that means hustling, bartering, or dressing in certain styles (devalued by the wider society)—that contribute to the ghetto's negative image. These behaviors and the values implicit in them are simply inconsistent with being mobile in the wider society. But to consciously reject the local system of cultural values is to place oneself at odds and even possibly at risk, both socially and physically, in one's own community. Hence, young people are often caught in a virtual catch-22. For instance, if and when one decides consciously to adopt those behaviors that might amount to capital in the wider society—speaking Standard English, reading books, or being a "good student," which many young people label as "acting White"—it places one at risk of losing social status among one's peers in the Black ghetto.

THE "TOKEN," THE "TOM," AND "THE HNIC"

As some Black people climbed to previously unreachable heights in society, the process of racial incorporation led to new places of encounter between Blacks and Whites, and thus to a proliferation of ways to make sense of the presence of Black people, including labels, such as the token, the Tom, and the HNIC, or the "head Negro in charge." As White and Black people gradually came to share space as coworkers, Black people who successfully integrated became associated with these labels. While the token, the Tom, and the HNIC are distinct, all three arose while that upstanding symbolic figurehead of the Black community known as the "race man" or "race woman" became harder to find, at least in the traditional form.

The generally accepted definition of a token is a symbolic representative of a group. Used as a label, the word implies that the person to whom it is attached is not just symbolic of a group but also that he or she is inconsequential as a person. Hence, throughout this process of inclusion, as Black people made their way into the larger society, they were often regarded by their fellow citizens as mere symbols of the ghetto. And often the positions they obtained were effectively reduced to sinecures in efforts to conserve the standard way of doing things and to "hold the line."

Tokenism is an example of how inclusion within the system was used selectively to resist the advancement of Black people on a larger scale. Many Black newcomers to the majority-White workplace were regarded by their White counterparts as mere tokens and were treated as such, necessitating an ongoing campaign for respect on the job. When a Black person rises or is suspected of rising beyond this traditional status, out of his or her "place" as a Black person, a measure of dissonance is created, especially for White people. But some Black people themselves occasionally raise issues concerning Black success and mobility. Because of their assumptions of the racist nature of the society, they worry that the successful Black person has in some way "sold out"—made a "deal with the devil"—and looks after the "White man's" interests more than the "natural" interests of the Black community, such as working against racial inequality, controlling errant police, and eradicating poverty. The notion is that the only way a Black person could move ahead is by selling out.

It is often the most alienated Black people who believe that successful Black people are out to do the "White man's bidding" at the expense of the Black community and are "race traitors." Within modern business organizations, this complex set of issues has given rise to an indelicate folk concept, the "head Negro in charge," or the HNIC. Often, unbeknownst to their White colleagues and bosses, successfully integrated Black employees risk being labeled "sellouts" and "Toms" by their own people, exemplifying their alienation and distance from other Black people. Alienation often leads to the inability of successful Black people to reach back and help their own, either through mentorship or by providing references or recommendations, leading to their designation as a "Tom" or "Uncle Tom," after the figure from Harriet Beecher Stowe's famous novel (although significantly modified in usage since then). This class of Black people is often severely criticized for not helping their own people, and Black activists often compare them negatively with well-situated members of other ethnic and racial groupings.

Typically, the HNIC is not chosen in any simple way. Those in power do not hold job fairs with the position advertised. Rather, the selection occurs quite naturally. The Black employee who gains the trust of his or her superiors is the successful Black person within the organization, the one who stands out for undeniably embodying and manifesting the organization's values. In other words, the HNIC demonstrates not only a certain amount of talent but also a certain degree of loyalty to the goals and identity of the organization.

Although it is a position of influence, the HNIC designation is not necessarily something one seeks out or campaigns for, and some Black people selected for it are genuinely surprised when they realize how much influence they have gained within the organization. Others within the organization, especially fellow Black employees, however, have often already taken notice of their peer's success. Strikingly, because the HNIC has earned this success, he or she is seldom someone who would "rock the boat." This is an unspoken rule, learned on the job through observation and by following one's intuition. It becomes second nature to never to do anything or to be party to activities that would embarrass the organization, especially the White superiors.

This process has grave implications for young Black employees. And for Black men who win—who "make it" in mainstream society—there is a certain distrust of the prize: their own success alienates them from the Black masses and also fails to win them true acceptance by the wider system. Those young middle-class Black men who acquire the resources to negotiate the wider system and who, in the process, work so hard to eliminate any potential confusion between themselves and their inner-city counterparts feel eternally in limbo between two extremes: the drug-dealing, gold-wearing street hustler who "disses" the conventions of the wider society, on the one hand, and the successful mainstream professional, on the other. Therefore, Black professionals must constantly struggle to define themselves on their own terms, in a society that both celebrates and demonizes them. All of this contributes to a certain precariousness of place that results from people's presuppositions about Black men. The Black man's color and maleness become his master status, calling into question anything else he may claim to be.

THE RACE MAN AND HIS FATE

The concept of the race man goes back to a time when the Black community was utterly segregated, a model of society that approached a caste system of racial organization, traceable to the era of slavery. The term itself was introduced in the classic ethnographic study of the Black community in Chicago carried out in the 1940s by Horace Cayton and St. Clair Drake, two Black sociologists at the University of Chicago, and published in their book *Black Metropolis*. By Cayton and Drake's definition, the race man (or, we might add, woman) was a particular kind of Black leader who not only lived within the segregated Black community but felt strongly responsible to Black people as a race, especially in their campaign for advancement and betterment. Often, the race man behaved as though he carried the weight of the whole race on his shoulders. In public, he embraced the need to put matters of "the race" first. Such a person was strongly committed to "advancing the race" by serving as a role model for young people, both to uplift the ghetto community and to disabuse the wider society of its often negative view of Black people.

In his efforts to advance the race against American apartheid, the race man assumed that every Black person he encountered was to be treated as a natural ally—a brother, a cousin, or a friend—in the face of White oppression. Moreover, everyone who was "anybody" in the community—not just professionals and politicians but the hardworking industrial union members, the "regulars" on the corner, and the neighborhood "grandmothers"—followed his lead, bound to become race men and women themselves. Implicit in this belief was a kind of assumed racial solidarity, a peculiar and exaggerated celebration of racial "particularism," putting matters of race above all other issues.

In this context, there were also community secrets that Black people shared only among themselves and perhaps with White "friends of the race." But in front of the White community in general, Black people were strongly expected to present a united front, to close ranks and be silent, and absolutely never to air "dirty laundry" in public or speak ill of another Black person to White people. Picking up on the figure of the race man but not grasping his full significance, well-meaning White people often referred to such a person as a "credit to his race."

Up through and after the civil rights movement, there existed a critical mass of race men and women in the segregated Black community, but their heyday was at a time when the racial caste system operated in the American culture as a whole, when a rigid wall of separation existed between Blacks and Whites that was expressed in terms of styles of life, behavior, culture, residence, and power. In this context, the race man and woman flourished.

Over the past several decades, as the racial incorporation process grew in the wider system and Black people became more diffuse in society, spreading throughout American culture, the rise in "colored immigration" has ensured that the Black community today is far from being a monolith, if it ever was one. Today, the Black community is highly complex. And in these circumstances, the race man of old loses his force, his power, and, of course, his ability to "speak for the race."

In their heyday, the race man and woman not only put the race's best foot forward; they defended the community in the face of adversity, actively promoting civil rights and making sure that the community got its just due politically from the municipal establishment. But as the educated Black middle class grows and members posture as assimilated middle-class citizens, their ideology comes to conflict fundamentally with that of the race man and woman. In other words, the more assimilated their people become, the less critical is the role of the race man and woman. Hence, in the past quarter century, American society has been experiencing on a large scale the emergence of a new type of Black professional, who divides their loyalties between their race and their profession, for their interests lie not just with the local folk but with their class or profession. These people tend to be more cosmopolitan in terms of their values and proclivities.

In many respects, this process is similar to that which the Irish, Jews, Italians, and other assimilated ethnic groups have undergone. At various periods in their histories, virtually all of these groups have had their race men and women, but as their fortunes have risen, as they have become better educated and enjoyed social positions consistent with their education, the social and political need for their respective race men and women has declined. Indeed, these groups experienced different kinds of leaders, people who in turn became increasingly more interested in their own professions and class positions. Such people do not necessarily forget their roots. But most often, the needs and requirements of their professions win out, and class issues take precedence over public displays of ethnic and racial particularism. This process has come to be expected as a normal consequence of an ethnic group's upward mobility in the United States.

Up to now, Black people, who have been dogged by the most virulent racism since the days of slavery, have been the exception. The realities of the Black community's unique history of racial injury, which still rears its head in modern dress, become profoundly consequential for the sporadic appearances of the race man in local and national politics. As Black people became better educated and as some applied themselves to working toward inclusion, many were rewarded with professional positions within the White-dominated establishment. As a result, many became upwardly mobile and were able to take part in the American dream, striving for the full rights, obligations, and privileges of middle-class Americans. And yet, many of these same people became frustrated when they found that even the best jobs and careers are not immune to powerful institutional racism. In the settings in which they have been incorporated, many of these people continue the struggle with their White colleagues' attempts to marginalize them and their kind. It is in this context of continual struggle that the race man and woman emerge and reemerge from time to time.

MORAL AUTHORITY

The negative images others take from the iconic ghetto conspire to negate or undermine the moral authority of the Black person in the larger society, and this is at no time more consequential than when he or she navigates the White space. When present there, the Black person typically has limited standing relative to his White counterparts and is made aware of this situation by the way others treat him. With a wealth of moral authority, others may empathize and one can experience acceptance, as well as an aura of protection against ritual offenses, including random acts of disrespect; without such authority, the Black person is uniquely vulnerable.

When respected, a Black person can exert a degree of moral sway that constrains, or checks, those inclined to show him disrespect, to offend him, or to mistreat him or her, for the possession of moral authority by the Black person places the potential offender on morally dubious ground. This can cause the person so inclined to pause, possibly constrained by what his offenses might mean for what others would think of him, or what he might think of himself if he follows his inclination. With his own esteem or self-concept in the balance, he might anticipate shame for himself and reconsider. But for the Black person, moral authority is truly actualized only when he is well integrated into the White space, and most often he is not.

When Black people lack moral authority, those who are inclined to offend them on the basis of their color may know no shame and face few sanctions. Thus, without such authority, the Black person moves through the larger society in a vulnerable state, which is particularly so when navigating the White space—a world in which he typically has limited social standing and, thus, limited respect. Indeed, it is in such settings that the Black person meets on occasion acute, racially based disrespect—or, as many Black people call it, the "n****r moment" (see Anderson 2011).

In navigating the White space, many Blacks regard such aggressions as inevitable and have learned to think of them as small and large (see Pierce 1970). Usually, they ignore the small incidents, considering them not worthy of the mental work and trouble that confronting them would require. But the large ones cannot be ignored, for typically they are highly disturbing, volatile, occasionally even violent, and capable of fundamentally changing one's outlook on life—not to mention the glossy exterior many Blacks display while negotiating the White space as part of their daily lives; when such a moment occurs, the person can feel humiliation, that he or she has been "put in their place."

In the general scheme of the White space, it matters little whether such acute disrespect is intended or unintended. The injury most often has the same effect: deflation and a sense of marginalization, regardless of the Black person's previous negotiations, achievements, or claims to status; the person is reminded of her provisional status, that she has much to prove in order to really belong in the White space.

The Black person's realization of her predicament may be gradual, as awareness often occurs in subtle and ambiguous ways over time, through what may seem to be the deceptively ordinary interactions and negotiations of everyday life. In the White space, small issues can become fraught with racial meaning, and small behaviors can subtly teach or remind the Black person of her outsider status, showing onlookers and bystanders alike that she does not really belong, that she is not to be regarded and treated as a full person in the White space. In time, she may conclude that the real problem she faces in this setting is that she is not White and that being White is a fundamental requirement for acceptance and a sense of belonging in the White space.

When Black people come to the realization that common courtesies will not be extended to them, that their White counterparts easily command them and they are not able to do the same, their faith in the putative fairness of the wider system—and the White space in particular—erodes, and they can become cynical. Such realizations do not occur overnight but are often gradual and may require many months or years of experience and observation before the Black person concludes that the "game is rigged" against him, chiefly because of the color of his skin. With an accumulation of race-based micro- and macro-aggressions, the person can hit a wall from which there is seldom a full recovery (Pierce 1970). When this point is reached, playing along, smiling, or laughing in the White space becomes more difficult. Gradually and effectively, he reaches an irreversible revelation that permanently impacts his consciousness—soon, he may depart.

With these understandings, many Blacks approach the White space ambivalently, and ostensibly for instrumental reasons. When possible, they may avoid it altogether or leave it as soon as possible. To obtain these rewards, Blacks must venture into the White space and explore its possibilities, engaging it to the extent that they can while hoping to benefit as much as possible. To be at all successful, they must manage themselves within this space. But the promise of acceptance is too often only that, a promise. All too frequently, prejudiced actors pervade the White space and are singly or collectively able and interested in marginalizing the Black person, actively reminding him of his outsider status to put him in his place.

KAYR'S STORY

A Foot in Two Worlds

While I was teaching at the University of Pennsylvania in the late 1980s and early 1990s, some friends and I sought out young Black men from the surrounding ghetto neighborhoods of West Philadelphia to mentor.

Specifically, we wanted to assist studious young men who were at risk from the typical urban ills like street gangs, drugs, and violence. Often these boys had no fathers in their homes. They lived with a single mother and her other children, typically a series of stepfathers or boyfriends, and at times a grandmother. Their households were impoverished, and many of these boys found the street much more attractive than school. We wanted to support those who were still interested in school and were motivated to excel.

KAYR was one of those boys. His childhood poverty, and the hardships he saw his siblings and neighbors undergoing, inspired him to seek a way out through education. Here is his story.

• • •

Okay. So, I'm KAYR (pronounced KAY-R), that's what I go by, and I grew up in Philadelphia with my six siblings in a single-parent household on public assistance—for those of you who don't know what that is, welfare—and my family, we moved around a lot. We rented a lot of houses throughout Philadelphia, and my family at one point did buy like one of the dollar houses from the city, and unfortunately that house caught on fire. And I remember vividly a point when we were so homeless, living in that house, that my elementary teacher brought us KFC, an eight-piece and some sides. And my family and I, we ate that food in the living room, and we were able to look at the stars through the ceiling because the whole third floor was missing. And so, at the time we were actually homeless, and then we went to live with various people in their basements and their extra rooms.

So that really hit me pretty hard, and created a burning desire in me. . . .

I remember that time period very vividly. It was something that never left my memory because it was so unbelievable and so surreal that I couldn't believe that we had to live like that, and had to go out and move around and live with various family members and friends.

I pretty much lived in every part of Philadelphia, and what's fascinating is that I actually have older siblings, two older brothers and two older sisters, and my sisters got pregnant. They were teenage moms, where I helped them raise children at a really young age, so they were like really young teenage moms, like fourteen or, what have you, fifteen. As a result, I was an uncle before I even made it to high school.

And I think that just made me mature, but the hardship, living through the hardship, seeing my family press on, and also seeing that my mother struggled with finances, and also, like, the local church and small Black businesses shutting down. . . . Like, on Fiftieth and Spruce, there used to be a restaurant called the Big George [West Philadelphia restaurant], and Bill Clinton actually ate there. It's shut down now.

Very early on, I wanted to know what was the root cause of all these financial issues. I just decided at the tender age of like fourteen to immerse myself in business books and self-help books, and I spent a lot of my free time when I wasn't working at Barnes and Noble at Thirty-Sixth and Walnut, where I would just read books and books on, like, how do you manage money? How do you grow money? How do you run a business? So that's where that passion for business and entrepreneurship came from.

And then, what happened in high school, I went to public school, I went to University City High School, which was on 3601 Filbert Street, and that's when I started to become really furious, looking at my sisters, saying that I wanted to have a better life. I remember my stepdad, and also other family members who were like, "Do what I say, don't do as I do," so they were like, "We haven't been disciplined in order to achieve our goals, but we know the right things to do." And so, I just wanted to apply what these people were telling me, like my stepdad and other professionals like you—if you apply yourself you can do much better.

In high school I worked really hard, working part-time, and also I became the captain of the track team, the cross-country team, the debate team, class president, school president, and graduated first in my class. And then I got into a program called Philadelphia Futures, where I was getting ready to apply to colleges. I was thinking about applying to a historically Black college, or going to an Ivy League college, but the counselor said, "KAYR, I don't want you to make a terrible mistake. I think that you should check out this school called Bowdoin College."

And what the counselor did is he called the admissions officer that was going to the big cities, trying to recruit students of color to come to Maine. And he came and met me and my mentor, who was a lawyer from Howard Law School, a young lawyer, and he said, "KAYR, we're going to fly you up for the weekend to Maine," and that was the first time I ever got on a plane in my whole life, and some of my siblings at this point had never been on a plane, and my mother hadn't been on a plane.

And I just said, "I'm going to go." And I went off to Brunswick, Maine, and I really, really was impressed with the facilities, like the library, the professors, the resources—the food at the time was ranked first in the country by Princeton Review—*it was like a whole new world. And I would tell my family members, "I really like Maine."*

And they said, "You might as well just go to Canada if you're going to go that far. We're not going up there—there're no Black people in Maine!" And one thing about my family, they kept their word. They never came up to visit me.

And so, I was like in a whole new world. And I really liked it, and I applied early decision, and I got the Chamberlain Scholarship, which was the most prestigious and also the presidential scholarship, and the college paid for everything.

I accepted the offer to go to Bowdoin College, and what I did is throughout the school year, I would hone my academic skills to fill in the gaps. I always tell people that when I went to college, I had to do everything you typically do in high school when I got to college, because I was playing catch-up. As a result, I worked extraordinarily hard and I was on the dean's list three out of my four years there—I had one too many Bs my freshman year. I had a 3.5 GPA; I should have done better.

And in the summers, I decided I wanted to explore the finance food chain. I got exposure to asset management at American Express my freshman year, then I got exposure to sales and trading at Prudential Securities on the precious metals desk, then I got exposure to investment banking at Credit Suisse and the Technology Group. And I got a full-time offer from Credit Suisse and a number of other banks, and New York, and I decided to accept an offer from Goldman Sachs, where I did investment banking in the Consumer Retail Group, where I got exposure to mergers and acquisitions, financing deals, and industry work.

What was fascinating about my work at Goldman Sachs is that after you finish your first year—and this is really exclusive, this doesn't happen, this is not normal at the firms—Goldman Sachs has the best clients on the buy side, hedge funds, private equity shops, and what they do is they recruit directly from Goldman Sachs's two-year analyst program, which is very prestigious. I think my class had three hundred people from around the world in the front office, and I think we prob-

ably only had like five African Americans, descendants of slaves. Maybe five, across three hundred. And it was really crazy, because after you finish your job, I was surprised—Goldman Sachs sent us an email, to all the analysts doing the program, saying these are all the external opportunities you can apply to, where you're going to be given prefer- ence because you went through the two-year Goldman Sachs analyst training program. And these are Goldman Sachs external clients.

I applied to work at Sirios Capital Management, a long-short equity hedge fund with three billion, and I was the only African American working there, where I covered financials and homebuilders, and I got an offer making a lot of money. So I went from Maine, where I was in college, then moved to New York to work for Goldman Sachs, and after two years I moved to Boston and I lived in the Devonshire on the twenty-second floor on Washington Street in downtown Boston right next to Faneuil Hall Marketplace.

And what's interesting was that I went from, let's say North Phila- delphia and Port Richmond when it was really tough, to Maine, living in this really fabulous dorm; and then going to New York City, living on the Upper East Side. But what was really interesting is that I went from Bowdoin College to . . . a part of my scholarship was that I had the option to spend five weeks at Phillips Exeter, to do a five-week program before I started college. That was the first time I learned how to play golf, I learned how to play tennis; that was the first time I had sushi, and the first time I was on a yacht. And that was just my eye-opener. That was the beginning stages to why I started to see the world from another perspective.

I had good mentors like you and Jesse from the nonprofit organiza- tion called the Great Young Society II and other people. . . . Like, when I was at University High School, I don't know if you remember, but I had braids and I had an Afro, and also facial hair and what have you. So, what I did was I cut my braids. I cleaned up my act, became more polished. I remember, when I was in University City, I'd probably have a pair of Jordans on, or something like that. And then, when

I went into Phillips Exeter, I befriended people and I started to figure out how do you fit in? And I went from, like, wearing Jordans to wearing New Balances, or I started wearing, like, boat shoes and khakis, and a Caesar haircut or a low fade.

And I think that what happened is that, for me, I realized that I wanted to be a part of this new world vs. being an outsider, or trying to challenge the system, so for me, I always believed that you could catch more bees with honey than you can with vinegar. And so, I said, "I have so many other things going against me, I just want to figure out how do I just put my head down, and I could focus, and not get distracted by all these other things that's beyond my control."

So, that's my approach from talking to, like, my own personal board of directors, which I include people like you, to help me just figure out how do you navigate this world. For me, that was my way of protest—the best protest is getting an A in the class, and getting the best internship, and increasing your net worth. So, that was my focus. I truly believe the best way to combat racism is living by this saying: Because I am a man of color, I must be two times as good to be half as good. I must be four times as good to be equal. I must be six times as good to be better. I reach for seven, not because I have to, but because I can.

With the suits, the really well-off kids, I didn't really go into detail about my background. So, we did not really have those in-depth conversations. I would be more interested in conveying my professional dreams, my intellectual prowess, or things of that nature, or talking about business. So, it'll be more because I already started to study the community and the way people act before I even got there, but I'm always one of those people who are, you know, in preparation vs. integration . . . or, not integration, intervention?

So, I said, "Let me look at how these people live, let me see how they operate. Now, I'm going to figure out what do they really like to do." So, for me, I made a conscious decision to really read Sports Illustrated once a week, to read The New Yorker, Time magazine, and watch 60 Minutes and 20/20, because I wanted people to see me more as their *peer vs. an outcast or someone from the 'hood. I wanted them to see me as, like, "Hey, look, he's just another middle-class Black kid from the Delaware Valley."*

I tried to fit in. And so, that's why I went from wearing Jordans to . . . Right now what's funny is I have like three pairs of New Balances in my apartment. I just didn't bring up the 'hood side of myself. I would connect with people. So, like, I would join, like, the Bowdoin Christian Association. When I was at Bowdoin, I would join, like, the Japanese Association or the Korean Association. I would join different affinity groups so that I could better understand different cultures and connect with people on a personal level.

I showed a different side of myself. It was a conscious decision. I always tell people, "When I was in Philadelphia, growing up in Philadelphia, I would eat a turkey ham sandwich in Philadelphia. And I would eat that with mayonnaise and American cheese, and on white bread, and I would also add a glass of whole milk to that. When I went to Bowdoin, by the end of my first semester at Bowdoin, I would eat turkey—not necessarily turkey ham, but turkey—with brie cheese, and also on a piece of whole wheat bread, and then I'd drink fat-free milk."

So, not only was I making a conscious decision about the way that I comport myself, but also the way I consume food. When I came home I would think that . . . I'm one of those people that believe "when in Rome, do as the Romans do." And so, you can just . . . you don't have to eat the same portions, or eat the same amount [as others eat] so, I'll just engage in that a little bit. But because my eating habits have changed, my stomach will get full and I'll just eat as much of the traditional low-income African American–type cuisine, because my stomach would just be full.

So, I basically worked to fit in with the crowd. And when I came back to, like, Philadelphia, I wouldn't wear the same outfit, or comport myself the same way that I did, like, in Hanover, New Hampshire. So, like, in Philadelphia, I will revert back to something that will make it feel more calming, like if you're a part of the community.

So, I code-switched, so to speak. 'Cause you don't want to be insulting to your family. Everybody at your family is eating that, and you're like, "I can't eat that," or, "I'm sorry, I can't engage in these activities, guys—they're so below me."

Oh, my family was incredibly impressed about my success and very happy, and encouraging. Some members didn't really know what it was, it was so foreign and so different, but overall I think that they were very happy to see that someone made it out [of the 'hood] and become successful. Like, when I made my money on Wall Street, my $10,000 internship, I was able to come home and buy my family members—my mother, my sister—something for her children or her house. So my success was actually helping the whole family. People encouraged me.

My junior year of college, I was happy to call my mother, and I just had got a big paycheck—they pay us big money when you're an intern on Wall Street. I went home and bought my sister Mara a new refrigerator and everything like this. I came back to New York for my internship, my mother said, "Call me."

I said, "What is going on?"

And she said, "Tony shot Mara five times in her face."

And my thought was like . . . I couldn't believe that, like that's impossible. Tony is the father of three of her children. And so, I went back to Philadelphia. So I'm in this White space where everything's perfect. In New York I'm getting paid good money; I think, nothing to worry about. But yet I'm getting drawn back. And actually, that week I had interviews coming up with other banks, so it's pulling me back to this Black space which could be tough, and so my mother says there's an emergency.

So, I go back to Philadelphia and find out that this guy Tony put my family on the hit list, and my family had to go move and hide from being endangered. And they eventually catch the guy, Maurice, but they catch him after he kills my sister and a taxicab driver. And luckily, he's in prison doing life for murder. But I had to make a decision. I could not just cancel all these interviews, so I mustered up the strength and I was able to go in and interview all these places and get jobs the following week.

*Another decision I had to make was . . . my college would say,
"KAYR, you can take the senior year off because of what happened
to your sister. You don't have to come back." But I was on a mission.
I was so determined, that burning desire from when I was young to
have financial freedom and to build a legacy that I wasn't going to let
nothing stop me. And so, I went back my senior year and I had my best
academic year. I think I had five As and three A-minuses, or something
like that—my best academic year! On top of that, I took accounting
courses at a local community college. And then I accepted an investment
banking job at Goldman Sachs and did investment banking. That was
definitely a very challenging time.*

*Another period that was really tough for me . . . The year that
I graduated from University High, my brother, who's one year younger
than me, actually went to prison for attempted murder. That was very
difficult—your brother that is one year apart from you. I'm getting
ready to go to this White space, I'm about to go off to Maine, get on a
plane, have a full scholarship and be spoiled, and go to Exeter, and
my brother is taking another path. He's going to the state penitentiary
for attempted murder, and he spent twelve years there. So, while I'm
in college in this White space, he's in college in this Black space, in
prison. It was a very fascinating experience to just maintain focus,
understanding.*

*I remember my brother writing me from prison—I think I may still
have the letter, where he says, "KAYR, I know what you're doing. Keep
your head up, stay focused. I'm proud of you, and I'm just going to
try to stay safe in here." And it's so interesting, because you read that
book,* The Other Wes Moore, *where the guy just has the same name
as a guy that's in prison, and he's writing it from the perspective of a
journalist. But when you actually have a blood relation, you grew up
in the same house, the experience is a lot deeper and richer.*

*I also had another challenging moment, when I was at Tuck my
second year, in the year of 2011, both of my parents, my biological
mom and biological dad, passed away in the same year. So that was*

another challenging moment. And I always joke, and I say, "Man! The Lord definitely is trying me. He must think I'm Job, the Black version, because He is taking everything from me."

As I was going through all these changes, meeting all these White people, I would try to keep everything secret, so I would not share this with a lot of people. So, even though I'm going through all this hardship and everything, I would keep it a secret. I would just smile and act normal, and they'd say, "Oh, KAYR, you getting ready for your year?" "Oh yeah, should be fun. I've been picking out my classes. You picking out your classes?" So, I would keep it like a secret and just keep it boxed up.

And what I learned to do, and I encourage others to do, is when I was at Bowdoin College I did take counseling. I encourage people who come from a family that is faced with a lot of drama to take counseling. The school offered it for free, so I definitely incorporated that.

My class at Bowdoin College, we had about 440 people in my class, and we had five African Americans. It was not a lot. And when I was at Tuck, my class had about 183, and that class only had about ten or eleven African Americans. So it's not like I'd ever been, at the age of eighteen, in spaces with a lot of Black people, in those types of situations. And so, even in my experience with those African Americans, my experience was so far removed from reality that a lot of them couldn't even relate to me, because it was so extreme—from my sister being murdered by the father of her three children, to my brother, one year apart, going to prison for attempted murder, to my mother being on welfare with all these children, to always moving around, our house burned down, being homeless at one point—it was so different from the other people that were at these colleges. I've never met anybody with a similar story.

Surprisingly, the kids that were there, the five African Americans, some come from real middle-class families, upper-middle-class families, or they're poor but they come from a stable home with two parents. Or they come from one parent that went to college that's stable, or they're Caribbean, or what have you, or African, so my experience was drastically different. I was surprised by how very few African Americans—like, slave-born African American descendants—were my classmates.

I had a good experience, but there were definitely some things about race that were offensive, or we had to have events on campus to talk about it—the traditional stuff, where people may spray-paint something that's inappropriate on the wall, or some people may have done something that really offended a whole group of African Americans and we had to have an event with the leadership of the school. Or you're having a party and somebody does something inappropriate at an African American party where they weren't invited. The issues that they have now on campus at these predominantly White schools, we had similar incidents back then, between 2001 and 2005.

Even some White people that I went to school with, if you put some of that stuff, they'd be like, "Oh my God, I never even knew all that stuff." It'll be so fascinating, like the old saying, "Never let them see you sweat," so people would be like, "Oh my God! How did he manage to just maintain his composure and be so stoic?"

What happened is I learned that for me to get support, it doesn't necessarily need for you to have the same background as me. What I wanted is support from people who share the same vibes as me. And so, when I look out for support, I don't really care about color or gender or what have you. It could be a White counselor who really cared about me at Dartmouth or Bowdoin College; it could be an African American counselor I used to talk to, cared about me a lot. So, what I do is I start putting together a team of people who have my best interests regardless of where they came from in life, because for me poor people, or people who come from extreme poverty, they don't have a monopoly on overcoming obstacles. A White kid, Irish kid who comes from Long Island who's well-off, his parents are divorced or who's just having self-esteem problems, he has obstacles he has to overcome, I have obstacles I have to overcome, and I try to find commonality. Where can we meet? And that's how I built the relationships on my support system.

My sister, my family, my siblings, they supported me when they could, but I supported a lot of them. I helped my nephews and put them in private schools.

My sister, the one that had four children and passed away, as soon as I was a freshman in college, I helped them financially. I helped with the funeral, I helped with school supplies, I'm the one that pays for them when they move into college, for transportation, I went to their football games, things of that nature, so I was helping them all along the way, and I still help them to this day. I give my niece a monthly allowance for college and my nephew a monthly allowance for college. I help with their rent, yup.

And my other siblings have children, and some of them I gave them jobs—actually, two of them work for me—the other one I gave first, last, and security to get into their own place. So, yes. It's always been an ongoing helping my family more than you would think the middle child would have to do.

I paid for multiple funerals for my family. I had to help pay for the funeral for one of my brothers, and I did come home for that funeral. But my other brother had a cremation, like a funeral, but I couldn't come home for that one. I paid for that as well.

Sometimes you need a little space, like James Baldwin in Paris, in order to think clearly and stay focused. I think that Baldwin's writing, when he came back and got more involved with the civil rights movement, became less focused and distracted. I think he was getting pulled in so many ways.

So, that's why I always tried to go to schools that are far away from my family, so that I can focus and really just grow, and be free, vs. being pulled down. That's why I didn't go to Temple University, or Drexel, or what have you.

One has to pick their battles because you're trying to win the war, and for me, the war was to get to [Wall Street]. There were always slights, where people will say indirect stuff, or act as though they're very uncomfortable with someone that looks like you or acts like you, but I would just overlook that and say, "You know, it's not even worth going down that path." Or I would read books like How to Win Friends and

Influence People *and implement that in my day-to-day life, so I would not let people get under my skin. And I would know that they treat you a certain way, or look at you in a certain way, or ask you even more questions than other people, are quick to judge you differently. And so I would say, in a very polite way, this is what I'm thinking.*

When I started at one job, I came in, and someone had said, "Excuse me, do you work here?"

And I said, "Oh yes, I'm the new Black guy." And then I showed them my ID.

And he said, "Oh, I'm so sorry!" But I'm like, they should have asked the White guy ahead of me the same thing.

So there will always be subtle things that I will have to deal with, where they ask you to do things other White people don't have to do. People would say things to question your qualifications, or question your intelligence on a certain subject matter. In the workplace, too, sometimes you have it, it can be a boss or something where they say something inappropriate.

And sometimes it'll be direct things, and so what I will do is I will step up and report them anonymously to HR if I feel as though they are treating me differently because of my race. But that's always a very tricky thing as well, where if you push too hard you'll get blacklisted, and people will say, "No one wants to work with that guy. He's a race guy."

You have to take it in stride—you can't let these situations paralyze you. One of my work friends, he had just been so fed up with his place of employment that he quit and became a teacher. He said he can't understand how I'm such a good actor, how I can put up with the crap. He probably had a boss that would give assignments to the White person, wouldn't give it to the Black person, and it happened a little too often, or they show favoritism, or you don't get invited out for drinks or something like that. You see a pattern, and you're like, "I don't want to keep on having to fight my way into everything," so I think my friend was exhausted.

I was very conscious of how the culture looked at a rising African American, so I was very cognizant of all different factors when I made decisions. *I will always read books from the left, perspective from the center, and also from the right so I can better understand how people perceive me, and then I will pick my battles very carefully so I stay focused. This is a whole way to navigate the system, to navigate the White space.*

You deal with it. It's more like . . . in the sixties, and North vs. the South, you know there are people who are racist, who have ill intent, but now they do it in a different way. They'll express their thoughts in a different way, a very subtle way, vs. out loud like how they used to do it in the South. It was really kinda weird things, like in the dorms, one of my friends was saying like how some White person was like, "Oh, can I touch your hair?" or they just have certain stereotypes, like you have a conversation with someone and they're like, "Oh, you don't act like a regular Black." And you can tell that they're kinda naive, nice people; it's not like they have ill intent, they'll just say, "Oh wow, you're not like a regular Black. Most of the Blacks I know, they do service around the house, or they play sports. You're kinda like very studious," or something like that.

So it's just like those conversations where people are intoxicated or unhappy, then they start to tell you what their real thoughts are, so you have those kinds of conversations. Or someone will tell you that one of their parents is not really big on Black people. Or you have certain actions where people treat you slightly different because of who you are.

You gotta have mentors, too. Well, I don't really say mentors; you gotta have sponsors. That is a big difference. Sponsors take a deep interest in you and they put their name on the line. A mentor just will advise you, but a sponsor is someone that goes beyond mentorship. They're willing to sponsor you and say, "Hey, he's with me," or, "She's with me," and that opens doors. That gives you, really, credibility.

There were a lot of good people [at Bowdoin], like the president of the college was very genuine and open to making everybody feel welcome. And the various deans at the college were so helpful to me—there were a lot of professionals that took a deep interest in my development that were White professionals, in addition to Black professionals as well.

Like we had certain people, Black and White, who reached out to me, so many good people helped me. So, there was a combination of White professionals and also Black professionals that had my best interests in mind.

There were also other students that I became really close with. There were upperclassmen, like Michel—he's Haitian, African American—and I had my own group of close friends that I made when I got on campus, that came from diverse backgrounds. White and Black.

That's something I learned in White space is very important. Some people are so focused on their day job that they forget that you need to find sponsors in the firm or at the bank, or in the business deals—you need those sponsors. They are even more important than if you're competent at your job.

I remember I used to have like a silver watch that I really liked. I had a chain with a cross on it, and a pinkie ring, a bracelet, and I thought that was so cool. But one of my mentors—or sponsors, I would say—told me, "KAYR, go get a Timex with a black leather band. Keep it very simple. Stay under the radar. Fit in. And wear that to work when you go in to Goldman Sachs."

Now I own over 105 rental units, and I have my own property management business, I have my own consulting business, and mo-tivational speaking business—we make well over a million dollars a year. I've retired from my Wall Street job, I'm teaching people about how to invest in real estate now, and so I'm in a place where I grew up extremely poor, worth a negative hundred thousand based on my parents' debts and everything, to now I'm a multimillionaire. And I'm thirty-seven years old.

I think that that's only possible because I have a track record of being successful throughout the years, and getting that stamp of ap-proval from various institutions and people, and also having powerful relationships with people like you and other people that have my best interests in mind, that help me move along in this world.

And then, the third thing . . . I think I have a reputation, and that reputation put me in a position to create real financial wealth in

America. I always think of America like three forms of capital. One, intellectual capital, and that is what you get from a classroom, from a coach, a mentor, a family member can teach you, a book; another one is financial capital—that's what you earn from a job or a business, or you get from a lender; and the third one is social capital, and that is the relationships that one forms over time to effect change, and so now I serve on three nonprofit boards. It's just been a privilege to really understand how America works, and for America to embrace someone with my background.

I just think I've had a fascinating journey from West Philly to where I am now, where I have people working for me, I have a bunch of tenants and properties with my name on it—it's very crazy.

• • •

KAYR's story points to a number of issues about what it means to be a Black person in White space. He's learned and honed this skill, and a large part of his success has come from the ability to maneuver between the worlds and code-switch.

His rise began in his Philadelphia neighborhood, where my friends and I recruited him and encouraged him, along with other promising young Black men who stood out from the crowd. They were studious, with a positive sense of the future, and they applied themselves to their schoolwork. Yet they were at risk of falling prey to "the street," which is highly seductive with its promise of adventure, love, and a lucrative way of getting what everyone knows as the "quick money" by what the street culture calls "getting legal" or "clocking," a flip on the meaning of legitimate work and civil law. Our mission was to save as many boys as possible.

I was joined in my efforts by people like Herman Wrice, who was a natural community leader. He and other "old heads" developed this group of "Renaissance men" to build a group of young men who could take their place in society, excel, and move into the system. Herman used to sit around with me and others and lament that even if we had jobs available for the young people in the community, we'd have a hard time filling them because they weren't ready. This was a constant refrain. The next question was how to get them ready.

In ghetto environments, good grades and studiousness were simply not valued, and for too many there was no payoff for such performance. Excelling at school or hitting the books was often branded as deviant behavior. On the streets and in the schools, a studious young man might be called a Poindexter, an epithet for a boy others made fun of or viewed as square or lame, a person who decidedly could not dance, could not fight, and could never qualify for the label hip or cool or down or attract the coolest girls.

When these young men joined us at Penn, we had a message for them. We encouraged them to stay in school and to study. We tried to reinforce to them the importance of academic work and place value on the Poindexters of the world—to let them know such young men were "going places." We encouraged them to excel. Our mission, informal as it was, was to support the Poindexter image, and sometimes we were successful.

KAYR was fortunate in that he was never called names for being studious or bullied for his academic efforts or achievements. On the contrary, he was celebrated for having good grades, perhaps owing to a generational shift. He and his peers decided to join the mentoring program because they wanted to find a purpose—to take ownership of their community and make it a better place.

I secured a seminar room at the Fels Institute at the university and held weekly meetings with the young men over lunches of pizza and sodas. On some Saturday mornings, I organized conferences in the ghetto neighborhoods. At some of the meetings, I distributed paperback dictionaries and lectured on the power of the word. Often we'd end our meetings with a testimonial from a young man who'd gone on to college or with a speech by a successful Black man who related his own story to the Poindexter theme.

At times I would assign them to write essays on vocabulary words like dignity or responsibility. We sometimes had animated discussions on Black leaders like Malcolm X, Martin Luther King Jr., Frederick

Douglass, or Denmark Vesey. We also discussed local politics, the idea of democracy, and the history and importance of Black voting rights.

I also recruited successful Black men to visit and tell their stories over lunch. Not surprisingly, their histories were not unlike the young men's. They would discuss the reasons for their success and tell how they'd had to apply themselves, but they'd also reveal that at some point in their lives they'd had to break away from peers who were up to no good.

KAYR was one of the boys we reached out to, and he was very receptive. His is a Horatio Alger story, one that validates and legitimates the wider system as open to the qualified regardless of race or ethnic background. Certain wealthy and not-so-wealthy White men love this story. It affirms them as wealthy people with no regrets: "Anyone can be where I am."

Along the way, KAYR had mentors and sponsors who encouraged him and looked out for him, but he was moving from the ghetto into a White space, so he had to know how to deal with it. And he learned to deal not only with Whites but with middle-class Blacks who were not from the iconic ghetto as he was. Not being born with a silver spoon or having a private school education, he needed all the help he could get. We tried to provide some of that help.

CHAPTER 12

GENTRIFICATION

Whites in Black Space

Perhaps no setting is more critical for appreciating social dynamics than the gentrifying, racially contested neighborhood. In the past, such Philadelphia neighborhoods have produced tightly knit communities with sometimes violent groups of young men who were quick to defend their space from the incursions of other ethnic groups, and especially any encroachment by Black people.

Now, certain ghetto neighborhoods, with their antique buildings and situated in close proximity to the city center, have become highly attractive, or "hot." White people, located in racially exclusive suburban communities far from "the action," suddenly want to live in the city. For much of urban history, Blacks and Whites have lived in distinct but overlapping housing markets, one "restricted" and the other "unrestricted," and both conditioned by the economics of race and housing. Because of their racial stigma, Black people typically operated in a restricted housing market, meaning they could sell their homes only to other Blacks; most Whites would never think of living near Blacks, except as a matter of last resort. White people, on the other hand, especially those who were well-off, operated in an unrestricted, or open, housing market, meaning they could theoretically sell to whoever was the highest bidder, for as much as the market would bear. Thus Whites might sell their property to a wide spectrum of buyers; such a market is theoretically unlimited. With gentrification, as White buyers begin to look to disenfranchised Black communities, they invest not only their financial capital but their racial capital, their White skin, increasing the value of the property simply by moving in. By investing themselves, they realize their own racial capital.

During the early 1900s, ethnic gangs fought one another for control of certain workplaces and the adjacent public spaces, which were often embedded in their neighborhoods. Certain ethnic groups claimed and often identified with certain factories or certain industries. The jobs in these places were often passed around to close relations, including sons, brothers, cousins, uncles, and nephews. Other ethnic groups were usually considered competitors and at times a threat to the local community's livelihood. In defending their turf, White ethnic groups sometimes fought pitched battles pitting one White group against another—for example, the Irish against the Italians. When Black people appeared, the warring groups were inclined to call a truce and focus on battling the Blacks, further contributing to the establishment of the ghetto (Davis and Haller 1998). These counteractions worked to dampen Black people's enthusiasm and aspirations. The apparent result was a certain containment and ghettoization, but not in the way many might think.

The actual process was more complex. When Black people first arrived in the city, they naturally gravitated to areas inhabited by other Blacks, seeking both comfort and familiarity with their "own kind." In time, as their numbers expanded, they began to seek accommodations in adjacent areas, breaching the turf of White ethnic groups (Davis and Haller 1998). Typically the Whites resisted Black people, and when they "crossed the line" or mistakenly entered what the Whites claimed as their turf, they were summarily discouraged. When a Black family bought or rented a home in the White space, White residents would publicly demonstrate, provoking local media coverage and publicly identifying the property beyond the line as contested space. Moreover, the White ethnics would pressure their neighbors not to sell or rent to Blacks (Reider 1987).

But in time some White people would break ranks because they needed money or because they were urged to sell by unscrupulous real estate agencies. These businesses would then exacerbate racial division and discontent by sounding the alarm and warning White residents of the impending arrival of "the Blacks" and the decline of their property values. The alarm provoked panic, and White families would sometimes sell their homes for below-market value in the "invasion and succession" classically described by Robert Park and Ernest Burgess about Chicago (Park, Burgess, and McKenzie 1925). As Black people moved into a neighborhood, property values fell and Whites sold out. Then the real estate agencies sold the homes to Black people at inflated prices.

This dynamic sequence occurred throughout Philadelphia, including parts of South Philadelphia and much of North Philadelphia, West Philadelphia, Germantown, and West Oak Lane. As Black people began to move into a White neighborhood, at first the Whites would nervously wait to see what would happen next. But because the Black migration to Philadelphia from the South was unrelenting, in time the edges of each White neighborhood were breached, precipitating "White flight." And as neighborhood change became imminent, Black people attracted more Black people.

As more and more Black residents arrived, there was always housing for them, since the housing market was in fact a market, with available housing going to the highest bidder. And to create more housing "stock," landlords and real estate agencies "cut up" once-elegant old homes into apartments. The highest bidders in many cases were part of the new influx, Black families in pursuit of the American dream. Once the Blacks arrived, these formerly White neighborhoods would seem "integrated," but only for a while. Soon the Whites would leave and the area would turn Black, segregated once again.

When the Whites departed too quickly, they left many vacant

houses in their wake, causing a sharp drop in local property values and making the area accessible to still lower-income Blacks. As these people moved in, the middle-class Blacks who had preceded them were motivated to leave, and local property values would fall even further. Soon the community would be dominated not only by Blacks but by the most impoverished Blacks. And so it went.

At other times the incoming Black people had the money but not the incentive to keep up their property, and their priorities, at least to members of the Black middle class, left much to be desired. For instance, some people saw no point in spending "good money" on maintenance. Elegant houses and grounds would "go to seed." Or the new homeowners might be easily scammed by aluminum-siding salesmen, installing cheap ornamental siding on a Greek revival house, embarrassing their more sophisticated middle-class Black neighbors. In time these more educated Blacks would distance themselves from the newcomers, disparaging those they deemed beneath them. They sometimes would try to bond with their White neighbors, who in time would move away leaving these middle-class Blacks feeling abandoned.

All over Philadelphia this pattern repeated itself. Apparently, Blacks were constantly on the move, chasing White people from neighborhood to neighborhood. In fact, though the Black people repeatedly sought better housing for their families, the iconic ghetto followed them. Their White counterparts presumed these Black people were from "the ghetto" no matter how accomplished and well-educated they were. They simply carried the stigma of being Black, marking them as permanently undesirable in the minds of their White counterparts.

Today a Black family wanting to buy a home in the suburbs may be aggressively courted by real estate agents and shown an array of choices within their means. This happens in part because it is now technically illegal to discriminate based on race. But the Black family is sometimes guided to an area where they "might be happy." And often, though not always, the setting where they "might be happy" is a small Black enclave to which other Blacks have been "steered" (Galster and Godfrey 2005). Since outright discrimination is now illegal, such practices have become more subtle. But a common result is that the suburban

Black enclave exists and in time expands, creating Black spaces in the suburbs. Of course, over time this practice affected housing values.

Given the history of racial segregation, as well as White attitudes about the "iconic ghetto," buyers with access to the "open" housing market would likely have little interest in investing in the Black enclave. On the "restricted" market, the value of housing is likely to remain stagnant, if only because of the limited capital available for home purchases in such a neighborhood. However, this market appeals to Blacks in part because the homes there are likely to be cheaper, but also because some Black people might prefer "being around their own kind" in spite of the limited rise in property values. Notably, if there are only Blacks in the pool of prospective buyers, the local housing market necessarily becomes narrower. If the Black home seekers buy in the "open" market, they could theoretically sell to anyone later on, and their homes would likely appreciate, selling for what the more general market would bear. Residential patterns notwithstanding, many Blacks have become upwardly mobile, assimilating the wider society's norms and values; of course many others have remained in the ghetto, in part because they are discouraged in the general market and encouraged to live among their own.[1]

Over time, through ethnic and racial residential succession, ghetto areas expand and contract. As they threaten to engulf nearby neighborhoods, economically better-off Whites and others tend to flee. Today, because many of these neighborhoods are located close to the city center, the edges of some of these Black ghetto communities appreciate in value. As values increase, Whites buy up the properties and move in, spurring on the process of "gentrification" (Anderson 1990).[2] Affluent young White people and "developers" have now "discovered" these communities. Strikingly, they premise their assessments on the hope and expectation that the impoverished Black residents will eventually depart.

And as the area gentrifies, Whites move in and impoverished Blacks move out. In time Blacks no longer can afford to live there; prices and taxes rise out their reach, and when leases are renewed on rental properties, Blacks are priced out.

As the process of gentrification gradually changes the neighborhood, what was potentially valuable land becomes increasingly attractive to adventuresome young White professionals and the developers who cater to them and often look out for their interests. In time, the city pays closer attention to their needs, especially in terms of city services, including police protection, public education, garbage collection, and building code enforcement. Also important, the banks and the insurance companies reverse their policies of redlining and begin to "green line" the area. In time, the neighborhood becomes perceived as informally "off-limits" to Black people, whom others associate with the iconic ghetto.

THE EARLY DAYS

I once lived in Southwest Philadelphia, at the outer boundaries of University City, where the University of Pennsylvania is located. I lived there for many years while conducting fieldwork for my books *Streetwise* and *Code of the Street* and teaching at Penn. The neighborhood has gone through a few transitions that I have been fortunate enough to participate in and to witness firsthand.

As gentrification progresses, one is struck by a neighborhood's transition from Black homeowners to newcomers who are increasingly White middle class to upper class. In my neighborhood, working-class people, both Black and White, had been living there when a group of middle-class gentrifiers moved in—again, both Black and White. To some extent, we gentrifiers were sponsored by the university, which helped with financing. We were a more cosmopolitan group than the old-time residents, more middle class and professional. As the same educated class of people, we got along well with each other, and to some extent we were then set against our working-class neighbors.

Although there was no real animosity between us, we could distinguish ourselves from them. We had more resources and were able to fix up these places, adding new kitchens, bathrooms, and other amenities the working-class people couldn't afford or didn't see the value in. As a sociologist, I could see the lines of demarcation. From time to time we would organize "progressive dinners," serving the first course at one house, then moving to other houses for following courses. We also held block parties, roping off the street. Kids played in the street, neighbors sat in lawn chairs and chatted, and sometimes a guy with a ukulele would turn up to entertain. Thirty to forty people might show up for barbecue and other potluck dishes, putting the diversity of the neighborhood on full display. Events like these built community and helped us know our neighbors better despite the class divisions.

However, it became clear that the area was growing more expensive and that the working-class people were on their way out. When my family moved into a house built in 1910, we understood that the property had passed through the hands of several types and classes of residents. When the previous owners bought the house they paid $4,000 to $5,000 at the most; we paid $47,000 for it in 1981. Our home was on Hazel Avenue at Forty-Seventh Street, which was then considered the border of the ghetto. People referred to it as the "edge" between University City and the ghetto—the racial boundary. Beyond this border lived a critical mass of Black working-class people mixed with "the poor." While the area was publicly regarded in this way, the reality was more complex, and one thing was clear—the neighborhood had the potential for growth, and this is what gentrification represented.

The area had many "unspoiled Victorian homes in need of reclaiming," as some of our gentrifying neighbors used to say. Our home was part of a row of Corinthian-style houses, mostly ten rooms and three stories, with postage-stamp backyards. Our block was striking in large part because all the homes were painted cream. This was dubbed the "Corinthian block," replete with faux Roman columns and dentil moldings. Inside were oak floors and dentil-laced woodwork, fireplaces, and truncated staircases typical of the Victorian style. At night the cream facades picked up the available light, so that at certain hours the block would take on an elegant air.

When my family moved in, some of the old-timers thought we lowered the neighborhood's status and perhaps even retarded its forward motion. When we arrived, the working-class families were divided along racial lines. As middle-class folks arrived, they improved the area through physical restoration and by paying more in property taxes. But because of our race, the neighbors' reactions to us were mixed at best. To many of these people a good block was homogeneously "White," and ours clearly was not.

In one house lived a Black family, including Jamal and his crack-addicted mom. Mrs. Carter and her son, who was known on the streets as "one of the biggest drug dealers in Philly," lived in another house—both were Black as well. In a house two doors away from mine lived Lou Washington, a Black working-class man who was often incapacitated by his diabetes. On occasion, he'd be found in a stupor, often brought on by his penchant for alcohol that invariably aggravated his medical condition. Lou's house was a dilapidated eyesore, and the neighbors often complained about him and his dwelling. In other houses on the block, one could find a White accountant and his wife, a business consultant, a White German professor (he was of German origin and also taught German) and his wife, an advertising executive at a Center City firm. The block also included two White Penn surgeons, a White medical student and his wife, a White male gay couple, a White female gay couple, a Black executive and his schoolteacher wife, and a White biology researcher studying viruses whose wife taught at a nearby racially segregated school, along with a contingent of working-class Whites.

We replaced Mrs. White, the wife in a White working-class family, whose husband had recently passed away. Mrs. White had moved to a working-class White neighborhood in New Jersey; I think she, like so many of the White people who had fled our neighborhood, thought she was escaping the "colored" influx. To her and her working-class neighbors, nothing could be worse than Blacks moving in, no matter what class they might be. They couldn't imagine why anyone would spend "so much money" to move into what was becoming a "Black neighborhood." It was all so confusing to them, for they often conflated Blackness and lower-class status. Such notions were persistent in this neighborhood, and the association of Blackness with low class and Whiteness with upper-class status died hard in our neighborhood, as well as in such neighborhoods throughout the city.

Moreover, we were thought of as the colored folks living in the Whites' house. When the past White owners of a home are beloved or well established in this neighborhood, they leave a positive aura regardless of who buys the property. Our house would always be "Mrs. White's house," and that was how the old-timers referred to it. My family and I were seen as interlopers, or "guests," and my established White neighbors were our "hosts." In other words, our various working-class neighbors had become socially invested in their many years on the block, and we represented a step backward, my position as a professor at Penn notwithstanding.

Our block, like many other blocks in West Philadelphia, was tended to by a variety of handymen who could be hired on the spot to handle almost any job, from simple plumbing to hanging wallpaper, plastering, and painting. They were like a cottage industry, both Black and White, who serviced our area. I soon learned that my neighbor across the street was one of these handymen. Stanton Andrews was a working-class Irishman who wore a bandanna around his white hair. He was proud that he could weld, plumb, and do carpentry, skills I could perform only in the most rudimentary way.

One cold November morning, my wife called my Penn office with the upsetting news that our basement water pipe had broken, creating a huge flood in the backyard. Thinking of the knowledgeable Mr. Andrews, she asked him for help. He came immediately, turned off the water, and applied a temporary fix. When I got home that evening, he came over and we went down to the basement. He began to describe the problem in an avuncular fashion, assuming I could know nothing about such matters and that it was his duty to teach me—or rather to show me—how to care for "Mrs. White's house." As we inspected the water pipes for other leaks, he said that his temporary fix would hold for now, but that some nice hot day in the summer he and I would need to make a more permanent fix.

"You can solder, right?" he asked.

I admitted I couldn't, so he began to instruct me on the ins and outs of soldering and repairing plumbing. I listened intently. After about an hour of instruction, he promised we'd make that permanent repair next summer, then he went home.

This was my first sustained interaction with Mr. Andrews, and it marked the start of our relationship. I'd been curious about him but had never had any excuse to get to know him. Now he was reaching out and had promised to help me repair my broken pipe. Over the next six months, I observed Mr. and Mrs. Andrews more closely. Their comings and goings were highly visible from my front window, and I was interested in them and in the neighborhood we were settling into. Of course the Andrewses could observe me and my family just as easily.

On occasion their middle-aged son would drive up in his broken-down car, rush inside, visit for a while, and leave. Whenever I encountered the younger Mr. Andrews on the street, he was brusque and would give me the evil eye. He always seemed in a hurry. We would look at each other but never speak. Every Saturday the Andrews family would go off to New Jersey as a kind of ritual, returning Saturday evening or Sunday. Mr. Andrews would tell me about those trips—New Jersey was the "promised land," much as it appears to have been for Mrs. White.

On a hot July day, Mr. Andrews made good on his promise. When we met on the street one Wednesday morning, he asked, "When are we going to fix that pipe?"

"Any time you want. What's a good time for you?"

"How about this Saturday?"

The last time we'd spoken about this matter, back in the winter, I'd promised to get a six-pack of beer for our project, so I asked what he liked. He told me and asked for fifteen dollars for the materials we'd need, including solder and epoxy. I happily complied.

About 1:00 p.m. that Saturday Mr. Andrews showed up at my front door and we headed for the basement. I turned off the water and we got to work. He was proud of his soldering skills and reminded me that

I had none. Then he spread a tarp on the floor and over the appliances. Soon he was busy with the task, instructing me along the way. I played the role of attentive helper.

About two hours and a couple of beers later, he had the pipe fixed—or so we thought. He motioned that the job was finished and said, "Okay, you can turn the water on."

I complied, and water sprayed everywhere.

"Quick, quick! Turn off the water!" he urged. I rushed to the main valve and turned it off. Mr. Andrews shook his head, saying he couldn't understand what had happened. He seemed embarrassed about this failure, in part because to him skills like soldering, plumbing, and carpentry were the measure of a man. Working-class White men like Mr. Andrews valued these skills and took them for granted: they were standards by which they measured themselves and other men. This failure left him feeling deflated.

We sat in my basement for a while and talked. He mentioned that he'd ask a couple of his friends from work to come over and get this thing fixed next week. "They're crackerjacks with the soldering." These were men he worked with from the "Northeast," a code for working-class, ethnic neighborhoods that were stereotypically anti-Black. These were the first men who came to his mind, but after more beer, he thought better of this plan. He mentioned the name of a "colored" guy he knew, and asked if I knew him, saying "maybe he could help me." I said I didn't know the man.

I could see why Mr. Andrews might hesitate to invite his buddies, working-class White men from the Northeast, to come to the aid of a Black man with whom he was friendly. When he suggested them, it didn't occur to him for a moment that I was Black. I realized he wouldn't want his friends to know he was so close to a Black man or to see him helping one. He would have been embarrassed. Mr. Andrews and I had a human connection, but it went only so far. I thanked him for his trouble. He thanked me for the beer and apologized again for not being able to help as he'd promised. Later I called a professional plumber to deal with my pipe. Mr. Andrews and I remained on good terms. From time to time, he'd invite me over for a beer, and we'd listen to tunes from the 1930s and '40s on his old phonograph. He'd talk about the old days. With his bandanna, he looked like an older hippie, which endeared him to me, and his wife reminded me of Edith Bunker. She was nice enough but steeped in working-class values. Once she crossed the street to complain because my two-year-old daughter was naked in the front yard.

Over time I learned from Mr. Andrews and others around the neighborhood and the city that racially integrated blocks, regardless of the social class of the Black residents living there, were viewed as compromising a neighborhood. Mr. Andrews tolerated me and made excuses for me, but even though I worked for the university, my main characteristic in his eyes was that I was "colored." In other words, the social class of Black people mattered much less than the fact that they were Black, and that because they lived there the neighborhood was no longer "White." Their presence undermined the value of the neighborhood, their middle-class status notwithstanding. This was my perception, gained through my years of fieldwork in the city. Many local working-class Whites think this way because of their own sense of group position, which is always above Blacks (Blumer 1958; Bobo and Hutchings 1996).

This was the nature of early gentrification, which continued to morph until the neighborhood consisted primarily of White middle-class homeowners, with fewer middle-class Blacks moving in. That went on until by today the "edge," or the boundary of the ghetto, has moved from Forty-Seventh Street to Fiftieth Street, and more and more White people are living in the area. Shops and businesses change along with the population shift, and the police respond differently. White people used their racial capital to make the place more valuable.

WHEN WHITES INVADE THE GHETTO

At Fiftieth Street and Baltimore Avenue in West Philadelphia sits an active brewery that includes a restaurant. The building was once a firehouse, and for decades the surrounding area was the center of a Black ghetto known as Southwest. Now that community is gentrifying. Its large Victorian houses have become highly attractive to developers and White home buyers. Just a few blocks from where I lived and conducted my fieldwork, I watched the place changing over time as the border between poor Black areas and mixed, middle-class areas moved deeper into the ghetto. The formerly Black area now has a growing number of young White professionals and students as well as a few Asian or Latino residents.

The brewery itself is viewed as a White space in the middle of the ghetto. Its clientele and workforce are overwhelmingly White, drawn mainly from the immediate neighborhood. I've visited this restaurant many times, and on one warm Saturday evening in August, I counted fifty-five Whites and two African Americans distributed among the four-top tables inside, at the bar, and on the sidewalk outside. The eleven employees included one Black male waiter, one Black male food preparer, two White male food preparers, three White male waiters, two White female bartenders, an Asian female cashier, and a White female host. Young to middle-aged White people congregate here to enjoy freshly brewed premium beer and a nondescript American cuisine of hamburgers, fries, pizza, and fancy green salads. The brewery has become an attractive watering hole for the young professionals and students who live nearby. But for many local Black residents, who are mainly working class or poor, the brewery represents the vanguard of a White invasion. They resent its presence, and few would think of patronizing it.

On this August evening, young Blacks walked stiffly past the diners on the sidewalk they once thought of as their own. Some marched right by, posing as indifferent while resenting what is clearly a significant racial symbol. Others were more direct, scowling as they passed. A few young Black men in small groups wore stern, almost angry looks. Meanwhile, the White clientele seemed generally comfortable. Some were oblivious of the mood of these passersby, while others directed annoyed looks at the Black "interlopers" who dared to disturb their meal. Invested in a posture of being at home in this environment, most brewery patrons displayed nonchalance and appeared unaware of the situational irony—that they had displaced the previous inhabitants from this historically Black space.

The fire station that originally occupied this space had previously been replaced by a farmers' market that catered to the neighborhood's increasingly diverse residents. On Saturday mornings the market buzzed with shopping and chatting as middle-class White and Black patrons joined working-class and poor Black customers. A wide array of fruits and vegetables and fresh fish and meats were on sale. A small interracial but predominantly White cadre of community activists had established the market and encouraged their friends and acquaintances to shop there.

When it first appeared, the market aroused curiosity and even wonder from the local working-class Blacks, but because it performed a vital community service, it soon earned the respect, goodwill, and protection of the local community. The market employed a good many local Black residents in a range of jobs, from butchering meat and tending produce to setting up the stalls each morning, then breaking them down and cleaning up at the end of each business day.

Perhaps most critically, the farmers' market served as a kind of community center where people of widely different backgrounds interacted across class and color lines. Friends frequently bumped into one another, catching up on the latest community news or gossip. The market was a prime example of what I call a "cosmopolitan canopy," an island of racial and ethnic civility. It served as a focal point of social and cultural convergence that afforded locals and outsiders an opportunity to observe one another up close, to meet, and to engage with people who were strange to them.

When the brewery bought out the farmers market, the whole enterprise became much more racially homogeneous, and Black residents now typically perceive it as a White space. The setting still provides people from different worlds with an opportunity, or an excuse, to come together or to check each other out in relative security, but the locals are seldom drawn into meaningful social intercourse with strangers. And those who come together here now are virtually all White.

Across the street from the brewery is a park where working-class Black residents occasionally gather for church picnics or bring their children to play. Idle Black men hang out there drinking and socializing, playing cards and checkers, whiling away their days and evenings. A liquor store across the street provides easy access to a "taste" whenever they feel like it or can get up the money. For much of the community, Black and White alike, the park is not a place to be at night, when homeboys, drug dealers, stickup boys, and others effectively claim the space. Over the past decade, this element has been checked somewhat by the local police patrols—which became more common as the neighborhood changed. Meanwhile, community activists have worked to clean up the park and have installed expensive play equipment. During pleasant weather, all kinds of people hang out in the park, at times with their families; occasionally, gentrifying Whites bring their children here. Some weekends there are outdoor jazz concerts, and all kinds of people are encouraged to come, though the takers are mainly local Blacks and a few Whites.

These changes have produced an uneasy mix of working-class Blacks and middle-class, racially tolerant Whites. In this setting, as well as on the neighborhood streets, the two groups tolerate one another, but—largely because of the huge class and race divide—rarely do they interact socially. Their interaction takes place primarily in these public spaces, which essentially are racially polarized.

Just a few years ago, Black people were the dominant presence in this area, and at night they still are, since in public Whites typically defer to Blacks, especially young males. The implication was that Blacks ran the public spaces and the Whites had to navigate them and watch out for those who didn't mean them well. The ones who most often came to mind were the "homeboys," and it wasn't simply racial animosity at work—it was the notion that these young males were dangerous. They were physically strong, and they could rob you. In people's minds, the dangerous person was fifteen to seventeen years old and looked fearsome, so they watched out for guys like that. But they often called them "kids," using that as a code for "these guys on the street."

The Whites realized they couldn't just leave their possessions outside. For instance, a tricycle left on the porch all night would disappear, as would a planted flowerpot, and once in a while a welcome mat.

Change from the console in your car would attract crack addicts who might break in, so you didn't leave it exposed. Whites were always concerned about being violated, and the violators were always Black: Black youths. This is what they understood, the way they thought of it.

By extension, when the Black families in the area were on the street, no matter what class they were, the Whites tended to keep a certain distance from them. This was most noticeable at the trolley stops or the bus stops, but also just in public places or walking down the street. For example, if a group of people were waiting at the bus stop, Whites who didn't know each other would strike up a conversation and leave out the Blacks. The Black people knew they weren't included, and they knew the White people didn't know each other yet were talking based on being White.

But now a beachhead has been established, and the local housing market beckons, attracting Whites as never before. The brewery and the park itself have become contested space, the cultural and economic manifestation of this area's ongoing shift from a Black space to a White space. As housing prices rise, the neighborhood marginally improves, and more White people become emboldened to move in and lay claim to a public space that for generations has been regarded as Black and relatively poor.[3]

WHITE SKIN AS RACIAL CAPITAL

When well-off White people move into Black neighborhoods, they raise the property values just by living there. Thus they invest not just their financial capital, the price they pay for the property, but also the capital of their White skin. They effectively gamble not only with their financial capital but also with their racial capital. This is typically a safe bet, given the wide availability of the housing stock of so many Black neighborhoods, there for the taking. Whites' presence in such lower-income areas becomes a virtual advertisement, a financial opportunity, for other Whites who are "courageous" enough move in and able to tolerate the racial and class elements of the areas they venture into. As Whites live in the community they adapt and become streetwise.

When the White friends, coworkers, or parents of gentrifiers visit, the homeowners may feel protective, as though they have to teach them the rules and emphasize that things are not as bad as they look. But to the outsider things look pretty bad. A White person, or a middle-class person of any race, has to make adjustments that wouldn't be needed in the suburbs, including being aware of their surroundings and realizing they could be stuck up and robbed. Some people dream of living close to the city and having all its amenities, but they don't always realize the price they'll have to pay. Usually they adapt and things work out, but not always.[4]

Developers and real estate people fan the flames, urging White prospects to buy and sell repeatedly. They're concerned less about who moves in than about the economic activity being generated. Suddenly Black people's homes in the ghetto are on the "open market" and may now be attractive to Whites who are willing to pay double and triple the prices of only a few years before.

My neighborhood had many unspoiled Victorian-style homes in need of reclaiming—just what gentrification represented. As Blacks moved into the community years before, the Whites had often felt compelled to move out. Realty companies and their agents had functioned as "blockbusters," opposed by quasi-government local agencies known as civil rights commissions that often supported integration in neighborhoods and were staunchly against such practices. In the early days, municipal agents investigated housing discrimination against Blacks and called the realty companies to account, at times successfully. They promoted "fair housing" and helped to make this into a national issue—in time Congress passed fair housing legislation, supported by a host of civil rights laws of the 1960s.

WHITES IN BLACK SPACE

These days, when Whites walk through the gentrifying community in Southwest, they make no eye contact with the Black people. They keep their heads down and act as though the Blacks are invisible. And it's this movement, this dance, that betrays their fear. They keep going, knowing that to some extent the law protects them. They don't expect to be confronted or threatened; in fact, most of the Blacks are quite tolerant of these Whites who clearly are just passing through their space. Still, the Whites tend to be wary, on edge; usually they just want to get from point A to point B, to pass Black people uneventfully. After dark they tend to stay inside or tense up when they see someone approaching. Their trips are purposeful; they move deliberately and seldom laugh or smile. They know they have safe passage, that they can get to their destination without being accosted, yet they're concerned not to make a false move.

The Black people have become inured to this presence. Publicly it's a Black space, but inside these big old Victorian homes live the White people. And clearly the Whites are biding their time, because they realize that at some point—at least so they hope—the neighborhood will change.

The Whites feel under siege, which is characteristic of the ghetto's edge. As you go backward toward the university you pass areas that have been secured by White professional types, and the White residents act freer in public than here on the edge. These are not racist people; they're just middle-class Whites who have moved into the space hoping for the best, trying to live their lives, much like Black people in White space, where the Whites are the hosts.

These Whites become survivors of a sort, trying to outlast the street crime and other problems in the community. They are living close to people who don't have much, who see that these new people have something and may want some of it. But in spite of this avoidance and these survival issues, my experience is that there's also a symbiotic relationship between the working-class Blacks in the community and the gentrifiers. This comes out especially during Halloween and after heavy snowstorms. On Halloween the little kids come around asking for candy, and Whites suddenly realize how many Black kids there are in the neighborhood. Some of the older kids don't even wear costumes. Halloween is a special time, of course, when you open your door to trick-or-treaters. But at a certain point these middle-class Blacks and Whites wonder, "Who are these trick-or-treaters?" For them, this is a question that almost answers itself—they are children and grown-ups from the nearby 'hood.

During snowstorms the neighborhood kids—who might be the same homeboys who could stick people up—come around with snow shovels. There's six to ten inches of snow that people need removed, so these boys make money off the gentrifiers that way.

Sometimes the women of the community clean or babysit for these new families, and people do make connections and may build lasting relationships that way.

As for the "edge," this imaginary line between the gentrifiers and the 'hood, the whole area is spotty. There's no fixed line showing where people live, because Black people may live near the university, and White people may live in what's considered the 'hood. It's complicated, and there are a lot of relationships going on.

That's how it was when I lived under the canopy, and to some extent that's how it is today. I believe the gentrifying people are not simply moving in and taking over; they're moving in and getting used to living with people who are diverse. They adapt and connect or they move out, especially when their kids are school age. So it's touch and go: those who survive keep on surviving, and they increase the number of middle-class people.

Property values go up, the police come when you call, and the area gets safer, but there are starts and stops along the way. Sometimes the White middle-class gentrifiers find out that living in this community is more than they bargained for, and they become demoralized. Sometimes there are victories and people hang together. They are hanging on to each other and to their properties and basically hammering out their own group position, which is a sense of Whiteness. This idea of White people surviving in Black space is in some ways not all that different from Black people surviving in White space. In this kind of community, the tables get turned.

CHAPTER 13

THE GYM

A Staging Area

Early one morning while I was exercising at a local gym, I observed an overweight White fellow in his mid-forties being instructed by an extremely well-built dark-skinned Black trainer in his early thirties. The scene was a study in contrasts as the White man nervously took instruction from the younger Black man, who appeared to be from one of the nearby ghetto areas. The White man lay on his back and tried to do crunches. The trainer knelt nearby and carefully coached him: "Now, ease up. You can do it! Careful with your neck, now! Come on, you can do it." It was clear that the Black man cared about the White man and wanted to help him.

The White man's brow was furrowed and his eyes darted apprehensively around the gym. But he was attentive as he gradually loosened up, with the Black trainer still firmly in control of the situation. Between repetitions, I overheard them making small talk as they exchanged intermittent smiles. They said little, but their close interaction signaled cooperation as they focused on the White man's workout. The Black man always appeared as the dutiful instructor, determined to get this rotund fellow into shape and on the road to better health. The difference in their skin color seemed irrelevant to their mission.

As the White man struggled to complete ten crunches, the Black man encouraged, nudged, and even pleaded with him to follow through. When he finally reached his goal, both men broke into smiles of triumph. These men, as well as the casual onlookers, treated the men's shared activity as ordinary. Yet this apparent ordinariness is precisely what makes the situation so significant ethnographically.

For the past decade, I've been engaging in fieldwork as a participant-observer in this fitness center, participating in normal gym activities while actively observing what occurs there. This chapter tells the story of the gym and its denizens, whose interracial interactions in this shared space are remarkable just because they are so ordinary. It is hard to imagine the gym operating now in the way I describe it in the following pages. Before the COVID-19 pandemic hit in 2020, I went to the gym regularly, and my descriptions are based on my observations of how it operated then. I assume that things will return to somewhat normal when the pandemic is over.

This setting aligns with my conception of the "cosmopolitan canopy," a diverse island of civility in a sea of racial segregation. Even people who might adopt an ethnocentric orientation in other places are careful to get along here despite their differences. As a commercial establishment, the gym is a public place open to anyone who can pay the membership fee or is the guest of a member.

This canopy-like space is neither Black nor White but ostensibly neutral and inclusive, though it strikes Blacks and Whites differently (see Anderson 2011). Some White members may view this space as too Black, and some Black people see it as still too White, or even as a White space. It's a matter of perspective. Some Whites see Philadelphia as a Black city, given the visibility and power of some of its Black citizens. Compared with what they are accustomed to, the gym may seem Blacker than it really is.

As a part of civil society, the gym is a setting where most people

expect that particularities like race, ethnicity, gender, and sexual preference may matter to an extent but will not be held against them. A
cosmopolitan orientation is typically assumed to rule, and those who
may be more ethnocentric know to keep that to themselves and defer
to the prevailing ethos. And for the most part everyone observes these
rules and even takes them for granted.

But all such spaces have hidden fault lines that become evident
from time to time and may even erupt in conflict. The most marginalized people can be subjected to acute disrespect based on gender,
sexual preference, ethnicity, or race. The social situation of Black
people is especially charged, given the history and continued salience
of Blackness in Philadelphia. Manifested in the way many people,
Black and White alike, associate anonymous Black people with the
iconic ghetto, Blacks collectively experience racial dynamics markedly
different from those that other non-White groups encounter. Black
people's history of racial injury has taught them to be wary of settings
where they may be discriminated against, marginalized, or excluded
and where others may seek to put them "back in their place." Black
people carry this burden everywhere, not only as they navigate White
spaces but also in cosmopolitan settings like the gym.

The gym's location defines it as neither White nor Black space. In
a strip mall in a northwest Philadelphia suburb, close to a number of
middle-class communities both White and Black, it is also accessible
from several ghetto areas, which nonresidents strongly associate with
poverty, crime, and danger. Locals commonly visit the mall to shop
at the large grocery store, eat at McDonald's, and use the full-service
public library, where diverse groups of grade school and high school
students gather to study, have homework dates, or simply hang out
with their friends.

Both Black and White people value the gym as a socially tolerant
and civil setting in which they can get a workout close enough to their
homes. These qualities keep both Blacks and Whites visiting despite
the racial diversity of its membership.

Although objectively the gym is a neutral space with a significant

Black presence, many Blacks are inclined to perceive it as a White space, mainly because they know that those who run it are White and so are most of its members. At the same time, many White Philadelphians might avoid the gym as "too Black." For those Whites who continue to visit, it has remained White enough, at least most of the time.

At present the gym is in a steady state, with a membership about 25 percent Black and 75 percent White and other. The proportion of Black and non-Black people there changes slightly throughout the day and evening.

For most Black people, this space is not what they consider "deep White," where Blacks are rarely found. When Black people enter such White spaces, they evaluate them; if there are no other Blacks, they can become uncomfortable, largely because they feel exposed and in need of allies, especially in an emergency. There's no such issue here.

About a quarter of the gym's staff consists of young people from nearby Black neighborhoods. People from a wide range of backgrounds are stationed at the front desk to check IDs. The cleaning crew is Latino, and the people who service the machines are often racially mixed—Latino, Black, and White. Beyond the desk and immediately to the right is an open expanse filled with virtually every kind of exercise equipment, including machines and free weights. To the left is a glass enclosure with stationary bicycles. Today's spinning class includes a mix of young, middle-aged, and older White men and women. Among the thirty-five people present, I see two Black men in their mid-forties.

Typically on the lead bicycle sits a fit-looking White woman in her mid-thirties who barks out orders for the spinners to follow. She provides them with a rationale for working out while she also encourages them: "Don't be afraid of people looking at you and being appalled at what they see." She coaches her charges to follow the script or the music. The constant background bass beat makes it relatively easy to follow along. After thirty-five to forty minutes and a number of speedups and slowdowns, the spinners go into "cooldown" mode, then stop and disperse. For most this is all they do, so they shower and leave for work, for home, for whatever.

People generally come to the gym because they want to improve themselves physically—to become healthy and strong. They share this overarching goal. Those who are weak, infirm, or less physically fit often feel they're falling behind, and others may reach out to help and encourage them. At least on the surface, everyone seems to be welcome. Diverse people get along and few discouraging words are heard. That members of different groups coexist amicably is featured in the gym's advertising brochure. For the most part, this description is accurate. The theme of civility is particularly striking in light of the city's past, since Philadelphia is known for its history of ethnic and racial strife. Some conflicts were political, such as the anti-draft riots early in the Civil War; others were ethnic turf fights.

When Black people migrated to the city, they were often resisted and physically kept out of certain White neighborhoods, schools, and workplaces. To live and work where they wanted, and to educate their children there, Blacks always had to campaign against the White people who collectively held them back. After fair housing legislation, the last passed of the measures advocated by the civil rights movement, some Philadelphia neighborhoods changed from White to Black. As middle-class Blacks "integrated" a neighborhood, its White residents would resist for a while, but ultimately they fled to the White spaces of the suburbs, where they made their stand. Then the class makeup of the neighborhood changed again, from middle class and working class to impoverished. These racial-ethnic turf struggles have created the contemporary geography of Philadelphia, the nation's sixth most segregated city as of 2010 (Logan and Stultz 2011).

The gym is in such a neighborhood, where local institutions are under almost imperceptible racial pressure to change. These accumulating changes leave in their wake aggrieved White residents who live with the increasing Black presence because they can do little about it. The wounds inflicted by exclusion are still fresh to Black Philadelphians. Although many Black people try to bury these racial injuries, they may also avoid situations that serve as reminders. The present state of race relations at the gym, with its unstable balance of civility and tension, is the result of this social history. But generally the denizens get along well together in civility.

THE GYM AS A STAGING AREA

The gym members today are a loosely knit collection of people who may arrive, exercise, and pass one another with no more than a greeting. Indeed, impersonality is one of the themes of the setting. People "see but don't see one another." Typically they pay what sociologist Erving Goffman (1971) called "civil inattention" to one another, each giving others their personal space.

When the regulars spot someone for the first time, they make mental notes. Over time they come to know one another, but seldom intimately. Most members recognize others but don't know their backgrounds, including their names or where they live. Personal details are not relevant to what goes on at the gym.

In another context, maybe across town or at a neighborhood event, a member might notice someone she's seen at the gym, and that person may have noticed her. But often both need to acknowledge each other (Anderson 1990). Such relationships are solidified at the gym, suggesting that more is going on than typically meets the eye or is publicly acknowledged.

As Shakespeare suggested and Goffman reminds us, human society is like a stage on which we each play a part. Consistent with this metaphor, social life consists of a front stage and a backstage. A person's "front" is her costume, and other people and objects may serve as props.

An important part of the social interaction here may be viewed as performance, involving "social gloss"—being polite and smiling and avoiding friction (see Goffman 1959). People negotiate past one another, "code-switching" as needed to maintain their dignity. With displays of body language, actors may sometimes "lie to tell the truth." Here people perform as men, as women, as Black people, as White people. There are all kinds, and anyone who can pay for membership is admitted.

The gym's staff and members are predominantly but not exclusively White. The people at the front desk are seldom all White, which promotes an image of diversity and signals to Blacks and other people of color that they are welcome. The attendants are often busy or distracted and just wave you in when you present your ID or key tab to the electronic monitor.

One Saturday morning I watched a Black woman trainer working with a White man, both of them appearing to be in their late forties. Overweight and sweaty, he looked out of shape and exhausted. He followed her from one piece of equipment to another, applying himself assiduously. The trainer carried a pad and pen and carefully checked off his achievements. He watched her closely and listened to every word. After completing each exercise, he looked at her expectantly and she nodded approval. The woman was a model instructor, and they showed mutual respect while working together, despite the color of their skins.

Meanwhile, other members worked out individually on their particular machines or took turns on the various pieces of equipment. When the gym is crowded, taking turns—"working in"—serves as a point of contact. Differences of race, ethnicity, gender, and age seem to be of little consequence. People are generally polite, even smiling, as they take turns in an orderly, rather ritualized manner.

The social gloss that eases interactions among relative strangers involves showing deference to others regardless of their color or apparent social standing. Men commonly treat women with particular deference. As they let women use the equipment they'd been waiting for themselves, they sometimes seem patronizing. Sometimes women come to the gym in twos and threes to work out or take classes, as protection in a male scene.

When an attractive woman in skintight workout clothes moves through the gym or works out, men typically "see but don't see" her— looking away and carefully respecting what they assume is her comfort zone. This common behavior may also be considered patronizing, implicitly defining the space as male-dominated: the men are the hosts and the women are reduced to visitors. In general, men are careful to seem to ignore women even as they watch them, at times using the wall mirrors to get a glimpse when they might be embarrassed to be seen looking more directly.

Some women regularly come with a male partner, and the two are regarded as a couple. They can become something of a spectacle, especially if the woman is attractive. Men regard women who wear revealing outfits as show-offs or exhibitionists and steal looks whenever they can, especially when a man actively claims the woman by sticking close to her, implicitly guarding her from other men.

At times a man even affirms his status by making eye contact with other males, encouraging them to look away, thus showing off his dominance. Together these men affirm the male-dominated character of the space. Women tend to be self-conscious, aware or suspecting that they are being watched. They may feel more comfortable if they come to the gym with a male partner or in a same-sex group.

For Black people, the gender dynamics are a bit more complex. The gym is generally considered a male-identified space, but in contrast to many other masculine domains, it typically includes Black males. Black men are generally highly regarded in the world of athletics, and many are treated as if their physicality is their "master status," along with their Blackness.

Whites generally defer to Black males when athletic prowess is involved, particularly if they are young and muscular. Civility prevails in this arena: even the most ethnocentric or racist people tend to keep these orientations in check. On the way out, strangers of another gender, race, or ethnicity may hold the door open for those entering and say, "Have a good workout."

The racial makeup of the gym is shaped by the membership fee, which can amount to $50 a month. Poor people, including many Black residents of local neighborhoods, don't have that much disposable income to spare. As recently as twenty years ago, such spaces were mostly White, and they excluded people not only because of race but also for their presumed religion and ethnicity. The Black presence in gymnasiums and health clubs is relatively new.

When unfamiliar Blacks appear at the gym, Whites may assume they come from the ghetto, although that isn't always true. White people are curious but are aware that they shouldn't show it. Black people generally keep their cool but know their presence is provocative.

As people play along, everyone acts as if the situation is normal, even if their own neighborhoods are less diverse. The setting encourages convergence for the shared purpose of getting fit.

RACIAL TIME-SHARING

Because of the clear racial divisions that mark contemporary society, various racial groups organize themselves into implicit time-sharing blocs. This practice is not systematic, planned, or certain, nor are the patterns stable over time. The order is emergent.

Use of the gym simply works this way, with visitors arriving according to their schedules while respecting racial preferences. Young, employed people exercise in the early morning and right after work. Older people, who may be retired, arrive between midmorning and midafternoon. These people are predominantly White, with a smattering of Blacks and other people of color. On late weekday afternoons and Saturday mornings, more than a fifth of the people who frequent this gym are Black.

Many of the White regulars grew up in working-class neighborhoods that over time have experienced an "invasion" of Black people who often are upwardly mobile. Because of this contentious history, many Black people are inclined to believe that the Whites here and elsewhere think of them as second-class citizens. Blacks tend to keep such thoughts to themselves, and most try to avoid becoming "racial." They are reluctant to express their sense of racial injury in the presence of Whites. In turn, White people typically behave with a surface politeness toward the Black people they encounter in passing at the gym.

Interracial relationships rarely go beyond the gym. Certain Black people are known to go out of their way to form friendships across the color line, but their advances tend to meet a gentle rebuff, rejected almost out of hand. Blacks sometimes appear to be given the benefit of the doubt and "chat it up" with their White counterparts, yet they understand that these relationships are on thin ice.

Most other Black people in this space couldn't care less what Whites think of them. They express themselves any way they want, at times "letting it all hang out," showing everyone that they have no obligation to please the Whites.

BROTHERS FROM THE 'HOOD

Amid the diversity of people there, the spatial dynamic of the Black and White racial binary that characterizes American society shapes the public perception of the gym. It also determines which race can continue to claim the space as its own. Significantly, that the gym is predominantly White helps put White members at ease and encourages their return.

About a quarter of the gym members are Black, and most of them are men thirty-five to sixty. Black women visit on occasion, but often, like White women, they bring the "protection" of a female or male gym mate or arrive in small groups. So the Black presence is well below the "racial tipping point" where the racial perception and definition of the space changes from White space to Black space (see Gladwell 2006).

White people typically avoid Black space, so if they perceive the gym as a Black space, they are likely to avoid it altogether, tipping the racial balance. If it becomes socially defined as a Black space, White people will stop coming.

Those who run the gym apparently appreciate this dynamic and want to maintain the status quo. Thus, for prominent staff positions, they hire and promote just the right numbers of Blacks, Whites, and others. One subtle but explicit way they maintain the atmosphere of the gym is with the music they choose. This music is always playing, and it's not blues or heavy metal or classical; each of these choices would turn off certain people. It's a kind of elevator music, with a slightly youthful touch. Although everyone tolerates it, the music could also be described as bland and inoffensively, albeit boringly, "White."

Inside the gym is a basketball court that attracts a mixed crowd of young men, a large number of them Black. Usually the court is unoccupied, but Black members sometimes shoot hoops and play pickup games, and they may invite their friends from Black neighborhoods to join them on guest passes. When these visitors enter the gym, especially in groups, the White members take special note. Suddenly the racial composition of the court area changes dramatically, transforming the court into the kind of playground normally found in the 'hood.

The Black male visitors from the 'hood not only play ball with one another but sometimes congregate and explore the rest of the gym between games. These "brothers" express themselves freely, often at high volume, attracting frowns from some of the White members. You can recognize visitors. The Black visitors don't follow the standard gym etiquette. They often wear street clothing, their pants hanging low and revealing their underwear. They talk loudly and curse. To the middle-class White people this is a spectacle—they're not necessarily angry, but they're surprised. Even some of the middle-class Black members who do observe the niceties of the gym are unnerved by this "ghetto behavior," because to the Black middle-class propriety is very important.

The Whites look on with interest, chagrin, and even deep curiosity. For some, this is their first real taste of Black culture, so they take the opportunity to see Black people up close with minimal risk. Sometimes they even engage with them, and the interaction, while delicate, is not negative.

When a group of Black basketball players claim White space within the gym, racial boundaries begin to materialize and solidify, and White space more clearly reveals itself. In a word, the gym reaches its tipping point and Whites may have second thoughts about its being their own. Well aware of this dynamic, the gym's management has considered closing down the basketball court, and Black members recognize the precariousness of this community space.

Other activities take place in the gym, many of them in the "backstage." Showers, restrooms, the steam room or spa, and to some extent the gateway to the pool are all parts of this backstage, where people cannot avoid more direct exposure to others. In these regions, people prepare for another front stage such as work or school. Here they change from gym clothes to street clothes or vice versa. They undress in front of strangers, not all of them kind. This is a moment of vulnerability. Black men often feel especially uncomfortable because they've noticed White men checking out the widespread myth about how well-endowed Black men are. Some Black men avoid the locker room. Those who are going to work afterward have little choice, or they may go elsewhere to shower and change. Others just ignore the White guys.

Even on the gym's front stage, people don't always look their best, as they huff and puff on the stationary bicycles, elliptical trainers, and treadmills or struggle to lift weights. The prevailing protocol is to pretend to ignore others' appearance in hopes that they'll ignore yours.

Another region of backstage intimacy is the steam room, where men may talk across social lines about almost anything or may just relax. Sometimes people have heart-to-heart conversations. You see White men in groups, sometimes including a Black guy. Over time these groups may evolve into something more.

SOCIABILITY AND THE RACIAL DIVIDE

When I go to the gym, I almost always see middle-class Black people I know from outside or friends I've made at the gym. Occasionally there are Whites I see repeatedly and know without really knowing them. They've become familiar faces.

Kim, the Black clerk at the juice bar selling smoothies, muffins, and protein-rich snacks, interacts freely with everyone. Because she lives in the nearby 'hood of North Philadelphia, she stands out, especially to Black folks, and with them she smiles, gives a special nod, and cracks jokes. Actually, she knows only a few of her customers, but because she's in a customer service position she is usually pleasant to everyone—Black or White, male or female. Toward Black gym-goers, she expresses a special racial communion, warm feelings that many Blacks convey to other Blacks they barely know. Although she claims to have known these Black people "for years," when pressed she doesn't know their last names or where they live. Yet through a form of ethnic bonding, she expresses familiarity whenever they appear.

Non-Whites at the gym come not only from traditional African American communities but also from various countries in Africa or the Caribbean. Black people who choose their friends based on skin color may distinguish between various types of Blacks as they consider initiating social bonds. White people tend to behave similarly, but their acknowledgment of one another is usually unremarkable and is perhaps subtly taken for granted.

All it takes is one "cultural broker" to start a trend of sociability. For instance, Bob, a White man, met Tom, a Black man. After three months, Tom introduced Bob to Mary, a White woman. Meanwhile George, a Black fellow, saw Bob and Mary conversing, and while George was in the presence of the two White people, Bob felt obligated to introduce him to Mary. George and Mary then started talking while Bob went off to continue his workout, leaving George and Mary alone together.

As they talked, Mary essentially interviewed George, asking where he comes from and how he knows Bob. She discovered that George is highly educated and writes a column for a local newspaper. In return, George essentially interviewed Mary. After a few minutes of conversation, they both left. They might never see one another again, or the germs of a relationship might grow. In this way the gym is knit into a community of folks, Black and White together, in a process often initiated by a cultural broker.

IKE

Ike, a heavyset, middle-aged Black man, was a prime example of a cultural broker; he facilitated social connections between all kinds of people at the gym. Ike was known and generally liked by virtually everyone, both Black and White. Until a few years ago, I had lost touch with Ike until we happened to meet at the gym. Around Philadelphia, relationships among the loose collection of local Black people of various class backgrounds seem to work in this manner—casually stopping or starting up with a chance meeting to "catch up," and then restarting with a casual conversation that may or may not go further.

Ike came to the gym throughout the week. He was quite affable, striking up conversations with almost anyone who wanted to talk, and many seemed open to such sociability, perhaps to delay the exertion of working out. Occasionally, I would have to break off our conversation to return to my workout; he'd then promptly look around for another person to talk to. I seldom saw him actually working out. While I'd known Ike for many years, it was only superficially. I never met his family, though he approached me, as well as others, as though we knew each other better than we actually did. Not only was Ike an affable fellow, but he always seemed prepared to introduce strangers to one another, including Blacks to Blacks, Whites to Whites, or Blacks to Whites. After an introduction, Ike might hold court, regaling others with his latest experience, then move on and continue to make his rounds.

Ike was born and raised in Philadelphia, and for many years resided in the ghetto of West Philadelphia. He attended college but never graduated and worked over the years in a succession of jobs, including selling insurance and used cars, and most recently at the city morgue. Ike told people his wife was a businesswoman and an excellent home-maker. One day, out of the blue, Ike interrupted my workout to hand me a jar of cooked lentils with which, he suggested, my wife might make soup. He said, "My wife fixed these lentils, and she wanted me to give them to you." Ike did the same with others too, and people had come to expect such gifts from him.

Ike also spoke of his two grown sons, successful doctors living in the Midwest. Ike presented himself to everyone, and especially the middle-class Black people who frequented the gym, as a family man with a middle-class lifestyle and, most important, as someone on their level. Everyone around the gym seemed to accept this version of him.

From time to time, to burnish his credentials as a "successful" person, Ike would speak knowledgeably about his investments in the stock market and cite financial news from articles he'd read in the *Wall Street Journal* and *Barron's*. Ike also discussed his local properties, saying he was a landlord of apartments in various local inner-city neighborhoods. One morning he invited me to have breakfast with him. I accepted and he insisted on paying for the meal. After breakfast, he drove me around to show me some of his properties. His supposed affluence was belied by his beat-up old car, which he said he drove because if his tenants thought he was doing well, they'd have incentive to delay paying their rent.

Then, a few years ago, Ike became very ill. He'd always seemed to have trouble controlling his weight, and he let others around the gym know he struggled with high blood pressure and diabetes. Later, it became clear that Ike had cancer, news that saddened many denizens of the gym, regardless of their race. After Ike was admitted to the hospital, his friends from the gym, Black and White alike, would visit him. Everyone assumed that because Ike's sons were doctors, and because he and his wife had means, he would receive quality care. However, one of Ike's closest friends at the gym, a Black man named Miles, told me he'd visited Ike at a Catholic facility for the indigent. When Miles arrived and asked about Ike, a nun said, "You must be from the gym," because most of Ike's visitors were from there.

During his illness, Ike's family never appeared. This seemed peculiar, and people began to talk. We learned that Ike was mostly alone except for us, his friends from the gym. With regard to his wife and sons, they didn't exist. We learned that Ike had been pretending all along. The gym members were astounded that Ike was not the person we thought he was. Everyone had been taken in by his story.

In essence, we all came to understand that we were his true family, White and Black. After Ike passed away, a number of us gathered at a local restaurant in his honor. During the luncheon, we discussed with amazement the way Ike had taken great care to present himself as middle class and "successful," with a loving family. Yet, he served as a true cultural broker, bringing all of us, people of different races and backgrounds, together at the gym.

The very charm and charisma that allowed Ike to sell his fictional life served to unite people who otherwise would never have interacted so closely. After the memorial luncheon, the diverse gathering never regrouped—the attendees simply faded away from one another, a fact that underscored the real reason we'd come together in the first place: to honor Ike, the friend we all had in common.

CONCLUSION

The Perpetual Stranger

What is driving the surge of incidents in which White people have called the police to report Black people who are simply going about their business—hanging out at Starbucks; birding in Central Park; or as was the case recently for a small group of middle-class Black women, talking too loudly on a train in California wine country? Part of the answer has to do with the ubiquity of cell phones, which facilitate rapid reporting of racial incidents to police and the news media, along with social media, which bring news of the same incidents to the public with nearly equal speed. Yet there is also a sociological explanation.

White people typically avoid the Black space, but Black people are required to navigate the White space as a condition of their existence. And many White people have not adjusted to the idea that Black people now appear more often in "White spaces"—especially in places of privilege, power, and prestige—or even just in places where they were historically unwelcome. When Black people appear in such places and do not show what may be regarded as "proper" deference, some White people want them out. Subconsciously or explicitly, these people want to assign or banish them to the iconic ghetto—to the stereotypical space in which they think all Black people belong, a segregated space for second-class citizens. A lag between the rapidity of Black progress and White acceptance of that progress is responsible for this impulse. And this was exacerbated by the previous presidential administration of Donald Trump, which emboldened White racists with its racially charged rhetoric and exclusionist immigration policies.

THE CIVIL RIGHTS REVOLUTION

The civil rights revolution upended long-standing notions of what spaces counted as "Black," "White," and "cosmopolitan." Over the past half century, the United States has undergone a profound racial incorporation process that has resulted in the largest Black middle class in history—a population that no longer feels obligated to stay in historically "Black" spaces or to defer to White people. When members of this Black middle class (and other darker-skinned Americans, too) appear in civil society today, and especially in "White" spaces, they often demand a regard that accords with their rights, obligations, and duties as full citizens of the United States of America. Yet many White people fundamentally reject that Black people are owed such regard, and indeed often feel that their own rights and social statuses have somehow been abrogated by contemporary racial inclusion. They seek to push back on the recent progress in race relations and may demand deference on the basis of White-skin privilege.

As these Whites observe Black people navigating the "White" privileged spaces of our society, they experience a sense of loss or a certain amount of cognitive dissonance. They may feel an acute need to "correct" what is before their eyes, to square things, or to set the "erroneous" picture right—to reestablish cognitive consonance. White people need to put the Black interlopers in their place, literally and figuratively. Black people must have their behavior corrected, and they must be directed back to "their" neighborhoods and designated social spaces. Not bold enough to try to accomplish this feat alone, many of these self-appointed color-line monitors seek help from wherever they can find it—from the police, for instance. The "interlopers" may simply want to visit their condo's swimming pool; or to sit in Starbucks or meet friends there before ordering drinks, something White people typically do without a second thought; or take a nap in a student dorm common room, make a purchase in an upscale store, or jog through a "White" neighborhood. For the offense of straying—for engaging in ordinary behavior in public and being Black at the same time—they incur the "White gaze," along with a call to the police. And we all know what can happen then. When the police have killed Black people, which seems epidemic, they have almost never been held accountable. The George Floyd case was an exception.

In times past, before the civil rights revolution, the color line was more clearly marked. Both White and Black people knew their "place" and, for the most part, observed it. When people crossed that line—Black people, anyway—they faced legal penalties or extrajudicial violence. In those times, to live while Black was to be American and nominally free but to reside firmly within a virtual color caste—essentially, to live behind the veil, as W. E. B. Du Bois put it in *The Souls of Black Folk*.

THE ROLE OF THE "ICONIC GHETTO" IN THE WHITE IMAGINATION

Social iconography is more complex today. Many urban dwellers now understand a city's public spaces to be a mosaic of Black space, White space, and "cosmopolitan space"—the last designation referring to virtual islands of racial civility in a sea of segregation, or what I have described in my previous book as "cosmopolitan canopies." In Philadelphia, for instance, where I have based most of my ethnographic studies over many years, examples of these cosmopolitan spaces are some large areas, such as the Reading Terminal Market and Rittenhouse

Square, local university campuses, and smaller areas, such as offices, department stores, restaurants, and certain coffee shops (including some Starbucks locations).

In this sociological context, the urban ghetto is presumed to be, descriptively, "the place where the Black people live." But it's also, stereotypically, a den of iniquity and insecurity, a fearsome, impoverished place of social backwardness where Black people perpetrate all manner of violence and crimes against one another. Between Black and White space, travel usually goes in one direction. Black ghettos, and Whites' attitudes about them, emerged after slavery and reinforced what slavery had established—that the Black person's "place" was at the bottom of the American racial order. For the White majority, ghettos helped to fuse inferior status with Black skin, and they became fixtures of mental as well as physical space. Each generation became socially invested in the lowly place of Black people; these White people understood their own identity in terms of whom they opposed, and this positionality was passed down from one racist generation to the next.

In practical terms, Whites know little about the iconic ghetto and the people who inhabit it. But for many White people, the anonymous Black person in public is always implicitly associated with the urban ghetto and decidedly "does not belong" in the White space. The link to the ghetto is so strong that it becomes the "master status" of the typical Black person, to use a term coined by the sociologist E. C. Hughes. It's the feature that most defines Black people in the White imagination. In this system, Black people move about civil society with a deficit of credibility; in comparison, their White counterparts are given a "pass" as decent and law-abiding citizens. Black people wage a constant campaign for respect, which is lost before it begins. The judges are most often the contestants who compete with Black people for place and position in our increasingly pluralistic and rivalrous society. Thus, the issue here is not simply the White supremacy of old. It's also a powerful new form of symbolic racism that targets Black people for being "out of their place" or, essentially, for behaving in ordinary ways, and especially in "White spaces," while being Black at the same time.

Strikingly, the iconic ghetto impacts the image of almost every Black person—especially as Black Americans increasingly inhabit all levels of the national class and occupational structure. They attend the best schools, pursue the professions of their choosing, and occupy various positions of power, privilege, and prestige. But for all Black people in public, the specter of the urban ghetto always lurks—it hovers over American race relations, shaping the public conception of the anonymous Black person.

• • •

Early on a cool weekday morning in spring 2021, I parked my car near the docks in Martha's Vineyard's tony Edgartown. In the middle of the pandemic, I wanted to get out and about and to enjoy the ocean view. After pulling up to a metered spot, I realized that one thing was missing: coffee. I had passed a bookstore with a sign that promised coffee, and now I wanted a cup to make the morning complete. I decided to walk the mile or so back to the shop to get one. Passing one establishment after another, I saw workers inside busily cleaning up or servicing the equipment. Most were not yet open for the season, and their roped signs said as much. The quaint streets of Edgartown were unusually deserted that day, but I spotted a White couple here and there, then an older White woman who was walking her Yorkshire terrier. As I passed her, she scowled at me. A young White kid on a bicycle sped by me, perhaps on his way to work.

When I reached the bookshop where I'd spotted the coffee sign, the front door was open and I stepped inside. The lights were on, but the shop itself was deserted. As I walked amid the rows of bookshelves, I called, "Hello! Anybody here?" Silence. I was feeling somewhat out of place, even a bit vulnerable, and thought I might be vaguely threatening in my jeans, sneakers, and black hooded sweatshirt. But I continued to walk around the apparently empty store, looking for a clerk. I was just about to leave when suddenly, a middle-aged White woman appeared, seemingly out of nowhere. "Can I help you?" she asked.

"Yes, I'd like a cup of coffee," I said.

"Oh, we're not quite open for coffee," she replied, despite the large sign outside to the contrary.

"Oh," I said, puzzled.

She began to tell me about a place down the street and around the corner where she thought I could get coffee. I listened intently. Then, graciously, she said, "Do you have a phone? I can Google it." With that, I pulled out my iPhone and handed it to her. She found the place's website and set me up with navigation. Pleasantly, we said our goodbyes, and I was out the door, continuing my search.

On the way up the street, I encountered a White man of about forty with a cup in his hand. "Excuse me," I said. I wanted to ask him where he got his coffee. "Excuse me," I said again. Clearly, he heard me, but looked away, ignoring my voice. I tried one last time, then gave up and proceeded on my way. In about ten minutes, I reached my destination, but the place was closed. I turned back to retrace my steps. On my way, I spotted the White man again, but this time, as he seemed to hurry along, a middle-aged White couple from across the street yelled to him, "Where'd you get that coffee?" This time, the man stopped. Politely, he engaged them, and then gave what seemed to be complicated directions to a place that was a ways off and too far for me, so I headed back to my car.

As I settled into my car, tension I hadn't been aware of released in me. This incident left me feeling uncertain, somewhat estranged, and possibly unwelcome on those streets, a "White space." The police could have been called on me at any point that morning, I thought. I was just lucky that they hadn't been.

POSTSCRIPT: WHAT BLACK FOLK KNOW

Almost every Black person has experienced the sting of disrespect on the basis of being Black. A large but undetermined number of Black people feel acutely disrespected in their everyday lives, discrimination they see as both subtle and explicit. In the face of this reality, Black people manage themselves in a largely White-dominated society, learning and sharing the rules of a peculiarly segregated existence. In White spaces, Black people are often tolerated, but seldom feel accepted or know exactly where they stand with the White people they meet. The persistent question is whether the White people in their presence are friends or foes, whether they mean them well or whether they are out to block them. However, this uncertainty is typically clarified by the onslaught of regular, everyday public racism, including occasional yells of n****r from White passersby or their strong encouragement to "go back where you came from"—the ghetto. Out of the blue, and from complete strangers, unknown Black people receive occasional scowls and dirty looks, or expressions of outright fear, especially on elevators, which some White people refuse to enter if only Black people are there, choosing to take the stairs instead. In upscale stores, young Black people—regardless of social class, and especially if they are male— are profiled and followed around. On the streets and in other public places, White people shun them or cross the street, and White women clutch their pocketbooks. Black men often feel they are regarded as criminals until they can prove they are not; one false move, and White people may call the police, and then, when the cops arrive, anything can happen.

Moreover, Black people generally are convinced that they must work twice as hard to get half as far in life. This sense of inequality is built into the working conception of the world that Black people share, providing a ready explanation of their relatively disadvantaged position in American society. And yet, they typically remain civil and are inclined to give the next White person the benefit of the doubt, while never really knowing for sure whether their trust was misplaced—at least until they are let down.

Upwardly mobile Black people who become professors, doctors, lawyers, and businesspeople are required to navigate a peculiar terrain. They are part of a prestigious class, but their Blackness marks them as stigmatized; and until they are able to prove themselves, they are burdened with a deficit of credibility. After successfully performing respectability, they may be granted a provisional status and, depending on their audience, they can always be charged with something more to prove. In the White-dominated professions, Black people often feel marginalized by their White colleagues, but are constrained to keep their concerns to themselves for fear of appearing "racial" or troublesome in the workplace. So they keep their complaints about race to themselves, while giving their White colleagues who might be encouraged to improve the environment the message that all is well and things are just fine. Meanwhile, backstage, among their Black colleagues and friends, they vent.

Among their own, Black people affirm and reaffirm this central lesson and, out of a sense of duty, try to pass it along to others they care about, especially to their children. The White majority, in large part, does not easily apprehend such lessons, because it has little ability to empathize with the plight of Black people, and also because many see themselves in competition with Black people for place and position.

For Black people, experience is a dear school; the cultural knowledge that Black people acquire is based largely on the experience of living while Black in a society that is dominated by White people. Strikingly, this cultural knowledge is most often inaccessible by White people, and when confronted with it, most Whites are incredulous. American society is ideologically characterized as open, egalitarian, and privileging of equal opportunity, but Black people are deeply doubtful. The everyday reality of Black people is that of being peculiarly subordinate in almost every way. In this social, economic, and political context, White people appear utterly advantaged, and Black people view themselves and their people as profoundly disadvantaged, and see White people—especially racist White people—as the source of their racial inequality. This reality becomes for many Black people their "working conception of the world," or their "local knowledge"—what they know as they go about meeting the demands of their everyday lives.

Systemic racism is an intractable condition of American life, a truth that Black folk know all too well, and too many White folk do not, or will not acknowledge. It is alive and well, and both subtle and explicit, a fact that is illustrated by the persistently segregated patterns of everyday life in American civil society, as well as the color-coded occupational structure, through which all Black people are racially burdened solely on the basis of their Blackness. Hence, racial equality is elusive, for no matter how decent or talented Black individuals are deemed to be, ultimately, they can usually attain only a provisional status—a place that is conditioned by the after-effects of the original sin of slavery centuries ago.

These effects are manifest in today's segregated civil society, and especially in the persistence of racial disparities in residence, education, health, and employment—racial inequality. Moreover, a strange, but powerful loop has been created. The iconic ghetto, the place "where the Black folk live," symbolically denigrates Black people as a population. White people typically accept and justify extant racial apartheid, which then works peculiarly to justify itself. Consequently, Black despair and alienation have become ever more entrenched. A self-fulfilling prophecy has been set in motion that defines Black people as inferior to White people, which then becomes "proven" by the sight of the existential condition of the most disenfranchised elements of the Black community.

The old racism of slavery and White supremacy created the ghetto. The civil rights movement opened its gates, and a new Black middle class emerged. But the new form of symbolic racism emanating from the iconic ghetto hovers, stigmatizing by degrees Black people as they navigate the larger civil society and, especially, the "White space."

NOTES

Prologue

1.   My "father" was actually my stepfather, who came into my life when I was two.

Chapter One

1.   Grounded in my ethnographic fieldwork, this analysis posits "White space" as a perceptual category. See my body of work, specifically *Code of the Street* (1999), *The Cosmopolitan Canopy* (2011), "The Iconic Ghetto" (2012), and "The White Space" (2015). See also the important work of Brunsma et al. (2019, 2020), Embrick et al. (2019), Hargrove (2009), Finney (2014), and Jackson (1999).

2.   For a provocative consideration of elite law schools as White space, please see Moore (2007).

3.   For an illuminating report detailing the special challenges that Black people face in isolated and unwelcoming White settings, see Rhonda Colvin's "Traveling While Black," *Washington Post*, January 26, 2018.

Chapter Two

1.   In his book *Ghetto: The Invention of a Place, the History of an Idea*, Mitch Duneier discusses the history of the term "ghetto" as it was used in Europe through the time of the Nazis, and the ways the term was later applied to

Black people living in poor inner-city communities in the United States. See also Lewis Wirth, *The Ghetto* (1928), which was the first real study of the ghetto. Wirth's book focused on Jews in Italy and in Chicago. While originally "ghetto" was used to mean poor Jewish communities throughout Europe, for most people today it implies poor Black communities. Duneier's book creates a link between the two.

2. For more on this complicated situation, see Bonilla-Silva (2015, 2017).

Chapter Four

1. See Douglas S. Massey and Nancy Denton, *American Apartheid: Segregation and the Making of the Underclass* (Cambridge, MA: Harvard University Press, 1993); Gilbert Osofsky, *Harlem: The Making of a Ghetto, Negro New York, 1890–1930* (New York: Harper and Row, 1996); Allan H. Spear, *Black Chicago: The Making of a Negro Ghetto* (Chicago: University of Chicago Press, 1967); "SW White Protest," *Philadelphia Inquirer*, 1985.

2. In my fieldwork, I came across many examples of elaborate kinship structures, strong female-centered households and Black churches and their associations, where people helped one another to survive. See, for example, Carol Stack's *All Our Kin* and Mary Lou Valentine's *Hustling and Other Hard Work*.

3. The situation is a bit more complicated for non-White immigrants, especially Caribbean Blacks. There is a growing body of literature on this subject, including the works of Tod Hamilton, Mary Waters, and Orly Clergé.

4. As a result of this dislocation, Blacks and Whites experienced spells of unemployment, but they tended to be longer for Blacks (Wilson 1987, 1996; Ong and Lawrence 1995).

Chapter Five

1. For an illuminating analysis of Blacks and Whites operating casually in the same space, see Reuben May's study *Urban Nightlife: Entertaining Race, Class, and Culture in Public Space* (2014).

Chapter Six

1. In "Busted," recorded in 1963, Ray Charles sang: "Well, I am no thief, but a man can go wrong when he's busted."

2. The songs of Tupac Shakur had a political edge as well as an obsession with violence, and he died after being shot at the age of twenty-five. Biggie Smalls died at twenty-four, in a shooting related to a feud between East and West Coast hip-hop artists; his former friend Tupac was on the other side.

3. Elijah Anderson, *A Place on the Corner: A Study of Street Corner Men* (1978; 2nd ed., Chicago: University of Chicago Press, 2003).

Chapter Eight

1. This over-policing is experienced as arbitrary and inconsistent by the Black people living in these communities, and it makes them reluctant to call the police unless as a last resort. Black people often think there is collusion between the police and the criminals, particularly drug dealers, and that when they call the police on community drug activity, the police will report them to the criminals. This makes Black people even more reluctant to call the police.

2. For more information on the racially discriminatory nature of all aspects of America's criminal justice system, see the Sentencing Project: www .sentencingproject.org/.

3. For more information about the school-to-prison pipeline, see Libby Nelson and Dara Lind, "The School to Prison Pipeline, Explained," *Justice Policy Institute*, February 24, 2015; and Russell J. Skiba, Mariella I. Arredondo, and Natasha T. Williams, "More than a Metaphor: The Contribution of Exclu- sionary Discipline to a School-to-Prison Pipeline," *Equity and Excellence in Education* 47 (2014): 546–64.

4. While these Black men are young, they are not minors. People under eighteen are processed through the Youth Study Center and then Family Court, not city hall.

5. In 2014 Eric Garner was killed by a police officer in Staten Island, New York, for selling loose cigarettes (Baker, Goodman, and Mueller 2015).

Chapter Nine

1. The material in this section is adapted from Anderson 1994, 1999, 2001, 2009, 2020.

Chapter Ten

1. For all of its problems, the ghetto can be a highly attractive place, with kin- ship ties and friendship networks that provide support for people in poverty and make it hard for them to imagine leaving.

Chapter Twelve

1. With regard to race and urban housing markets, please see Molotch's early conceptions of "the dual market," including his notions of "restricted" and "unrestricted" markets in South Shore, a neighborhood in Chicago (1972) and the earlier discussion of neighborhood change by Taeuber and Taeuber (1965).

2. See also Loretta Lees, Tom Slater, and Elvin Wyly, eds., *The Gentrification Reader* (New York: Routledge, 2010), and John Joe Schlichtman, Jason Patch, and Marc Lamont Hill, *Gentrifier* (Toronto: University of Toronto Press, 2017)

(the authors discuss their personal experiences in several cities including Philadelphia).

3. The process of gentrification follows the outlines I described for Powelton Village, the subject of *Streetwise* (Anderson 1990). Similar racial dynamics appear to be at work in this area today—the property values are double and triple those of just six years ago.

4. White parents often come to this sense of "buyer's remorse" when their children reach school age. For an example of how this affects Black children, see the story about Malik in chapter 9.

REFERENCES

Adams, Carolyn, David Bartelt, David Elesh, and Ira Goldstein, 2008. *Restructuring the Philadelphia Region: Metropolitan Divisions and Inequality*. Philadelphia Voices, Philadelphia Vision. Philadelphia: Temple University Press.

Alba, Richard D. 2020. *The Great Demographic Illusion*. Princeton, NJ: Princeton University Press.

Alba, Richard D., John R. Logan, and Brian Stults. 2000. "How Segregated Are Middle-Class African Americans?" *Social Problems* 47:543–58.

Albright, Alex, et al. 2021. "After the Burning: The Economic Effects of the 1921 Tulsa Race Massacre." NBER Working Paper 28985. DOI 10.3386/w28985.

Alexander, Michelle. 2010. *The New Jim Crow: Mass Incarceration in the Age of Colorblindness*. New York: New Press.

Anderson, Carol. 2016. *White Rage: The Unspoken Truth of Our Racial Divide*. New York: Bloomsbury.

Anderson, Elijah. 1978. *A Place on the Corner: A Study of Black Street Corner Men*. Chicago: University of Chicago Press.

Anderson, Elijah. 1980. "Some Observations on Youth Employment." In *Youth Employment and Public Policy*, edited by Bernard Anderson and Isabel Sawbill. Englewood Cliffs, NJ: Prentice Hall.

Anderson, Elijah. 1990. *Streetwise: Race, Class, and Change in an Urban Community*. Chicago: University of Chicago Press.

Anderson, Elijah. 1996. Introduction. In *The Philadelphia Negro*, by W. E. B. Du Bois. Philadelphia: University of Pennsylvania Press.

Anderson, Elijah. 1997. "The Precarious Balance: Race Man or Sellout?" In *The Darden Dilemma: 12 Black Writers on Justice, Race, and Conflicting Loyalties*, edited by Elis Cose. New York: HarperCollins.

Anderson, Elijah. 1999. *Code of the Street: Decency, Violence, and the Moral Life of the Inner City*. New York: W. W. Norton.

Anderson, Elijah. 2000. "The Emerging Philadelphia African American Class Structure." *Annals of the American Academy of Political and Social Science* 568:54–77.

Anderson, Elijah. 2001. "Going Straight: The Story of a Young Inner-City Ex-Convict." *Punishment and Society* 3 (1): 135–52.

Anderson, Elijah, ed. 2008. *Against the Wall: Poor, Young, Black, and Male*. Philadelphia: University of Pennsylvania Press.

Anderson, Elijah, ed. 2009. *Against the Wall: Poor, Young, Black, and Male*. Philadelphia: University of Pennsylvania Press.

Anderson, Elijah. 2011. *The Cosmopolitan Canopy: Race and Civility in Everyday Life*. New York: W. W. Norton.

Anderson, Elijah. 2012a. "The Iconic Ghetto." *Annals of the American Academy of Political and Social Science* 642:8–24.

Anderson, Elijah. 2012b. "Reflections on the Black-White Achievement Gap." *Journal of School Psychology* 50:593–97.

Anderson, Elijah. 2012c. "Toward Knowing the Iconic Ghetto." In *The Ghetto: Contemporary Global Issues and Controversies*, edited by Ray Hutchinson and Bruce Haynes, 67–82. Boulder, CO: Westview.

Anderson, Elijah. 2014. "What Caused the Ferguson Riot Exists in So Many Other Cities, Too." *Washington Post*, August 13, 2014. http://www.washingtonpost.com/posteverything/wp/2014/08/13/what-caused-the-ferguson-riot-exists-in-so-many-other-cities-too/.

Anderson, Elijah. 2015. "The White Space." *Sociology of Race and Ethnicity* 1:10–21.

Anderson, Elijah. 2018. "Race Relations since the 1960s Riots." In *Healing Our Divided Society*. Edited by Alan Curtis. Philadelphia: Temple University Press.

Anderson, Elijah. 2020. "Black Folk and COVID-19." *Penn Institute for Urban Research*. April 17.

Anderson, Elijah, Duke Austin, Craig Holloway, and Vani Kulkarni. 2012. "The Legacy of Racial Caste." *Annals of the American Academy of Political and Social Science* 642:25–42.

Appelrouth, Scott, and Laura Desfor Edles. 2008. *Classical and Contemporary Sociological Theory: Text and Readings*. Thousand Oaks, CA: Pine Forge Press.

Armour, David. 1978. "White Flight, Demographic Transition, and the Future of

School Desegregation." RAND Paper Series. Santa Monica, CA: RAND Corporation.

Armour, David. 1978. "White Flight, Demographic Transition, and the Future of School Desegregation." RAND Paper Series. Santa Monica, CA: RAND Corporation.

Asbury, Herbert. (1927) 2008. *The Gangs of New York: An Informal History of the Underworld*. Reprint, Vancouver, WA: Vintage.

Auletta, Ken. 1982. *The Underclass*. New York: Random House.

Baker, Al, J. David Goodman, and Benjamin Mueller. 2015. "Beyond the Chokehold: The Path to Eric Garner's Death." *New York Times*, June 13.

Baker, Peter. 2018. "Bush Made Willie Horton an Issue in 1988, and the Racial Scars Are Still Fresh." *New York Times*. December 3.

Bearak, Bany. 1997. "Between Black and White." *New York Times*, July 27, sec. 1, p. 1.

Becker, Howard S. 1973. *Outsiders: Studies in the Sociology of Deviance*. New York: Free Press.

Blacher, Mitch. 2021. "Philly Police Less Likely to Arrest Suspect When Murder Victim Is Person of Color." NBCPhiladelphia.com. May 13.

Blumer, Herbert. 1958. "Race Prejudice as a Sense of Group Position." *Pacific Sociological Review* 1:3–7.

Bobo, L. 1999. "Prejudice as Group Position: Micro-Foundations of a Sociological Approach to Racism and Race Relations." *Journal of Social Issues* 55:445–72.

Bobo, Lawrence, and Vincent L. Hutchings. 1996. "Perceptions of Racial Group Competition: Extending Blumer's Theory of Group Position to a Multiracial Social Context." *American Sociological Review*, December 12: 951–72.

Bonilla-Silva, Eduardo. 2013. *Racism without Racists: Color-Blind Racism and the Persistence of Racial Inequality in America*. New York: Rowman and Littlefield.

Bonilla-Silva, Eduardo. 2015. "The Structure of Racism in Color-Blind, 'Post-Racial' America." *American Behavioral Scientist* 58 (11): 1358–76.

Bonilla-Silva, Eduardo. 2017. "What We Were, What We Are, and What We Should Be: The Racial Problem of American Sociology." *Social Problems* 64:179–87.

Brunsma, David L., et al. 2020. "The Culture of White Space: On the Racialized Production of Meaning." *American Behavioral Scientist* 64 (14): 2001–15.

Brunsma, D. L., N. G. Chapman, and J. W. Kim. 2019. "The Culture of White Space, the Racialized Production of Meaning, and the Jamband Scene." *Sociological Inquiry* 90 (1): 7–29.

Carter, Stephen L. 1991. *Rejections of an Affirmative Action Baby*. New York: Basic Books.

Clark, Dennis. 1982. *The Irish in Philadelphia: Ten Generations of Urban Experience*. Philadelphia: Temple University Press.

Clark, Kenneth B. 1965. *Dark Ghetto: Dilemmas of Social Power*. New York: Harcourt, Brace.

Coates, Ta-Nehisi. 2014. "The Case for Reparations." *Atlantic*, June. www.theatlantic .com/magazine/archive/2014/06/the-case-for-reparations/361631/.

Coates, Ta-Nehisi. 2017. *We Were Eight Years in Power: An American Tragedy*. New York: One World.

Cobb, Jelani, with Matthew Guariglia, eds. 2021. *The Essential Kerner Commission Report*. New York: Liveright.

Coleman, James S. 1988. "Social Capital in the Creation of Human Capital." *American Journal of Sociology* 94:S95–120.

Collins, Sharon M. 1997. *Black Corporate Executives*. Philadelphia: Temple University Press.

Conley, Dalton. 1999. "Getting into the Black: Race, Wealth, and Public Policy." *Political Science Quarterly* 114 (4): 595–612.

Cose, Ellis. 1993. *The Rage of a Privileged Class*. New York: HarperCollins.

Covert, Bryce. 2019. "The Myth of the Welfare Queen." *New Republic*. July 2.

Cox, Oliver. 1948. *Caste, Class, and Race*. New York: Doubleday.

Crenshaw, Kimberlé W. 2017. *On Intersectionality: Essential Writings*. New York: New Press.

Cucchiara, Maia Bloomfield. 2013. *Marketing Schools, Marketing Cities: Who Wins and Who Loses When Schools Become Urban Amenities*. Chicago: University of Chicago Press.

Darity, William. 1982. "The Human Capital Approach to Black-White Earnings Inequality: Some Unsettled Questions." *Journal of Human Resources* 17:72–93.

Davis, Allen F., and Mark H. Haller, eds. 1998. *The Peoples of Philadelphia: A History of Ethnic Groups and Lower Class Life, 1790–1940*. Rev. ed. Philadelphia: University of Pennsylvania Press.

Davis, Allison, and Burleigh Gardner. 2009. *Deep South: A Social Anthropological Study of Caste and Class*. Columbia: University of South Carolina Press.

Dobbin, Frank, and Alexandra Kalev. 2017. "Are Diversity Programs Merely Ceremonial? Evidence-Free Institutionalization." In *The Sage Handbook of Organizational Institutionalism*. Edited by Royston Greenwood et al. London: Sage.

Dollard, John. 1957. *Caste and Class in a Southern Town*. New York: Doubleday Anchor Books.

Drake, St. Clair, and Horace Cayton. (1945) 1993. *Black Metropolis: A Study of Negro Life in a Northern City*. Reprint, Chicago: University of Chicago Press.

Du Bois, W. E. B. (1903) 1995. *The Souls of Black Folk*. Reprint, New York: Dutton.

Du Bois, W. E. B. (1899) 1996. *The Philadelphia Negro*. Reprint, Philadelphia: University of Pennsylvania Press.

Duck, Waverly. 2015. *No Way Out: Precarious Living in the Shadow of Poverty and Drug Dealing*. Chicago: University of Chicago Press.

Duneier, Mitchell. 2000. *Sidewalk*. New York: Farrar, Straus, and Giroux.

Duneier, Mitchell. 2016. *Ghetto: The Invention of a Place, the History of an Idea*. New York: Farrar, Straus, and Giroux.

Eason, John M. 2017. *Big House on the Prairie: Rise of the Rural Ghetto and Prison Proliferation*. Chicago: University of Chicago Press.

Edelman, Peter B. 1997. "The Worst Thing Bill Clinton Has Ever Done." *Atlantic Monthly*, March, 43.

Embrick, D. G., S. Weffer, and S. Dómínguez. 2019. "White Sanctuaries: Race and Place in Art Museums." *International Journal of Sociology and Social Policy* 39 (11/12): 995–1009.

Emirbayer, Mustapha, and Matthew Desmond. 2015. *The Racial Order*. Chicago: University of Chicago Press.

Esper, George. 1985. "Racial Protest Splits Urban Neighborhood: Philadelphia Black Couple Forced to Move; Interracial Pair Plans to Stay Despite Threats." *Los Angeles Times*. December 29.

Evans-Pritchard, E. E. (1940) 1969. *The Nuer: A Description of the Modes of Livelihood and Political Institutions of a Nilotic People*. Reprint, London: Oxford University Press.

Fagan, Jeffrey, and Richard B. Freeman. 1999. "Crime and Work." *Crime and Justice* 25:225–90.

Feagin, Joe. 2006. *Systemic Racism: A Theory of Oppression*. New York: Routledge.

Feagin, Joe R. 2013. *The White Racial Frame: Centuries of Racial Framing and Counter-Framing*. 2nd ed. New York: Routledge.

Feagin, Joe R., and Melvin P. Sikes. 1994. *Living with Racism: The Black Middle-Class Experience*. Boston: Beacon Press.

Finney, Carolyn. 2014. *Black Faces, White Spaces*. Chapel Hill: University of North Carolina Press.

Franklin, John Hope, and Evelyn Brooks Higginbotham. (1947) 2021. *From Slavery to Freedom: A History of African Americans*. 10th ed. New York: McGraw-Hill.

Frazier, E. Franklin. 1939. *The Negro Family in the United States*. Chicago: University of Chicago Press.

Frazier, E. Franklin. (1957) 1962. *Black Bourgeoisie: The Rise of a New Middle Class in the United States*. Reprint, New York: Scribner.

Galster, G. C., and E. Godfrey. 2005. "By Words and Deeds: Racial Steering by Real Estate Agents in the U.S. in 2000." *Journal of the American Planning Association* 71 (3): 1–19.

Gans, Herbert. 1996. *The War against the Poor*. New York: Basic Books.

Geertz, Clifford. 2000. *Local Knowledge: Further Essays in Interpretive Anthropology*. 3rd ed. New York: Basic Books.

Gladwell, Malcolm. 2016. *The Tipping Point: How Little Things Can Make a Big Difference*. Boston: Little, Brown.

Glazer, Nathan. (1975) 1987. *Affirmative Discrimination*. Reprint, Cambridge, MA: Harvard University Press.

Glazer, Nathan. 1997. *We Are All Multiculturalists Now*. Cambridge, MA: Harvard University Press.

Goff, Philip Atiba, et al. 2014. "The Essence of Innocence: Consequences of Dehumanizing Black Children." *Journal of Personality and Social Psychology* 106 (4): 526–45.

Goffman, Alice. 2014. *On the Run: Fugitive Life in an American City*. Chicago: University of Chicago Press.

Goffman, Erving. 1959. *The Presentation of Self in Everyday Life*. New York: Anchor Books.

Goffman, Erving. 1961. *Strategic Interaction*. Indianapolis: Bobbs-Merrill.

Goffman, Erving. 1963. *Stigma: The Management of Spoiled Identity*. Englewood Cliffs, NJ: Prentice Hall.

Goffman, Erving. 1971. *Relations in Public: Microstudies of the Public Order*. New York: Basic Books.

Gotham, Kevin F. 2000. "Urban Space, Restrictive Covenants and the Origins of Racial Residential Segregation in a US City, 1900–50." *International Journal of Urban and Regional Research* 24:616–33.

Graham, Lawrence O. 1999. *Our Kind of People: Inside America's Black Upper Class*. New York: HarperPerennial.

Green, Victor H., and Nat Gertler. 2019. *The Negro Motorist Green Book Compendium*. Camarillo, CA: About Comics.

Hacker, Andrew. 1995. *Two Nations: Separate, Hostile, Unequal*. New York: Ballantine.

Hagedorn, John. 2017. "Gangs, Schools, and Social Change: An Institutional Analysis." *Annals of the American Academy of Political and Social Science* 673:190–208.

Hargrove, M. D. 2009. "Mapping the 'Social Field of Whiteness': White Racism as Habitus in the City Where History Lives." *Transforming Anthropology* 17 (2): 93–104.

Hassanein, Nada. 2021. "Young Black Men and Teens Are Killed by Guns 20 Times More than Their White Counterparts, CDC Data Shows." *USA Today*. February 23.

Hepp, John Henry, IV. 2003. *The Middle-Class City: Transforming Space and Time in Philadelphia, 1876-1926*. Philadelphia: University of Pennsylvania Press.

Higham, John. 2002. *Strangers in the Land: Patterns of American Nationalism, 1860-1925.* Rev. ed. New Brunswick, NJ: Rutgers University Press.

Hinton, Elizabeth. 2017. *From the War on Poverty to the War on Crime: The Making of Mass Incarceration in America.* Cambridge, MA: Harvard University Press.

Hinton, Elizabeth. 2021. *America on Fire: The Untold History of Police Violence and Black Rebellion since the 1960s.* New York: Liveright.

Hinton, Elizabeth, LeShae Henderson, and Cindy Reed. 2018. *An Unjust Burden: The Disparate Treatment of Black Americans in the Criminal Justice System.* New York: Vera Institute of Justice.

Hirsch, Arnold R. 1983. *Making the Second Ghetto: Race and Housing in Chicago, 1940-1960.* Chicago: University of Chicago Press.

Horowitz, Ruth. 1983. *Honor and the American Dream.* New Brunswick, NJ: Rutgers University Press.

Houston, Ellen, and Jared Bernstein. 2000. *Crime and Work: What We Can Learn from the Low-Wage Labor Market.* Washington, DC: Economic Policy Institute.

Hughes, Everett C. 1945. "Dilemmas and Contradictions of Status." *American Journal of Sociology* 50:353-59.

Hughes, Everett C. 1964. "Good People and Dirty Work." In *The Other Side: Perspectives on Deviance,* ed. Howard S. Becker. New York: Free Press of Glencoe.

Hunter, Marcus Anthony. 2013. *Black Citymakers: How the Philadelphia Negro Changed Urban America.* Oxford: Oxford University Press.

Hutchinson, Ray, and Bruce Haynes, eds. 2012. *The Ghetto: Contemporary Global Issues and Controversies.* Boulder, CO: Westview.

Hyra, Derek S. 2017. *Race, Class, and Politics in the Cappuccino City.* Chicago: University of Chicago Press.

Ignatiev, Noel. 1995. *How the Irish Became White.* New York: Routledge.

Jackson, Ronald L. 1999. "White Space, White Privilege: Mapping Discursive Inquiry into the Self." *Quarterly Journal of Speech* 85:38-54.

Jaynes, Gerald D. 2004. "Immigration and the Social Construction of Otherness: Underclass Stigma and Intergroup Relations." In *Not Just Black and White: Historical and Contemporary Perspectives on Immigration, Race, and Ethnicity in the United States,* edited by N. Foner and G. M. Fredrickson. New York: Russell Sage.

Johnson, Hannibal B. 2014. *Tulsa's Historic Greenwood District.* Charleston, SC: Arcadia.

Jones, Nikki. 2004. "'It's Not Where You Live, It's How You Live': How Young Women Negotiate Conflict and Violence in the Inner City." *Annals of the American Academy of Political and Social Science* 595 (1): 49-62.

Jones, Nikki. 2010. *Between Good and Ghetto: African American Girls and Inner-City Violence*. New Brunswick, NJ: Rutgers University Press.

Kamin, Deborah. 2020. "Black Homeowners Face Discrimination in Appraisals." *New York Times*, August 25.

Kasinitz, Philip, et al. 2009. *Inheriting the City: The Children of Immigrants Come of Age*. New York: Russell Sage Foundation.

Katznelson, Ira. 2006. *When Affirmative Action Was White: An Untold History of Racial Inequality in Twentieth-Century America*. New York: Norton.

Kendi, Ibram X. 2016. *Stamped from the Beginning: The Definitive History of Racist Ideas in America*. New York: Bold Type Books.

Kennedy, Randall. 1997. "My Race Problem, and Ours." *Atlantic* 279 (5): 55–66.

Kerner Commission. 1968. *Report of the National Advisory Commission on Civil Disorders*. Washington, DC: Government Printing Office.

Kirschenman, Joleen, and Kathryn Neckerman. 1991. "'We'd Love to Hire Them, But . . .': The Meaning of Race for Employers." In *The Urban Underclass*, edited by Christopher Jencks and Paul E. Peterson. Washington, DC: Brookings Institution.

Kohler-Hausmann, Issa. 2019. *Misdemeanorland: Criminal Courts and Social Control in an Age of Broken Windows Policing*. Princeton, NJ: Princeton University Press.

Lacy, Karyn. 2007. *Blue-Chip Black: Race, Class, and Status in the New Black Middle Class*. Berkeley: University of California Press.

Ladson-Billings, Gloria. 2017. "'Makes Me Wanna Holler': Refuting the 'Culture of Poverty' Discourse in Urban Schooling." *Annals of the American Academy of Political and Social Science* 673:80–90.

Landry, Bart. 1988. *The New Black Middle Class*. Berkeley: University of California Press.

Lane, Jeffrey. 2019. *The Digital Street*. New York: Oxford University Press.

Lee, Jennifer. 2002. "From Civil Relations to Racial Conflict: Merchant-Customer Interactions in Urban America." *American Sociological Review* 67, no. 1 (February): 77–98.

Lepoutre, David. 2017. "Street Culture and Social Control in Different Types of High Schools in Working-Class and Immigrant Neighborhoods in France." *Annals of the American Academy of Political and Social Science* 673:251–65.

Lewis, David L. 1984. "Parallels and Divergences: Assimilationist Strategies of Afro-American and Jewish Elites from 1910 to the Early 1930s." *Journal of American History* 71:543–64.

Lieberson, Stanley. 1981. *A Piece of the Pie: Blacks and White Immigrants since 1880*. Berkeley: University of California Press.

Lincoln, C. Eric, and Lawrence H. Mamiya. 1990. *The Black Church in the African American Experience*. Durham, NC: Duke University Press.

Loewen, James W. 2005. *Sundown Towns: A Hidden Dimension of American Racism*. New York: New Press.

Logan, John R., and Brian Stultz. 2011. "The Persistence of Segregation in the Metropolis: New Findings from the 2010 Census." Census Brief prepared for Project US2010.

Logan, John R., and Charles Zhang. 2010. "Global Neighborhoods: New Pathways to Diversity and Separation." *American Journal of Sociology* 115:1069–109.

Loury, Glenn. 1976. "A Dynamic Theory of Racial Income Differences." Northwestern University, Center for Mathematical Studies in Economics and Management Science, Discussion Papers, no. 225.

Loury, Glenn C. 2002. *The Anatomy of Racial Inequality* (The W. E. B. Du Bois Lectures). Cambridge, MA: Harvard University Press.

Lybarger, Jeremy. 2019. "The Price You Pay: On the Life and Times of the Woman Known as the Welfare Queen." *The Nation*. July 2.

Madigan, Tim. 2003. *The Burning: Massacre, Destruction, and the Tulsa Race Riot of 1921*. New York: St. Martin's.

Majors, Richard, and Janet Billson. 1993. *Cool Pose: The Dilemmas of Black Manhood in America*. New York: Simon and Schuster.

Marglin, Stephen A., and Juliet B. Schor. 2011. *The Golden Age of Capitalism: Reinterpreting the Postwar Experience*. Oxford: Oxford University Press.

Massey, Douglas. 2007. "Building a Better Underclass." In *Categorically Unequal: The American Stratification System*. New York: Russell Sage Foundation.

Massey, Douglas S., and Nancy A. Denton. 1998. *American Apartheid: Segregation and the Making of the Underclass*. Cambridge, MA: Harvard University Press.

Massey, Douglas S., and Karen A. Pren. 2012. "Unintended Consequences of US Immigration Policy: Expanding the Post-1965 Surge from Latin America." *Population and Development Review* 38:1–29.

Matza, David. 1969. *Becoming Deviant*. Upper Saddle River, NJ: Prentice Hall.

May, Reuben A. B. 2014. *Urban Nightlife: Entertaining Race, Class, and Culture in Public Space*. New Brunswick, NJ: Rutgers University Press.

McIntosh, Peggy. 1989. *White Privilege: Unpacking the Invisible Knapsack. Seeking Educational Equity and Diversity*. Wellesley, MA: Wellesley Centers for Women, 1989. www.wcwonline.org/images/pdf/Knapsack_plus_Notes-Peggy_McIntosh .pdf.

McGee, Heather. 2021. *The Sum of Us: What Racism Costs Everyone and How We Can Prosper Together*. New York: One World.

McLeod, Jay. 1995. *Ain't No Makin' It: Aspirations and Attainment in a Low-Income Neighborhood*. New York: Routledge.

McWhorter, John. 2000. *Losing the Race: Self-Sabotage in Black America*. New York: Free Press.

Merton, Robert K. 1957. *Social Theory and Social Structure*. New York: Free Press.

Mincy, Ronald, ed. 2006. *Black Men Left Behind*. Washington, DC: Urban Institute Press.

Monk, Ellis P., Jr. 2015. "The Cost of Color: Skin Color, Discrimination, and Health among African-Americans." *American Journal of Sociology* 121:396–444.

Monk, Ellis P., Jr. 2021a. "Colorism and Physical Health: Evidence from a National Survey." *Journal of Health and Social Behavior*, 1–16.

Monk, Ellis P., Jr. 2021b. "The Unceasing Significance of Colorism: Skin Tone Stratification in the United States." *Daedalus* 150 (2): 76–90.

Moore, Wendy L. 2007. *Reproducing Racism: White Space, Elite Law Schools, and Racial Inequality*. Lanham, MD: Rowman and Littlefield.

Morris, Aldon D. 1984. *The Origins of the Civil Rights Movement: Black Communities Organizing for Change*. New York: Free Press.

Moynihan, Daniel Patrick. 1965. *The Negro Family: The Case for National Action*. Washington, DC: Office for Planning and Research, US Department of Labor.

Moynihan, Daniel Patrick. 1970. *Maximum Feasible Misunderstanding: Community Action in the War on Poverty*. New York: Free Press.

Muhammad, Khalil Gibran. 2011. *The Condemnation of Blackness: Race, Crime, and the Making of Modern Urban America*. Cambridge, MA: Harvard University Press.

Myrdal, Gunnar. 1944. *An American Dilemma: The Negro Problem and Modern Democracy*. New York: Harper and Row.

Ness, Cindy D. 2004. "Why Girls Fight: Female Youth Violence in the Inner City." *Annals of the American Academy of Political and Social Science* 595 (1): 32–48.

Ogletree, Charles. 2010. *The Presumption of Guilt: The Arrest of Henry Louis Gates Jr. and Race, Class, and Crime in America*. New York: Palgrave Macmillan.

Oliver, Melvin, and Thomas Shapiro. 1995. *Black Wealth/White Wealth: A New Perspective on Racial Inequality*. New York: Routledge.

Omi, Michael, and Howard Winant. 2014. *Racial Formation in the United States*. New York: Routledge.

Ong, Paul M., and Janette Lawrence. 1995. "Race and Employment Dislocation in California's Aerospace Industry." *Review of Black Political Economy* 23: 91–101.

Orfield, Gary, John Kucsera, and Genevieve Siegel-Hawley. 2012. *E Pluribus . . . Separation: Deepening Double Segregation for More Students*. Los Angeles: Civil Rights Project/Proyecto Derechos Civiles, University of California, Los Angeles.

Osofsky, Gilbert. 1996. *Harlem: The Making of a Ghetto; Negro New York, 1890–1930*. 2nd ed. Chicago: Ivan R. Dee.

Pager, Devah. 2003a. "Blacks and Ex-Cons Need Not Apply." *Contexts* 2 (4): 8–59.

Pager, Devah. 2003b. "The Mark of a Criminal Record." *American Journal of Sociology* 108 (5): 937–75.

Pager, Devah. 2007a. *Marked: Race, Crime, and Finding Work in an Era of Mass Incarceration*. Chicago: University of Chicago Press.

Pager, Devah. 2007b. "The Use of Field Experiments for Studies of Employment Discrimination: Contributions, Critiques, and Directions for the Future." *Annals of the American Academy of Political and Social Science* 609 (1): 104–33.

Pager, Devah. 2009. "Discrimination in a Low-Wage Labor Market: A Field Experiment." *American Sociological Review* 74:777–99.

Pager, Devah, and Lincoln Quillian. 2005. "Walking the Talk: What Employers Say versus What They Do." *American Sociological Review* 70 (3): 355–80.

Pager, Devah, Bruce Western and Naomi Sugie. 2009. "Sequencing Disadvantage: Barriers to Employment Facing Young Black and White Men with Criminal Records." *Annals of the American Academy of Political and Social Science* 623:195–213.

Painter, Nell Irvin. 2010. *The History of White People*. New York: W. W. Norton.

Palmer, Chris. 2021. "Philly's Violent Year: Nearly 500 People Were Killed and More than 2,200 Shot in 2020." *Philadelphia Inquirer*. January 1.

Park, Robert E., Ernest Burgess, and Rod McKenzie. 1925. *The City*. Chicago: University of Chicago Press.

Parker, Kim, et al. 2015. *Multiracial in America: Proud, Diverse and Growing in Numbers*. Washington, DC: Pew Research Center.

Pattillo, Mary. 2005. "Black Middle-Class Neighborhoods." *Annual Review of Sociology* 31:205–29.

Pattillo-McCoy, Mary. 2013. *Black Picket Fences: Privilege and Peril among the Black Middle Class*. Chicago: University of Chicago Press.

Pennsylvania Human Relations Commission. 1968. *Memorandum of West Philadelphia Schools Committee concerning Relevance of Facts as to Lower Quality of Teachers and Staff at Predominantly Black Schools in the Philadelphia School District*. Philadelphia: West Philadelphia Schools Committee.

Pettigrew, Thomas. 1980. *The Sociology of Race Relations*. New York: Free Press.

Pfeffer, Fabian T., and Alexandra Killewald. 2019. "Intergenerational Wealth Mobility and Racial Inequality." *Socius: Sociological Research for a Dynamic World*, March 21.

Philadelphia Comptroller. "Mapping Philadelphia's Gun Violence Crisis." 2021. Office of the Comptroller, City of Philadelphia. controller.phila.gov/philadelphia -audits/mapping-gun-violence/#/2021.

Pierce, Chester. 1970. "Offensive Mechanisms." In *The Black 70's*, edited by F. B. Barbour. Boston: Porter Sargent.

Portes, Alejandro, and Min Zhou. 1993. "The New Second Generation: Segmented Assimilation and Its Variants." *Annals of the American Academy of Political and Social Sciences* 530:74–96.

Rainwater, Lee. 1967. "The Revolt of the Dirty Workers." *Transaction* 5 (November): 2.

Riddle, Travis, and Stacey Sinclair. 2019. "Racial Disparities in School-Based Disciplinary Actions Are Associated with County-Level Rates of Racial Bias." *Proceedings of the National Academy of Sciences of the United States of America* 116 (17): 8255–60.

Rieder, Jonathan. 1987. *Canarsie: The Jews and Italians of Brooklyn against Liberalism*. Boston: Harvard University Press.

Rifkin, Jeremy. 1995. *The End of Work: The Decline of the Global Labor Force and the Dawn of the Post-Market Era*. New York: Putnam.

Rios, Victor. 2011. *Punished: Policing the Lives of Black and Latino Boys*. New York: New York University Press.

Robinson, Eugene. 2010. *Disintegration: The Splintering of Black America*. New York: Doubleday.

Robinson, Eugene. 2011. *Disintegration: The Splintering of Black America*. New York: Penguin Random House.

Roediger, David R. 1991. *The Wages of Whiteness: Race and the Making of the American Working Class*. London: Verso.

Rose, Peter I. (1973) 1990. *They and We*. Reprint, New York: Random House.

Rothstein, Richard. 2017. *The Color of Law: A Forgotten History of How Our Government Segregated America*. New York: Liveright.

Ryan, William. 1976. *Blaming the Victim*. New York: Random House.

Schlesinger, Arthur M., Jr. 1992. *The Disuniting of America*. New York: Norton.

Schneider, Eric C. 2020. *The Ecology of Homicide: Race, Place, and Space in Postwar Philadelphia*. Philadelphia: University of Pennsylvania Press.

Sears, David O., and P. J. Henry. 2003. "The Origins of Symbolic Racism." *Journal of Personality and Social Psychology* 85:259–75.

Sharkey, Patrick. 2014. "Spatial Segmentation and the Black Middle Class." *American Journal of Sociology* 119 (4): 903–54.

Shaw, Julie. 2021. "A 16-Year-Old Was Killed Outside a 7-Eleven after Looking at a Man Who Took It the Wrong Way, Police Say." *Philadelphia Inquirer*, February 24.

Shedd, Carla. 2015. *Unequal City: Race, Schools, and Perceptions of Injustice*. New York: Russell Sage Foundation.

Shibutani, Tamotsu. 1961. "Social Status in Reference Groups." In *Society and Per-*

sonality: An Interactionist Approach to Social Psychology, by Tamotsu Shibutani. Englewood Cliffs, NJ: Prentice Hall.

Skrentny, John, David. 1996. *The Ironies of Affirmative Action*. Chicago: University of Chicago Press.

Sohoni, Deenesh, and Salvatore Saporito. 2009. "Mapping School Segregation: Using GIS to Explore Racial Segregation between Schools and Their Corresponding Areas." *American Journal of Education* 115 (4): 569–600.

Spear, Allan H. 1969. *Black Chicago: The Making of a Negro Ghetto, 1890–1920*. Chicago: University of Chicago Press.

Stack, Carol. 1997. *All Our Kin: Survival Strategies in the Black Community*. New York: Basic Books.

Steele, Shelby. 1990. *The Content of Our Character: A New Vision of Race in America*. New York: St. Martin's.

Strmic-Pawl, Hephzibah. 2016. *Multiracialism and Its Discontents: A Comparative Analysis of Asian-White and Black-White Multiracials*. New York: Lexington Books.

Stryker, Perrin. 1953. "How Executives Get Jobs." *Fortune* 48 (2): 117ff.

Sugrue, Thomas J. 1996. *The Origins of the Urban Crisis*. Princeton, NJ: Princeton University Press.

Sylvester, David Hale. 2011. *Traveling at the Speed of Life*. Philadelphia: e-book published by the author.

Taeuber, Karl E., and Alma F. Taeuber. 1965. *Negroes in Cities: Residential Segregation and Neighborhood Change*. Chicago: Aldine.

Taylor, Keeanga-Yamahtta. 2019. *Race for Profit: How Banks and the Real Estate Industry Undermined Black Homeownership*. Chapel Hill: University of North Carolina Press.

Thomas, William I. 1969. "The Definition of the Situation." In *Symbolic Interaction: A Reader in Social Psychology*. New York: Allyn and Bacon.

Tonry, Michael. 2010. "The Social, Psychological, and Political Causes of Racial Disparities in the American Criminal Justice System." *Crime and Justice: A Review of Research* 39:273–312.

Valentine, Betty Lou. 1980. *Hustling and Other Hard Work*. New York: Free Press.

Valentine, Charles A. 1968. *Culture and Poverty: Critique and Counterproposals*. Chicago: University of Chicago Press.

Venkatesh, Suhir Alladi. 2009. *Off the Books: The Underground Economy of the Urban Poor*. Cambridge, MA: Harvard University Press.

Wacquant, Loïc. 2007. *Urban Outcasts*. Malden, MA: Polity Press.

Wacquant, Loïc. 2012a. *Punishing the Poor: The Neoliberal Government of Social Insecurity*. Durham, NC: Duke University Press.

Wacquant, Loïc. 2012b. "Repenser le ghetto: Du sens commun au concept sociologique." *Idées économiques et sociales* 167, no. 1 (2012): 14–25.

Welch, Kelly. 2007. "Black Criminal Stereotypes and Racial Profiling." *Journal of Contemporary Criminal Justice* 23 (3): 276–88.

Wellman, David T. 1977. *Portraits of White Racism*. New York: Cambridge University Press.

Wherry, Frederick F., Kristin S. Seefelt, and Antony S. Alvarez. 2019. "To Lend or Not to Lend to Friends and Kin: Awkwardness, Obfuscation, and Negative Reciprocity." *Social Forces* 98:753–93.

Wicker, Tom. 1968. *U.S. Riot Commission Report: Report of the National Advisory Commission on Civil Disorders*. New York: Bantam.

Wideman, John Edgar. 2010. "The Seat Not Taken." *New York Times*, October 7, 39.

Wiese, Andrew. 1995. "Neighborhood Diversity: Social Change, Ambiguity, and Fair Housing since 1968." *Journal of Urban Affairs* 17 (2): 107–29.

Wilkerson, Isabel. 2020. *Caste: The Origins of Our Discontents*. New York: Random House.

Williams, Terry. 1989, *The Cocaine Kids: The Inside Story of a Teenage Drug Ring*. Boston: Addison-Wesley.

Wilson, William Julius. 1978. *The Declining Significance of Race: Blacks and Changing American Institutions*. Chicago: University of Chicago Press.

Wilson, William Julius. 1987. *The Truly Disadvantaged: The Inner City, the Underclass, and Public Policy*. Chicago: University of Chicago Press.

Wilson, William Julius. 1996. *When Work Disappears: The World of the New Urban Poor*. New York: Random House.

Winant, Howard. 2002. *The World Is a Ghetto: Race and Democracy since World War II*. New York: Basic Books.

Wirth, Louis. 1928. *The Ghetto*. Chicago: University of Chicago Press.

Woldoff, Rachael A. 2011. *White Flight/Black Flight: The Dynamics of Racial Change in an American Neighborhood*. Ithaca, NY: Cornell University Press.

World-Changing History. 2020. *Tulsa Race Massacre of 1921*. ebook.

Zweigenhaft, Richard L., and William Domhoff. 1991. *Blacks in the White Establishment?* New Haven, CT: Yale University Press.

INDEX